Lefty Kreh's Fly Fishing in Salt Water

Third Edition

LEFTY KREH

Foreword by Blane Chocklett

Illustrations by Rod Walinchus

LYONS
PRESS

Essex, Connecticut

This book is dedicated to my wife,
Evelyn,
who has been a great partner and
for more than thirty-five years has supported me
in everything I've tried to do.

An imprint of Globe Pequot, the trade division of
The Rowman & Littlefield Publishing Group, Inc.
4501 Forbes Blvd., Ste. 200
Lanham, MD 20706
www.rowman.com

Distributed by NATIONAL BOOK NETWORK

Copyright © 1986, 1997, 2003 by Bernard "Lefty" Kreh
First edition published 1986

Foreword to this paperback edition copyright © 2023 by Blane Chocklett

Illustrations © 1997, 2003 by Rod Walinchus
Designed by Joel Friedlander Publishing Services, San Rafael, CA

British Library Cataloguing in Publication Information available

The Library of Congress has cataloged the hardcover edition of this book as follows:

Kreh, Lefty.
    Fly fishing in salt water / Lefty Kreh: illustrations by Rod
Walinchus. —3rd rev. and fully augmented ed.
        p. cm.
    Includes index.
    1. Saltwater fly fishing.   I. Title.
SH456.2.K73   1997
799.1'6—dc21   97-8225
                                CIP

ISBN 978-1-4930-7200-2 (paper : alk. paper)
ISBN 978-1-4930-7519-5 (electronic)

∞™ The paper used in this publication meets the minimum requirements of American
National Standard for Information Sciences—Permanence of Paper for Printed Library
Materials, ANSI/NISO Z39.48-1992.

Contents

Foreword

I would like to start out by saying, in my opinion, there has never been such an ambassador for the sport of fly fishing as Lefty. He embodied the spirit of sharing in spreading his knowledge of the sport, especially fly fishing in salt water. Lefty's love of sharing knowledge and his tireless life's work show in all his books. There are many people all over this world who Lefty has touched and helped in some way. And there are also several much closer friends of Lefty who are more deserving than me to write this foreword. I am truly honored and humbled to be able to write this because Lefty was and is a big part of my life. He guided me through my career and I feel so lucky to have had one of my heroes be a friend and mentor.

I first found out about Lefty when I was a young man still in high school, when he appeared on *The Walker's Cay Chronicles* hosted by Lefty's good friend Mr. Flip Pallot. Flip always spoke highly of Lefty on other episodes before having him on a particular episode. Flip's referencing of Lefty throughout his show, asking "What would Lefty do?," intrigued me, so I set out to learn more about this man. Back then Google did not yet exist, so I went to my school and local libraries to find some of his books. Seeing Flip share his saltwater world really sparked my interest in saltwater fly fishing. So, to my surprise and delight, I came across THE quintessential book on the subject, *Fly Fishing in Salt Water*, by the man himself, Lefty Kreh. This book opened up a new world to me not only for saltwater fly fishing but also for my home waters in the mountains of Virginia. It let me know about the importance of sinking lines and how to use them, but also delved into streamers and their use.

Learning about the streamers and sinking lines helped shape my career very early on and set me up to where I am now. I didn't know it then but it was the beginning of a lifelong career. I got to meet Lefty about seven to eight years later at a trade show in Denver after I opened my fly shop in Roanoke, Virginia. As I would find out, I wasn't the only person starstruck from meeting a hero; admirers always surrounded him. I got my chance to meet him as he walked by and smiled, and I introduced myself. As he always did, he treated me like a long-lost friend and was very humble, which left me feeling at ease and important. Just a few years later in North Carolina my life would change forever with another meeting with Lefty.

During the fall in the Southern Outer Banks, a special migration happens, and during the late 1990s it became the place to be in the fly-fishing community. During this time, I had been developing my Gummy Minnow flies and Sili Skin material. I hadn't tried these new patterns yet but I knew I could make these flies match exactly and look like the prey items that the false albacore fed on, such as bay anchovies and silversides. I tied several hundred flies of different sizes and colors in anticipation of the fall migration. I always set aside the first part of November to host trips down to the sleepy town of Harkers Island along the shores of Cape Lookout in North Carolina. Along with the fishing, Tom Earnhardt and Jones Brothers Marine would have a party/pig picking in honor of the migration. This event brought the who's who of fly fishing. Knowing this, I planned my trip down there during this time. Along with that, I also could unveil my new creations to many well-known tiers and anglers like Bob Popovics, Bob Clouser, and Lefty. On my arrival I purposely sought out Bob Popovics because of his out-of-the-box thinking on fly design.

I showed Bob my flies and he was very kind and interested in these new patterns. We spoke about the realism, movement, and how the public would react to these nontraditional flies. He felt very confident that they would work well and be widely accepted, much like his Surf Candy patterns. Bob asked me to hold on for a second as he wanted to take these flies to someone and show them. After about fifteen minutes or so Bob came back and asked me to follow him because he wanted me to meet someone. This, as I said, was a party outside and many people were enjoying the evening as the sun set. Bob and I weaved through the crowd and ended up in the middle of the party where everyone was crowded around. It seemed like the seas parting and in the middle of it all was Lefty. He was holding my new flies and immediately told me how much he liked them and how well they would do, not only for fishing but also in my career as a tier.

Lefty asked me many questions about how I designed them and how long they took to make. He then asked me if I had heard of Umpqua Feather Merchants. I told him I had and that just earlier that year I had my first pattern accepted by them: my Disc slider and popper series. Well, Lefty said that this will be an instant classic and asked if he could have some. I, of course, was very flattered and asked him to take as many as he wanted. He, unfortunately, was leaving the next morning but he said he would share them around. This was before cell phones, at least for me, and the party was on a Saturday night. The next two days I got to fish them and was very happy with the results. On Monday evening after my day of fishing, I had a message from my wife that the Fly Czar from Umpqua wanted me to call them.

That evening I called (can't remember his name at this time) and he told me sight unseen that Lefty had called him telling him about my new pattern. Lefty told them they absolutely wanted this fly and it would be an instant classic. He told me that evening they wanted six colors, three sizes to start, which was a big deal since they hadn't even seen it yet. That's how much Lefty has meant to the fly-fishing world—he understood the sport and the industry, always wanting to make it better. He selflessly helped me because he saw the potential in me and wanted to help cultivate that.

This brings me back to this book. Lefty has been there and done it all over the world. He fished most of the all-fresh and saltwater destinations and was a student of the game. His desire to help grow this sport and push it forward shows in his books and his life's work. This book is a must-read for those who have been life-long anglers interested in saltwater fishing as well as those who have been doing it their entire lives. I guarantee that you will gain more knowledge by flipping through these pages. The book is iconic, much like the man who wrote it, Mr. Bernard "Lefty" Kreh. It changed my life way back when and I know it will do the same for you. As Lefty would always end saying, "All the Best!"

Blane Chocklett

Fly Fishing in

Salt Water

PART ONE

The Lure and Tackle of Saltwater Fly Fishing

 # The Lure of Saltwater Fly Fishing

Why would a man want to fly fish in salt water? There are many reasons, some obvious, others understood only by those who have actually tried this kind of fishing. The sea has always been a fascination to me, and the creatures in it offer the greatest challenge a fly rodder will ever know. The solitude on a mountain brook is a taste of the real solitude of wading along the shore or on a shallow flat in search of trophy fish.

Saltwater fish are much stronger than their freshwater counterparts. The freshwater fly rodder worries that a fish may break his leader—the saltwater man occasionally wonders if he owns enough line to hold the fish streaking through the water with his fly in its mouth. No one can really describe the run of a bonefish, the slugging battle of a jack crevalle, the mighty leap of a tarpon; these things have to be experienced. Once they are, the freshwater angler is never the same.

Anyone who has hooked a tarpon of more than 100 pounds and seen it emerge from the surface like a silver rocket, throwing water like a broken fire hose, appreciates fly fishing at its best. To watch a billfish, enraged because it cannot get the teaser, suddenly charge your fly as it trails in blue water behind the transom will thrill you as no freshwater fishing moment can. I once hooked a fifty-pound Allison tuna in 150 feet of water on the Challenger Banks off Bermuda. Nothing, literally *nothing*, has ever stripped line from my reel with the speed of that fish—it was awesome. And when, twenty minutes later, I had that magnificent game fish lying fifteen feet off the transom, exhausted but still beating its tail, I was completely overjoyed. Minutes later the line had somehow tangled in the rudder and the fish was lost; but the memory of that great fish and the battle that it gave was worth the game.

No stocked fish roam the seas. These are fish straight from God's hand, and they are in prime condition. There is little cover in the sea, and since almost every sea creature feeds upon something smaller than itself, the only way the pursued can escape is to go away—fast. Species that did not learn

The author finds the most fun in fly fishing when poling across a shallow flat searching for fish.

to swim quickly did not endure. When a saltwater fish hits your fly, its speed is evident as it strains your tackle in its natural attempt to escape.

Unlike fresh waters, the sea is wide open to anyone who has a boat or cares to wade. And, while fresh waters are diminishing at an alarming rate, there has been only a slight decrease in the areas good for saltwater fly fishing. In fact, new saltwater fishing areas are being discovered all the time, as adventurous fishermen test new waters.

The brown trout may frustrate you, but a permit will drive you mad. I kissed the first one I caught; it weighed only five pounds. The permit is an extremely strong fish, perhaps one of the strongest in the sea. It is endowed with keen eyesight, and it's as wary as a cat in a dog pound, ready to flee at the least disturbance.

A ten-pound striped bass offers little resistance on a rugged surf-spinning stick, but that same fish on a light fly rod and leader is another experience. Somehow, a sea fish caught on fly tackle is that much more rewarding.

There is a bonus thrill, too: fishing over huge schools of feeding fish. Anyone who has ever approached a school of savage bluefish or jacks tearing into frantic baitfish, and tossed a fly into the carnage, wants to keep repeating this experience forever. The excitement of the chase—getting there before the school goes down, and then catching as many as you can— is difficult to describe.

Saltwater fly fishing often combines the best qualities of hunting and fishing. Such is bonefishing, seeking permit or tarpon, searching for big cruising sharks on the flats, looking for heavy stripers that move up on the mud flats to feed, or trying to stalk a big shark in the shallow water. Sight fishing is one of the ultimate thrills for the true angler, and many like this type of angling so well that they do no other kind.

Where it is tailored to the fishing, as for dolphins, bonefish, tarpon, and other fish that take flies well, the fly rod is really the most efficient tool for the sport.

As an outdoors writer for more than forty years, I have fished for everything from giant tuna to bluegills, with anglers who have sampled every area of fishing. I have never met a single fisherman who did not prefer a fly rod to any other type of tackle.

You need not justify the lure of saltwater fly rodding to those who have tried it.

 # Saltwater vs. Freshwater Fly Fishing

Nearly three-quarters of the earth is covered by salt water, most of it relatively unexplored by fly fishermen. Naturally, the high seas are not considered fly-fishing waters, even though anglers do fish with flies many miles from shore. But somewhere, at any time of the year, saltwater fishing is at its peak. Bluefishing on the northeastern coast is at its best in the late spring, summer, and early fall; Florida bluefishermen like the winter period. The traveling angler can find his sport somewhere—whenever he can get away.

Much of the potential of saltwater angling is yet to be discovered. Central America, South America, Africa, and Australia offer fishing better than most of us have ever experienced. I've waded flats in Central America where I've seen more bonefish in a week than I do in a year in Florida, and the fish were just about as wary.

As new areas open to pioneering anglers, tackle is improved, and better techniques are developed, we will find the fishing even more exciting.

Freshwater angling has few real physical frontiers anymore (but plenty of room for refinement in technique); saltwater fly fishing is still in its infancy, and there are a lot of "growing" years ahead.

The oceans are vastly different in terms of their underwater geography, and of the fish species that inhabit them. The fish in northern coastal waters eat different foods and live in a different environment from their cousins in tropical waters—and require different fly-fishing approaches and techniques.

Few significant insect hatches occur on the seas as they do on fresh waters. The saltwater fish exist primarily on smaller fish, crustaceans, and other bottom life. Exact imitation is relatively unimportant, except in a few cases.

Freshwater fish are minor-league swimmers compared to the wahoo, the kingfish, and the barracuda. To the uninitiated, the ferocity of a barracuda's strike, its prodigious leaps, and its sheer strength will be startling. Gene Utech, a fine trout fisherman, hooked a twenty-pound barracuda the first time he went fly fishing in salt water with me. The cuda jumped over a small mangrove bush on its first run, breaking the leader in the process; the expression on Gene's face was something to behold.

Saltwater fish are, with a few exceptions, much stronger than freshwater fish. We all like to think of the bass and the trout as real battlers, but we scale down our tackle to give the fish a chance. An albacore or a jack crevalle needs no handicap—they can slug it out on *any* tackle. Fishing near the Dry Tortugas with an angler friend several years ago, I located a school of permit on a wreck in shallow water. He had hooked several fish, but they had repeatedly broken his line. Finally, determined that he would land one, he locked the drag on a heavy-duty trolling reel loaded with fifty-pound monofilament. He cast to a school of thirty-pounders, and they swarmed to the surface. He sat down in the front of the boat, and waited for one of the fish to take the crab. He felt the line come tight and struck; the rod bent like a question mark. Straining, neither he nor his drag would yield; the big permit began to beat its sickle tail in an effort to get back to the wreck below and safety. Slowly, very slowly, my friend was pulled from the boat seat to his knees. Then the fish dragged him and the rod the entire length of the boat. When he came up against the fish locker at the back of the boat, the rod bent even deeper.

My friend was a husky guy, and he hung on.

Suddenly, like a firecracker exploding, the fifty-pound monofilament broke, and my friend fell into the bottom of the boat. The fish had escaped. No thirty-pound freshwater fish can drag a man the length of an eighteen-foot boat and break a fifty-pound line in the process. Saltwater species are tough, and the fly rodder new to this fishing will learn quickly to appreciate their strength.

Saltwater tackle must receive extreme care. Guides must be securely attached; the rod must have casting *and* lifting power. When a 100-plus-pound tarpon is lying eight feet below the boat, the angler must forcibly lift the fish with his own muscle and the latent power of the rod. If the rod doesn't respond, the angler will lose the fish. In fact, some rods are designed primarily for fish fighting, with casting of secondary importance.

Reels must be able to sustain high-speed runs, and the drags have to be whisper smooth. All metal parts of tackle must be resistant to saltwater

Doc Robinson and Captain Lefty Reagan developed the method of teasing billfish to the fly. Here Doc is working his fly in front of a billfish.

corrosion. And proper cleaning and care of tackle is much more important than in the case of freshwater gear.

Every effort is made to get the utmost from tackle; knots come under intense scrutiny—just attaching a fly to a leader won't do. Knot strength is paramount, but if you attach a fly to a 100-pound shock leader, the knot must allow the fly to work properly. Both braided and solid wire are used, and special knots must be learned. Accomplishment in building a leader for

Big fish can be taken on fly rods. This tarpon was boated at Homosassa, Florida, by the author long before it became known as the best U.S. site for giant tarpon.

saltwater fish comes when the angler can make one so that all knots are stronger than the weakest material used in building that leader—and this is possible.

The serious fly fisherman need know only half a dozen knots to get by—but the advanced angler will use as many as a dozen for special situations. To fish in salt water the angler must understand how to tie knots in Dacron (for backing), fly lines (attaching the backing and the leader butt), and monofilament and wire for leader construction. If any of these knots fail, so will fishermen.

While many saltwater fish are taken on small flies, a lot of them take flies that wouldn't even fit in a freshwater fly box. A streamer with twenty saddle hackles is not unusual, and popping bugs with faces more than an inch in diameter are used to excite amberjacks into striking; anything less will receive little interest from the fish.

Hooks must be different. Stainless steel is rapidly becoming the preferred material, and special sharpening techniques have been developed. It takes an incredibly sharp hook to penetrate the tough, raspy mouths of many saltwater fish.

In many cases the physical stamina of the fisherman becomes a factor. This is not always true, of course, but a fight with a bluewater fish may last from thirty minutes to more than two hours. During that entire time you are attempting to regain your line and keep a deep bow in the rod. Even fishing for bonefish with a six-pound tippet takes stamina. You can't stand all day long on the forward platform of a boat, searching for the wily fish, without your legs giving out occasionally, and your back telling you that you are not used to this. Conditioning is a serious matter if you plan to do a lot of saltwater fly fishing.

Boats used for fishing should be able to travel a long distance at high speed. Fishermen must often search for schools of fish. They shut down the boat's engine when the fish are located and either drift or pole the boat to the fish. But this often requires miles of running before fish are located. And the experienced angler often knows that he has the last two hours of the tide to fish bluefish, tarpon, or stripers on a certain bar; then he must get to another location quickly to catch the first part of the incoming tide. To do so, he needs a fast boat. In tropical areas, as well as much of southern Florida, the angler may travel 100 miles a day in search of the fish he desires. Fortunately, boats are now being constructed to meet all these requirements.

Two totally different kinds of saltwater fishing are possible. Inshore fishing requires specific techniques, tackle, and knowledge; offshore angling, a different set of procedures. For example, depth finders are rarely used inshore, but become vital for serious offshore angling; wrecks, of little importance to the man who wades, will harbor all sorts of trophies for deep-water anglers; drifting debris might mean dolphins offshore and indicate nothing to the inshore angler.

There are subtle differences, too. Trout and bass fishermen, panfish and steelhead fishermen all use different tackle and techniques; similarly, the procedures for catching a bonefish, a snook, a channel bass, and a shad all vary. Each fish is a different subject. The fish's habits, the temperatures it prefers, the food it eats, and where it will appear must be considered before the angler can successfully fish for the various species with a fly.

One basic problem the fly fisherman new to salt water must face is mastering the breeze. The temperature variance between the land and the sea causes air masses to move. It is a rare day, except in the dead of summer heat, that the angler does not have to solve a wind problem when fishing the salt. This calls for the use of tackle that can overcome the wind, and an angler used to swinging a small trout rod will have to polish his casting before he can perform as well with the larger saltwater sticks.

Except when casting to a rising trout, or locating a salmon in its lie, the freshwater angler usually is "blind casting," hoping that his fly will move before a hungry fish. Anglers even hang several flies on a leader in hopes of better attracting their unseen quarry. In much of shallow saltwater fly rodding, you must actually hunt the fish; and only after it is sighted do you make your cast. This requires special skills and tools; but the added flavor of actually searching for and then finding your quarry before you cast makes the fishing much more thrilling.

Saltwater fly rodding can be inexpensive. It all depends on where and how you want to fish. The man who has a bass fishing outfit is already equipped to fish the shallows for redfish and bonefish. The man with a small aluminum or fiberglass boat can cruise protected waters and catch many species, and certainly no one can fish with less expense than the man who seeks shad as they run up our rivers in the spring.

Of course, there is the other extreme, too. Some saltwater fly fishermen fly to distant lands, charter offshore cruisers, and spend days seeking specific types of game fish. This type of fly rodding takes money. Guides are expensive, but it should be said in their defense that their operating costs are so high that few ever make what most people would consider a good salary.

How much money you spend on your saltwater fly fishing will be determined by your taste as well as your finances. If you are satisfied with local fishing from relatively small boats, the cost is low, and the excitement can be high.

There is another way in which saltwater fly fishing differs greatly from freshwater fishing, one that lends much excitement to the sport. The fresh-water angler fishes for a solitary trout, perhaps a single salmon lying on a gravel bar, or one bass lurking under an overhanging tree limb. In saltwater fishing, huge schools of fish are frequently encountered; I have seen acres of calm water turn into a froth from savage jack crevalles tearing into tiny sardines. I have seen the surface water around a marker actually change color as a school of cobia appeared; mackerels and bluefish, prey and preda-tor, are sometimes so packed together it is difficult to understand how they can swim.

The fly rodder on the Chesapeake Bay in the fall can thrill to the sight of breaking bluefish that number in the hundreds. They can be seen from some distance tearing into baitfish. Much of the angler's thrill in this kind of fishing is the mad chase across the water, with one hand gripping onto the boat and the other grasping the tackle.

Not only are the schools of fish often enormous, but some of the fish themselves are massive. Many times a fly rodder battling a fish has been amazed when an amberjack, cobia, or large grouper appeared out of the depths and simply inhaled the hooked fish. Teasing a big amberjack or sail-fish with live bait right at boatside, then throwing a large popping bug or streamer fly at the fish, which takes it with a splash that fills your face with salt water, is a tremendous thrill.

Fishing salt water is different in many ways from fresh water, perhaps the greatest being the fact that you can often tangle with what appear to be unlimited numbers of fish—and opponents so powerful that unless you follow a careful plan, the fish will win, and even destroy your tackle.

CHAPTER 3

 # Tides

Perhaps the greatest adjustment that a fresh-water angler will have to make is learning about tides. In freshwater fishing, temperature and clarity of water are the two most important factors. If the water temperature is acceptable to trout or bass, and the streams and lakes are not roiled by rains, the angler can usu-ally fish successfully. This is not true in salt water.

Temperature is important, of course, but turbidity in salt water is rarely a factor. Sometimes water will muddy from wind or wave action, and bot-tom-feeding fish like mullets and bonefish create mud, but these waters almost always clear on the next tide.

Few people who fish really understand much about tides and how they can affect angler success. Thus an angler not familiar with a specific area should either hire a guide or at least inform himself about tidal effects on local waters.

One of the major reasons why knowing about tides is vital to fishing success is to also understand the baitfish that the predator species feed on. Unlike many saltwater species, baitfish don't have a home. They may be here today and gone tomorrow. They don't fight tidal currents. Rather, they allow the tide to take them along. Predator species know this and ambush the baitfish in places where the tide will make them available.

The tide causes many changes. One important to the angler is a tem-perature change. Shallow water that has lain under a hot sun will become

Knowledge of the tides is essential for wade fishing. Here an angler is working a bar for striped bass on Long Island.

uncomfortable for fish. As the tide rises, it brings cooler water from the deeper area, and with it will come the larger fish. Conversely, during a cool night and a low tide, flats become chilled. As water flows in over these chilled banks, they act like refrigerator coils, drastically cooling the water. This drop in temperature will force fish into deeper water. Sometimes it can be severe enough to cause a fish kill.

The tide can also have an enormous effect upon water clarity. A flat can be so stirred by the wind that the water looks like soup. Yet a tidal change can suck all that dirty water away, exchanging it for clear water on the next tide. On a high tide, grass, small sticks, and other floating debris are carried in among the mangrove roots or deposited along the shoreline. Should a higher tide occur, it will free all this debris, which is then drained away on the next falling tide. This is a condition that can ruin fishing until the debris is washed out of the area.

Rising tides can cause fish to move into a specific area or to be widely scattered. Low tides can cause fish to concentrate in deep pools in the shallows for safety. Common sense helps in analyzing tidal effects: if there are wide, shallow flats with a deep, narrow channel cutting through them, on low stages of the tide you would certainly expect most fish to be in the channel. Another basic tidal situation that any fly fisherman can easily understand and take advantage of is an inland bay or lagoon. If such a body of water is tide-drained through a narrow creek, fish will obviously feed on the bait funneled through the creek. The place to fish is on the down-tide side of the mouth of the creek—or at the mouth of the funnel.

River mouths are in most cases best fished on a falling tide. Some have underwater bars that become feeding stations for predator species when the tide rises. Baitfish will go with the incoming tide, seeking the shallows and safety. When the water falls the baitfish try to remain in the security of the shallows as long as possible. Any ditches or drainages on the lower stages of a tide are the places they will finally have to come out. Predators establish feeding stations at such outlets.

So the most important fact for fishermen to know about tides is that the tidal currents carry the small baitfish to and fro. Larger fish understand this very well, and if the angler can apply this information he can cast his fly to feeding fish.

Even people with some understanding of the tides mistakenly think they are caused entirely by the gravitational pull of the moon. The National Oceanic and Atmospheric Administration (NOAA) employs thirty-seven variables in figuring its tidal predictions. The key word is *predictions*, because they are not always borne out.

The wind is an important factor in relation to tides. For example, on the West Coast, when the prediction is for a high tide at 6:00 P.M. but there is an exceptionally strong west wind blowing against the shore, high tide will occur a little earlier, and it will certainly be higher than was predicted. The warming of northern seas in the summer can cause higher tides. Atmospheric pressure can affect a tide's height. Even a flexing of the earth's surface can affect tide.

But the moon and the sun cause the major effects. If the angler has some basic understanding of these two bodies, he can better relate his fishing to the tides. It takes twenty-eight days (scientists say the time is a little less), or roughly a month, for the moon to travel along an elliptical path around the earth. At points in its orbit the moon is farther away, and this reduces tidal effect.

The moon exerts nearly two and a half times as much gravitational pull on the earth as does the sun. As the moon goes around the earth the water

In many areas an incoming tide is best for bonefishing. Here two anglers are fishing a Florida Keys flat as the tide is rising.

is pulled toward it. Naturally, the "bulge" in the earth's water always lags behind the pull of the moon as it orbits the earth.

There is a seven-day period when the moon is closer to us than at any other time during a twenty-eight-day span. During this time both the sun and the moon are in near direct line with the earth. The corresponding positions of the three bodies increase the gravitational effects, causing the tides to rise higher and to fall lower than at any other time during the month. These are called spring tides. At this time the moon is said to be in perigee (usually indicated on tidal charts).

As the moon continues to orbit the earth, there will only be a slight rise and fall in tide during the next seven-day period. When minimal tides occur, they are referred to as "nip" tides, properly called neap tides.

The next seven days will have another period of spring tides, but they will not range quite as high or low as the first set of spring tides. Following this will be another week of neap tides, and then the whole cycle is repeated.

Broken into a simple pattern, what the fisherman can expect during a twenty-eight-day period is a week of spring tides, a week of neap tides, another week of spring tides, and, finally, a second week of neap tides.

How can you quickly determine what kind of tide will be occurring where you're fishing? Simple: if you see a full moon or a new moon (no moon or a very thin sickle) there is a spring tide condition. If the moon is in one of the quarters, there will be a neap tide.

One complete tidal cycle ranges through two high and two low tides during a span of twenty-five hours. This means that every day the tides will be one hour later if all weather factors are roughly the same. To utilize this information in your fishing let's use an example. Let's say that you are fishing San Francisco Bay around the pilings for big striped bass on a spring tide. Note the time when the action really gets hot, and for the sake of illustration it starts at 10:00 A.M. If you return tomorrow the action should start one hour later, at 11:00 A.M. But remember that every two weeks tides also repeat themselves and that reverse tides occur a week apart. Thus, if you

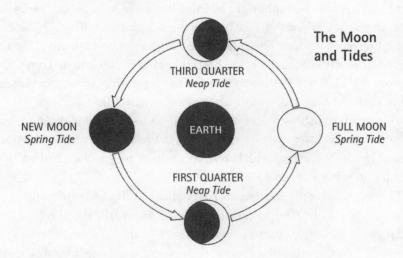

THIRD QUARTER
Neap Tide

The Moon and Tides

NEW MOON
Spring Tide

EARTH

FULL MOON
Spring Tide

FIRST QUARTER
Neap Tide

were fishing a high, rising tide on Rum Bottle Bank on the tenth of the month at ten o'clock in the morning—and you did great—don't go back seven days later (the seventeenth) because tidal conditions will be exactly the opposite. Instead, return two weeks to the day and hour, and unless there is a major weather or wind change, conditions should repeat themselves. Remember, too, that radical changes in weather can affect the fish so much that tides could become reduced in their importance to angling success.

How can you determine what kinds of tides will occur where you are fishing? There are a number of ways. Local newspapers along the coast carry daily tide tables. Regional fishing magazines almost always list the tides for the issue period. Two books published by the NOAA give the tides throughout the Western Hemisphere. These books are available by ordering them from NOAA, U.S. Department of Commerce, Washington, D.C. The titles of the two books are *Tide Tables—High and Low Water Predictions for the East Coast of North and South America* and *Tide Tables—High and Low Water Predictions for the West Coast of North and South America* (specify the year for both publications).

Remember a very important point about reading a tide table: the listed time is for a specific area. If you want to know the tidal conditions some distance from that point, you must look for a tidal correction. Here is an example: if the tide begins to rise at the mouth of Barnegat Bay, New Jersey, naturally it will be higher at the inlet before it reaches the same stage farther up the bay at Tom's River. And as the tide falls, it will reach the lower stage first nearer the inlet. The tidal correction tables will indicate that there is a three-hour difference between high tide at the inlet and at Tom's River. Therefore if a high tide occurs at noon at the inlet, the correction table will indicate that the high tide is due at Tom's River at 3:00 P.M.

Marine charts show water depths, and although the water depths are indicated slightly differently on the East and West Coast charts, the figures are reliable. Unlike maps, which tell you where to go, charts most of the time tell you where *not* to go.

There are some places, such as parts of the Gulf of Mexico, where only one tide occurs daily. And in certain parts of the world there is practically no tidal rise and fall. Pensacola, Florida, sees practically no tidal effect! If two people ride the ends of a seesaw, they rise and fall considerably, but the center of the board remains at one point. Pensacola is in a position comparable to the center of the seesaw.

The fly fisherman who goes fishing in the salt must learn the basics about tides—or hire a good guide—if he is to succeed.

CHAPTER 4

Tackle

When selecting tackle, you must first consider the fly that will draw the strike and the specific fishing conditions. You don't want to throw a tiny bonefish fly to a king mackerel, or thump an amberjack popping bug on the still waters of a flat, spooking every permit in the area. A fly can be compared to a bullet: the size of each is a vital consideration when seeking your quarry.

FLY LINES

Most hunters would first talk about guns rather than the game they seek. While the type of fly you cast should determine to a large degree the type of tackle used, I would prefer to start this tackle discussion with fly lines. It is the line that transports the fly to the target, and then takes it to the proper depth. If a properly sized fly is cast on an improperly sized line, disaster will follow. For example, bonefish are best pursued with light lines (sizes 6 through 8) in most situations. A size 11 line will get the fly to the fish, but the impact of that heavy line crashing to the surface of the water is going to frighten away any wary fish. On the other hand, if you are trying to push a large, wind-resistant popping bug to a cobia cruising around a marker, a light line simply won't take it there.

It's best to start with an understanding of fly-line shapes. There are four basic ones: level, double-taper, weight-forward, and shooting taper (frequently called a shooting head). For nearly all saltwater fly fishing you'll need only two of these tapers, the weight-forward and the shooting head, as level and double-taper lines do not lend themselves well to this kind of angling. **Weight-forward** means that most of the line's weight is concentrated in roughly the first thirty feet of the line; behind this portion is a thinner running line. The angler will work the heavier portion outside the rod tip, then make a forward cast. At the end of the stroke, he releases the running line, which is easily carried forward a good distance by the heavier front portion. An advantage of this line is that it can be retrieved until only the weight-forward section is outside the rod tip. The angler can then make a quick backcast and, with a single forward cast, shoot the fly to the target and begin another retrieve. The larger-diameter portion of the line is referred to as the belly. The length of the belly section varies with different manufacturers, but most of them make a belly approximately twenty feet long, with a long taper in the front and a short back taper leading to the running line.

There is one special weight-forward line called a **saltwater taper.** It has a shorter-than-average belly, which allows the angler to hold most of the heavy portion of the fly line outside the rod guides. When a fish is located, the angler can quickly throw all the heavy line into the air and, with a single false cast, usually shoot to the target. For people who are poor casters, the saltwater taper may be an asset in getting into action quickly. A saltwater taper (which should really be called a speed-cast taper) has so much weight concentrated at the front end of the fly line that too much energy is carried forward. This often causes the line to "dump over" or crash to the water, creating a poor presentation. This sounds great, but in actual practice it doesn't work that well. For anyone moderately capable in their casting, a conventional weight-forward taper is the better choice.

The standard weight-forward taper has a more even weight distribution over a greater portion of the line. It forms a smoother casting loop, slows down faster, and doesn't dump at the end of the cast. *The thinner, lighter front taper results in a more delicate fly landing.* The larger diameter of the saltwater taper also makes the line more wind resistant and thus more difficult to cast on windy days.

When casting with a weight-forward taper of any design, the caster should start with as much of the heavy portion outside the rod tip as possible. This reduces the number of false casts before shooting the line. When retrieving, try to keep the weighted part of the line outside the guides; this allows you to pick up and make a better cast. The angler who is not sure of the best pickup length can install a nail knot in the line at the point most comfortable to him. Use six- or eight-pound monofilament for the knot. *Be sure to draw the knot well down into the finish.* This never interferes with casting, and you can easily feel this knot under your fingers as you strip in line. When you do, make your backcast.

The other line design that is very useful in many areas of saltwater fly fishing is the **shooting taper,** sometimes called a single taper, shooting head, or just head. Nearly all of the weight of this line is concentrated in the first thirty feet. Commercial lines usually have a heavy Dacron loop attached to the rear of the shooting head. To this you connect either monofilament or an extra-thin fly line called a running or shooting line (usually a size 2, 3, or 4 fly line).

The casting concept is basically the same as with a weight-forward line. The heavy thirty-foot front portion is held outside the guides, and on the final forward cast the line is released. The much thinner shooting line is easily pulled through the guides for a considerable distance to the target. Shooting heads allow you to make much longer casts than with any other kind of line taper. They are often the best choice when you need to search a great deal of water with your fly. But, you must use some caution concerning your commercial running or shooting lines. Some of them test less than fifteen pounds—and your leader may be stronger than that! However, stronger lines with a bit thicker diameter are available.

You can connect shooting heads to shooting lines by making a loop in the rear of the shooting head, and another in the shooting line, then loop-to-looping them together. This permits the angler to detach the head and exchange it on the scene for a different head. If you are going to use loops, they should be as small as possible, so that the connection flows smoothly through the fly-rod guides. To make this connection, I use the whipped loop (see chapter 5 for tying instructions). If you use commercial braided loops, don't depend upon the small plastic ring that is heat-shrunk to hold the loop in place. Instead, make a nail knot or whipped loop to secure commercial braided loops.

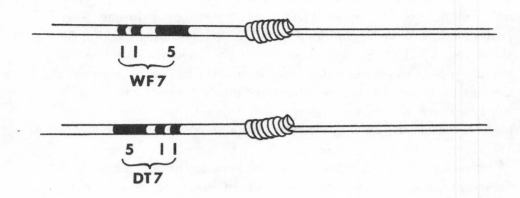

Fly-Line Sizes

Most fly fishermen will end up with a number of fly lines. Sometimes it becomes confusing to determine the size of a line. There is a simple method of marking fly lines (with a large permanent marker) so that you always know their weight. A long, circular mark (half an inch in length) means a number five and a short ring around the line means a one. If the circular mark is placed to the front, as illustrated, the line is a weight-forward. If the small marks are positioned in front, the line is a double-taper.

FLY-LINE DENSITIES

Fly lines (including shooting heads) come in various densities. Some float, some sink slowly, some sink faster, and some sink at a very rapid rate—a few even have a portion that floats and a part that sinks. The **floating line** is the most useful. It's the one line that a saltwater fly rodder should always consider having with him. But, it can be more difficult to cast into a breeze because it contains buoyant materials (glass bubbles filled with air) and is larger in diameter than other lines. A floating line is used when fishing in water less than six feet deep. Because it floats, the line is the easiest to lift from the water for the backcast. It is the line to use with any surface lure such as a popping bug.

Another line that has become exceedingly popular with many experienced saltwater fly rodders is the **intermediate** or **very slow-sinking line**. This line will cast better into a breeze, and it barely sinks—both great advantages. It also allows you to get the fly deeper a little quicker than with a floating line. When floating grass and debris litter the water's surface, a floating line "funnels" the grass down to the leader and fly on the retrieve. The intermediate line is retrieved just below the surface, however, and picks up less debris. On choppy days, a floating fly line rides up and down on the surface, giving the fly an unnatural motion, while a line that is a little below the surface eliminates the problem. Because of all these advantages, the intermediate line has become extremely popular. *But, I feel that the Scientific Anglers Wet Cel II line is a better choice.* This line sinks a little faster than an intermediate, casts a bit easier into a breeze, and yet can be fished almost like an intermediate. If you haven't tried a Wet Cel II, I suggest that you do.

A **sinking-tip** is a very useful line on the flats, when seeking species such as redfish, seatrout, stripers, bluefish, flounders, and many others. The first ten feet of the line sinks and the remainder floats. Manufacturers also make sinking-tip lines so that the tip sinks at various rates. This line is perhaps the most unpleasant of all fly lines to cast, and those with an extra-fast-sinking tip are even more difficult to handle. It is best to try to make an open-loop cast with all sinking-tip fly lines to get a better presentation. Yet, despite the undesirable characteristics of the line, it is the best choice for many kinds of fishing. Because the tip sinks and the rest of the line floats, it is easier to make a backcast than it would be with a full-sinking line.

Two other fly lines are used in the salt effectively: the **super-fast-sinking lines** made by Cortland and Scientific Anglers. They are required when you are trying to get the fly down deep, such as offshore over a reef, or where the current is powerful. Both of these lines are difficult to cast until you have mastered their special properties. *Once the simple technique is mastered, however, they are usually easier to throw than other lines.* The extra-fast-sinking lines, such as the Scientific Anglers Deep Water Express, are conventional fly lines loaded with tungsten dust (much heavier than lead dust) in the coating so that they bomb toward the bottom. They can be purchased as shooting tapers or as weight-forward lines. The lead-core shooting head (usually about thirty feet of lead-core trolling line attached to 100 feet of shooting line) will drive a fly deeper than almost any other type of fly line. Some anglers attach monofilament on the lead head, but when the fast-traveling head is released on the forward cast it tends to lift the entire mass of monofilament off the deck, jamming it in the guides. These specially designed shooting lines made by Cortland and Scientific Anglers work much better. Dan Blanton, who knows as much about shooting heads as

Fly-Line Weight

Sinking lines can be cast on a greater range of fly rods than floating lines. With floating lines, it's a good idea to match the rod to the line. For example, if you are casting with a rod that calls for an 8-weight line, it's best to use an 8-weight floating line. But, the same rod can easily cast a 9- or 10-weight sinking line.

This same technique applies to shooting heads. Because heads are usually shorter, it's best to use a head at least one size heavier than the rod calls for. For example, use at least a nine-weight line on a rod calling for an eight-weight line.

anyone alive, says that if the boat deck is kept wet, monofilament line will shoot almost trouble-free most of the time. It's a good tip that I have used to my advantage.

A line that has revolutionized much of saltwater fly fishing is the **Teeny series.** They are really an improved, or modified, shooting head. Jim Teeny designed these lines after he realized that almost all sinking fly lines were designed with a front taper. The thinner front portion did not sink as fast as the heavier belly. This caused the fly line to swim deeper in the water column than the fly. Jim designed the entire forward sinking portion as a level line. That meant that the front taper sank at the same rate as the belly. This carried the fly much deeper than conventional fly lines.

Jim went farther in the design, too. He made the entire rear of the fly line float. Full-sinking lines never shoot as well on the forward cast. Floating lines shoot better. With a stroke of genius, Jim Teeny made the sinking portion one color, and the thin shooting line another color. When the line was retrieved, the angler knew exactly when the sinking portion arrived at the rod tip on the retrieve, thus knowing to begin his backcast.

The weight of a Teeny line is easy to identify. Different-weight lines have a different color for the floating portion. Each line is identified by a number from 200 to 650. For example, a Teeny 300 means that the sinking portion of the line weighs 300 grains. All of the Teeny sinking lines that end in a round number (200, 300, 400) are eighty-two feet long, with a belly never longer than twenty-seven feet. All Teeny sinking lines that have a number ending in 50 (350, 450, 550) have a thirty-foot sinking head and are longer than eighty feet.

The Teeny lines have virtually replaced lead-core shooting heads. In fact, I have found that the 650-grain Teeny line actually sinks faster than a lead-core line.

Many people try using a lead-core shooting head or a sinking line (such as the Teeny) and give up. They complain that it is the most difficult line to cast. The truth is that if they modify their casting a little, it becomes the *easiest* of all fly lines to cast.

When casting sinking lines, you shouldn't cast them the same way you do a floating fly line. That's when the problem occurs. With a floating line we are taught to throw a tight loop and a fast backcast, which eliminates slack and allows us to make a better forward cast. *A tight loop and a fast backcast are the last things you want to do with a sinking line.* Instead, you want to throw as slow a cast behind you as possible, and here's the catch—*with a wide loop.*

The problem with sinking lines is that a fast backcast means that the line is flying away from the target. Then a forward cast is made and the abrupt change in the direction of the cast causes shock waves, tangles, and knots. But, by making a slow backcast with a wide loop you are able to change direction slowly—thus you get a smooth cast. Imagine the way a boat trailer follows a car around a curve—that's what you want to do with the backcast. The leader and fly should swing around a curve. Once the backcast straightens behind you, you can make a good, normal forward cast. Once the car and trailer round the curve, the car can safely accelerate!

Here is how you accomplish this. As the retrieve ends, you simply can't yank a sinking line out of the water for a backcast. Instead, make a roll cast and lift the line into the air. Generally, a backcast is made while the line is roll casting in the air in front of the angler. That demands making a fast backcast—and trouble! Instead, use what is called a water haul. Many writers have suggested a water haul is used to achieve an even better loading of the fly rod. But, you use the water haul for a totally different reason—*to make the slowest backcast possible.*

A water haul is made this way. The sinking line is retrieved to the rod tip. Then a roll cast lifts the line out of the water. Allow the line to unroll on the surface. *When the end of the fly line touches down on the surface, make a slow drawing of the fly line to the rear.* Because the sinking fly line will remain on the surface as long as you make a slow-drawing motion, a very gentle, slow backcast can be made. When you're ready to throw the line behind you, deliberately make a large loop. When the backcast straightens behind you, make your normal forward cast. Perfect this and you'll find that sinking fly lines and heavy flies (such as heavily weighted Clouser Minnows) can be cast easier than floating lines. That's because the weight of the line, once you get it moving, actually aids in getting distance on the cast.

RODS

There is no one fly rod that will do it all in the salt. In many saltwater situations the rod must cast the fly well and also be designed to fight big fish. The size range of flies in freshwater fly fishing is not great. But, in salt water it may take a huge popper to entice a cobia or a fly as large as a brook trout to interest a seven-foot billfish. Yet, for bonefish, the angler will be required to drop a tiny, size six, sparsely dressed fly delicately enough on the surface to prevent spooking his quarry.

Another problem unique to salt water is the *lifting power* that must be built into rods for many fish-fighting situations. For example, when you have an amberjack, tarpon, or tuna down deep, the only way to bring the fish up to the boat is by physically lifting it with the line and rod. Freshwater rods do not need this kind of muscle.

Rod length is an important consideration. An offshore angler battling tuna on conventional heavy trolling tackle would never consider using a rod longer than seven feet. There has been a myth among fly fishermen that the shorter the rod, the more sporting the angler. Nothing could be farther from the truth. The shorter the rod, the greater the leverage that can be applied against the fish. The most effective fish-fighting rod I've ever owned was an

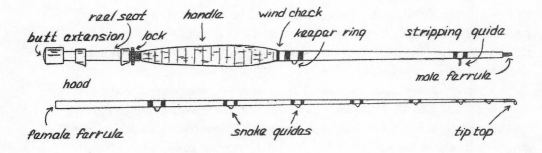

ROD NOMENCLATURE

eight-foot spinning rod originally used for deep jigging that I converted to a fly rod. It cast like hell, but it would kill a fish faster than anything I've ever used.

For general fish fighting of larger species, both offshore and in the shallows, a rod of nine feet offers good leverage and casting qualities. A nine-footer is also good for wading on flats (such as those in Texas) for redfish and seatrout. It helps get the fly off the water easier and keeps the backcast up. My all-time favorite for bonefish is a four-piece nine-footer that casts an eight-weight line. Rods longer than nine feet are very tiring when you must make many long casts. Fortunately, rod builders are now aware of our problems and a number of excellent rods for various saltwater fly-fishing situations are now available.

Bamboo is simply not practical for saltwater fly fishing. Glass rods dominated the saltwater scene for years, and improved "S" glass blanks today are still exceptionally good tools and cost less than graphite. Graphite, when it first appeared, did poorly, mainly because it did not have good hoop strength and broke under the strain of big fish. But, when combined with glass—and new designs in the scrim (hoop strength)—it makes rods that

You need a fly rod with a stout butt to land a bigger shark, as John Abplanalp is doing here.

are state of the art. Almost any graphite rod made today is going to do a good job.

If you're concerned about selecting a rod for giant tarpon or an off-shore species, where lifting power is a necessity, you can make a simple check. Run the line through the rod guides until six inches extend beyond the tip; attach a five-pound weight. Lift the rod—if the butt section bends deeply, the rod is too soft. There should be a good bit of straightness left in the butt under such treatment. Many of the modern rods have a fast tip that aids in casting and a stiffer butt section that aids in fighting larger fish. For years there was a trend to use only 12- and 13-weight fly rods for giant tarpon. But, unless you plan to fight tarpon exceeding 150 pounds (and few will), a modern 10- or 11-weight rod will be adequate. The best part about using 10- and 11-weight rods is that they are lighter and cast so much better. This is so helpful to fly fishermen who don't have much experience, because if you can't get the fly there, the game is lost.

FLY-ROD GUIDES

The hardware that comes with a rod is a vital consideration in saltwater fly fishing. The type and size of guides is important. Most fly rods today carry one or more space-age ceramic guides on the butt section. One company for which I helped design a rod constructed a casting machine to test rod performance. We determined that a fly line doesn't enter the guides smoothly like a slithering snake going down a hole, but instead often forms coils of line that strike the guides and overlap before finally going through. This overlap reduces the effective casting distance. Based on the results from the machine, we worked out that the smallest stripping- or butt-guide size for all fly rods carrying a seven line or larger is sixteen millimeters. Because of this I do believe that one modification should be made to all fly rods that are used in the salt. Just about any commercial fly rod has a stripping guide that's too small. Saltwater fly rodders have to shoot a lot more line than their freshwater buddies. All line shot at the target must first enter the stripping guide. I believe that a twenty-millimeter guide is the *smallest* that anyone should consider for rods 7-weight and larger. For 9- through 12-weight rods I favor twenty-five millimeters. Such a large guide allows line to almost always get through. But, a guide this big doesn't look attractive in the store and can affect sales. I think for this reason rod manufacturers are reluctant to install them. However, any competent fly shop has someone who can replace a smaller guide with a larger one.

Many times when a fish takes off after the strike the line has a knot when entering the guides. For that reason, saltwater rods should be armed with the largest snake guides possible—and a large tip-top. While all knots won't go through, the larger the guides, the better your chances. Every fly fisherman will eventually strike a fish that will escape, causing a knot to develop in the running line. If the rod is held in the normal position, that line is supported on the guides. That means as the knot gets well up on the rod, it will catch on each of the snake guides. That's when the leader breaks. To avoid this, if you see a knot approaching the guides, *turn the rod upside down*. The line and knot will run along the rod blank—where there is the largest possible space. You'll be amazed at how many times a knotted line slithers through the guides with the rod held upside down.

FIGHTING GRIPS

Fighting grips on rods used for tarpon and offshore species are really not necessary, but some anglers find them helpful. However, the grip should not be so large that it stiffens the blank and interferes with casting efficiency. The problem with gripping the fighting butt while battling a fish is that all of the rod below the grip is not used in the battle. This bottom section is the most powerful part of the rod. For maximum leverage on the fish, you need to slide the hand holding the rod in front of the cork handle. However, unless you have had long experience at fighting big fish, this can be a tiring method of holding the rod. People who don't have much experience, or are not very strong, can use the fighting grip not so much for the battle but for breathing periods, so the hand can relax a bit.

FIGHTING BUTTS

Sometimes a fighting butt is called for. This is a short length of material that juts out from the bottom of the rod. The idea is that it can be positioned against the body during the fight. This serves as a pivot point when pumping the fish and helps keep the reel a bit away from the body when winding line. Yet, there are also disadvantages to a fighting butt. A butt too long will snag the fly line on the shoot. Few seasoned saltwater anglers use a butt extension longer than two inches, finding that length to be more than ample for their efforts. The shape of the butt is also important. Butts that have a sharp edge can bruise the stomach. The best-designed butts have a large rounded end, usually made of soft neoprene. Some rod builders make an extension butt of threaded aluminum. Corrosion soon makes these useless. The best butts are generally made of the same noncorrosive material as the rod and are built up to give a comfortable rounded end. Rods with butt extensions also have the advantage of being easily storable in boat rod holders.

ROD HANDLES AND REEL SEATS

There are various shapes of rod handles; the Half Wells and Full Wells are the only ones most of us consider good shapes for saltwater fly fishing. The Phillippe Cigar and Hardy shapes have the front of the handle tapering away from the thumb when casting. The Half and Full Wells have a swelling at the forward end of the handle where the thumb is pressed during casting. This gives good support and aids in casting.

Most reels have a foot length of about 2½ inches, but one manufacturer insists on making his 2⅝ inches long. Be sure that the reel seat on your rod will accommodate the reel you plan to use. The best hardware for the seat is still chrome-plated brass, although many aluminum seats with good anodizing are excellent and lighter.

CARING FOR YOUR ROD

After fishing, the reel should be removed from the rod and washed in warm water to get rid of any salt accumulation. A piece of panty hose pulled

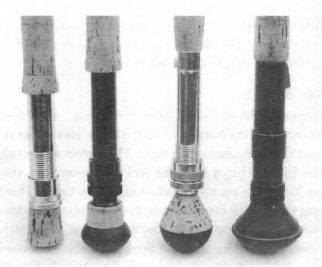

There are various extension butts used on saltwater fly rods. The left butt has sharp edges and would be uncomfortable; the larger and rounder the butt cap (within reason), the more comfortable it is.

through a guide will catch on any crack or burr, indicating that the guide should be replaced. Rod handles can get slimy and hard to handle, so clean them routinely with warm water and soap. On board a boat, rods should always be stored in their holders. To prevent excessive wear at the ferrule and to prevent tips flying off on a cast, lubricate the male portion of a glass, graphite, or boron rod with a candle.

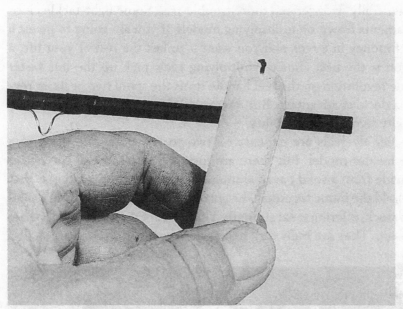

The male portion of a modern fly-rod ferrule occasionally requires lubrication to keep it from coming apart. Just a few strokes with a candle will do the job.

 **REELS**

Many modern-day catches would be impossible to handle on the reels designed for freshwater fishing. While many people regard the reel as a line-storage device—and that's true for much of freshwater fishing—it should certainly not be regarded so in salt water.

For many years saltwater fly fishermen had only two companies that made reels they had confidence in. If you wanted to fish seriously for salt-water species, you bought either a Fin-Nor or a Seamaster. I have several models of these reels that are more than thirty years old—and they perform as well today as they did when I first got them. But, fortunately, in the past few years a number of truly outstanding fly reels have been developed, so that the angler can now select from a wide variety, choosing the one that best suits his purpose.

There are three basic types of fly reels: automatic, single-action, and multiplying. **Automatic reels** are useless for the serious fly fisherman. They have no drag to speak of, carry too little line, and salt water corrodes them almost overnight. **Single-action reels** are preferred by saltwater fly rodders. They are generally stronger and more trouble-free. Some light-tackle clubs and tournaments frown on multiplying models. If you are going to invest a good bit of money in a reel, and you want it to last the rest of your life, a single-action is the best choice. **Multiplying reels** pick up the line faster because one revolution on the reel handle turns the spool two or more revolutions—a decided advantage. But, the necessary gearing and design often cause a slight sacrifice in durability.

Saltwater fly reels are expensive—two to ten times the price of a decent freshwater model. But there are justifications. Most of the better reels are made from a solid bar of aluminum, turned out on a lathe so that no screws hold the frame together. The spools are also produced from a solid aluminum stock, offering great strength. The reels are then anodized to prevent corrosion. They are built very precisely—most reel makers are skilled

Modern heavy-duty saltwater fly reels are usually made from a solid section of aluminum, which is then plated to resist corrosion. Shown here are the steps in making a Billy Pate fly reel.

machinists who got hooked on fishing and transferred their efforts. These reels are the jewels of the machinist's trade.

There are some guidelines that you can use to select a top-flight saltwater fly reel that will stand up to a lifetime of use. I think that almost all serious fly rodders will agree that the fewer moving parts a reel has, the better. One of the greatest compliments I've heard about a current model came from a competitor who grumbled, "Hell, that reel doesn't have anything in it." The fewer parts, the fewer failures you can expect on the fishing grounds; that's why many salmon reels have never been popular in the salt.

Some people put too much emphasis on reel weight, claiming they want the lightest reel made. But, fly reels get knocked around in boats, and in rough seas they can be dropped. Light reel frames are going to bend, so buy a reel that will be rugged.

There are many fine reels available to saltwater fly fishermen today. Shown here are just some of the popular models:
Top Row—Tibor.
Middle Row (left to right)—Ross, Orvis DXR, Islander, and Billy Pate.
Bottom Row (left to right)—Lamson, Catino, Sage, and Scientific Anglers.

The handle on the reel is important. The better-designed reels carry only one handle. Its shape can mean aggravation or comfort. One of the best handles for an antireverse reel is on the Billy Pate model. It's a flat handle, one inch long, with a textured gripping surface.

Handles on direct-drive reels should be designed totally differently. A direct-drive reel, when you wind it, recovers line. When the fish pulls out line, the handle spins. That can mean some banged-up fingers. I've witnessed fly fishermen using direct-drive reels on fast-running fish, where they barked their knuckles so much that their blood was splattered on their shirts. A handle on a direct-drive reel should be short—no longer than three-quarters of an inch—and it should taper, allowing the short handle to be released quickly.

A reel should have only drag or resistance when the fish takes out line. A few reels require cranking against the drag setting, which can be very tiring. Also, check the reel for sharp edges; some can be painful to hold during a fight.

Reels come in various sizes. The largest have spools of about four inches in diameter. Such reels pick up line incredibly fast and are terrific when fighting fast-running fish like sails and big tarpon, but are really too big for perhaps 80 percent of saltwater fly-rodding situations. They work fine, but you simply don't need reels that large and heavy. However, at least one current model has a spool that is hollow in the center, with the line held on the outer portion. This allows the angler the benefit of high-speed line recovery, which smaller-diameter spools don't have.

Fly reels for the salt can probably be placed into two categories: those that will hold 250 yards or more of thirty-pound backing, and those that will hold about 200 yards. These smaller reels generally need only be loaded with twenty-pound backing for most saltwater situations. A good bonefish reel, for example, should hold about 150 yards and a size 8 line. Few inshore species are going to run off half that much line. But, for big tarpon and some of the offshore species, the larger model is a decided advantage.

A wide spool offers additional line capacity without making the total reel seem much bigger. But, be careful—even the best anglers will sometimes, in the heat of battle, forget to spool the line on evenly. If it begins pulling on one side, it can suddenly collapse and the tangle can mean the loss of a good fish. Most seasoned anglers prefer spools that are narrow with wide arbors, rather than a wide reel with a small arbor. Don't forget that as line diminishes on the spool, drag increases. This is an important point to consider when fighting long-running fish.

RIGHT VS. LEFT HAND

There is a never-ending debate whether the reel should be worked with the left or the right hand. Let me emphasize a point: if you are right-handed, you will probably do better reeling with your right hand. The major problem in fighting long-running fish is not whether you can raise the rod on the pump, but how well and fast you can recover the line for extended periods of time. It takes more dexterity to turn that tiny handle many revolutions than it does to lift the rod. The argument that you have to shift hands to start reeling doesn't hold water, for on a long-running fish you have plenty of time to shift hands. A right-hander who uses spinning tackle will wind the reel with his left and. But, the same right-hander will reel a plug-casting reel with his right hand. Why is that? First, it is very difficult to buy a left-hand-wind plug reel, since most reels are sold to right-handers. Second, a spinning-reel handle turns in fairly wide circles, and people have no trouble doing this with their nondominant hand. But, a plug-casting reel turns in tiny circles, and a right-hander will almost always be smoother and more efficient if he uses his right hand.

There is another and surer way to convince any right-hander which hand he should wind with. Use two fly reels that are the same. Pull off all the fly line and about fifty feet of backing from each reel. Make sure you have the same amount of line off each spool. Then, have a friend look at his watch and begin to wind as quickly as you can. Time the period it takes to spool all the line onto the reel with one hand. Then, with the second reel, use the other hand to repeat the experiment. In my fishing seminars I find that regardless of how long a right-hander has been winding line with his left hand, he can make better time with his right hand.

DRAG

Aside from the strength of construction found in saltwater reels, the major difference between a freshwater and a saltwater fly reel is the drag. Drag doesn't mean much in most freshwater angling but it means everything in many saltwater situations. Some reel manufacturers are proud that they can put twenty or forty or even more pounds of drag on their reel. That's nonsense! In most fish-fighting conditions you will want less than a pound of drag and the better the angler, the less mechanical drag is required.

The skilled fisherman brings his fingers and hands into play. One writer/angler made a great point about catching a large fish on a reel without a drag, but he had a click built into the reel that required one pound of force before the spool would revolve. It was all the "drag" that he needed—or wanted! What is critical is that the drag release line smoothly. A leader is almost always broken when a jerk occurs against it—and I like to say that the jerk is usually at the reel end. If the drag is smooth throughout the first few pounds of adjustment it will probably serve you well.

An easy way to test a drag's smoothness is to tie the leader to a car bumper and have the car move off at about ten miles an hour against a drag setting of about a pound. While holding the rod tip at about 45 degrees, watch the tip. If it jumps around like a conductor's baton, the drag is not releasing smoothly.

One other factor is critical concerning drags. Some reels carry a very small drag-adjustment nut that only needs to be turned a short distance to go from minimum to maximum setting. That's dangerous in a fish fight, for it is too easy to overadjust the drag. The adjustment nut should be large enough to change pressure over a fairly wide range.

Harry Kime, a pioneering saltwater fly fisherman on the West Coast and one of the most innovative anglers I know, developed years ago one of the neatest drags for reels with a rim control. By attaching a paddle-shaped piece of belt leather to the brace on the bottom of the reel he can get the drag he needs by pressing the leather paddle, which puts pressure against the revolving rim of the spool. The best features are that it can be released instantly if the fish should bolt away, and that it can be easily added to any rim-control reel.

I am constantly amazed at how reel manufacturers keep coming up with new brake materials. Airline brake disks have been used, along with a huge variety of other materials. There is a very true saying: "If it ain't broke—don't fix it." When Fin-Nor produced the first quality saltwater fly reel decades ago, these reels carried a type of drag that has certainly stood the test of time. Fortunately, it is still the most commonly used. This drag is a large, single disk of specially designed cork composition that is glued to the spool and contacts another large surface in the reel. A large washer such as this enables you to obtain a wide range of smooth pressure, and it has enough surface to eliminate heat and reduce wear. There are numerous guides who have used a reel with such a drag for ten or more seasons without changing it. The only maintenance needed is a small amount of lubricant applied to the cork disk. Use the lubricating material recommended by the manufacturer.

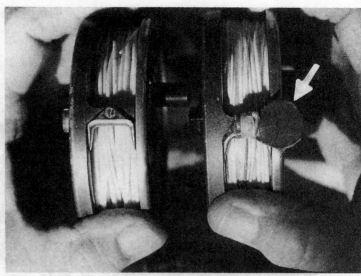

The most important thing to understand about fly reels is that those with soft washers in the drag system—and that's nearly all—need the drag pressure to be released, every day after fish-

Reels that have the rim of the spool exposed—so you can push against it to obtain drag—can be modified simply (as shown) to create a great drag. Use a piece of an old belt for the leather drag pressure plate. Zane Grey used a leather pad on his ocean reels to subdue big fish before the days of modern drags.

ing, to prevent crushing the washers' elasticity and ruining the drag's performance. *Unless you release the pressure at the end of the day, the compression will eventually squeeze the life out of the soft washers, and your drag will deteriorate.*

CARE OF REELS

Even the finest anodized fly reels can eventually be marred or even ruined by saltwater exposure. A small amount of care after each fishing trip is recommended and will ensure a lifetime of good service from the high-quality reels.

Setting a fly rod and reel on the dock and then turning a hose on it is not a good idea. The heavy flush of water drives salt inside the reel, where it can go to work on the internal parts. Preventive measures are always better. Simply don't let your reel get a good spraying of salt water if it can be helped. And, never sit a fly reel down in the dirt—or worse, the sand. Don't delay in cleaning it when you return to the dock.

Cold water will only rid the reel of a small amount of dried salt. Salt is more soluble in warm water and a little soap. Dip a rag or small sponge in the warm soapy solution and wipe off all reel parts. On occasion it's a

Some reels, such as the inexpensive Pflueger Medalist, originally designed for freshwater use, can easily be modified for some saltwater situations. In this case, the drag is not sufficient for many fish. To correct this, cut out a portion of the reel (as shown). Be careful not to damage any of the insides of the reel. Smooth the edges and replace the spool.

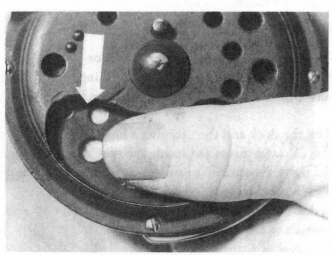

By routing out a portion of the Pflueger Medalist reel (as shown), the thumb can be pushed against the reel spool to apply needed drag pressure. Some large fish can be caught this way.

good idea to use a toothbrush to tease the soapy water into the hard-to-clean places, such as where the foot is positioned on the reel. After the reel is dry, you can lightly oil it, but I prefer to use hard, paste, car wax. A good coating of wax rubbed on all reel surfaces will resist salt corrosion better than anything I know.

Occasionally oil the handles; there may be times when you will have to remove the handle, clean the shaft, and give it a light coating of good grease. If a fish has made a long run into the backing, it's a good idea to clean it (see page 63). Finally, it bears repeating that you should, after each day's fishing, back off the drag-adjustment nut so that the compression doesn't ruin the soft washers.

Some Available Reels

Reel Name	Spool Diameter (inches)	Weight (ounces)	Capacity	Comments
AARON				
SS78/TR78	3.25	7.6	250 yds 20 lb + 7 line	direct-drive and rim
			225 yds 20 lb + 8 line	control
			190 yds 20 lb + 9 line	
SS910/TR910	3.67	10.9	275 yds 20 lb + 8 line	direct-drive, antireverse,
			250 yds 20 lb + 9 line	and rim control
			200 yds 30 lb + 10 line	
SS101/TR101	3.85	10.3	325 yds 30 lb + 10 line	
			300 yds 30 lb + 11 line	
SS121/TR1213	3.85	12.5	450 yds 30 lb + 11 line	
			425 yds 30 lb + 12 line	
			400 yds 30 lb + 13 line	
ABEL (all Abel reels feature rim control)				
Model 2	2.75	7.8	225 yds 20 lb + 8 line	direct-drive
Model 3N	3.375	8.3	190 yds 20 lb + 9 line	direct-drive
Model 3	3.375	10.0	250 yds 30 lb + 10 line	direct-drive
Model 4	3.375	11.5	300 yds 30 lb + 12 line	direct-drive
Model 5	3.375	14.5	800 yds 30 lb + 12 line	direct-drive
(Note: models with "A/R" are antireverse style)				
Model 3N A/R	3.375	8.8	150 yds 20 lb + 10 line	
Model 3 A/R	3.375	10.0	375 yds 20 lb + 10 line	
Model 4 A/R	3.375	12.0	300 yds 30 lb + 12 line	
Model 4.5 A/R	3.920	13.0	400 yds 30 lb + 13 line	
ATH				
S1	3½	6.9	300 yds 20 lb + 8 line	direct-drive
S2	3¾	7.7	350 yds 20 lb + 9 line	direct-drive
Rainbow	3½	10.9	300 yds 20 lb + 10 line	direct-drive
Stu Apte (bonefish–permit)	3½	11.2	350 yds 20 lb + 9 line	
Stu Apte (tarpon–sailfish)	4½	13.3	500 yds 30 lb + 12 line	
L. L. BEAN				
TideMaster (all models have rim control and direct-drive)				
Model #1	3.33	7.8	150 yds 20 lb + 8 line	
Model #2	3.73	8.9	200 yds 20 lb + 10 line	
Model #3	3.95	11.3	275 yds 30 lb + 11 line	
BILLY PATE (these four reels come in antireverse and direct-drive)				
Bonefish	3.125	8.5	300 yds 20 lb + 8 line	
Salmon	3.25	8	200 yds 20 lb + 9 line	
Tarpon	3.5	13	350 yds 30 lb + 10 line	
Marlin	4	15	600 yds 30 lb + 12 line	
CHARLTON				
Signature Series (all models are direct-drive with rim control; Signature series Titanium add 3.7 ounces to Model 8500 and 8600 weights)				
Model 8400—1.2	3.00	9.9	150 yds 20 lb + 8 line	
Model 8400—1.6	3.00	10.6	200 yds 20 lb + 10 line	
Model 8500—8	3.75	11.6	240 yds 20 lb + 8 line	
Model 8500—1.2	3.75	12.3	450 yds 20 lb + 10 line	
Model 8500—1.6	3.75	13.2	375 yds 30 lb + 12 line	
Model 8600	4.75	15.9	425 yds 30 lb + 12 line	

CORTLAND (all models have antireverse and rim control)			
AR-6	$2\frac{3}{4}$	6.6	150 yds 20 lb + 8 line
AR-8	3	7.8	200 yds 20 lb + 8 line
AR-10	$3\frac{1}{4}$	8.6	250 yds 20 lb + 10 line
FIN-NOR (can be ordered in direct-drive or antireverse; all have rim control)			
Model #2	$3\frac{3}{8}$	8.75	200 yds 20 lb + 8 line
Model #3	$3\frac{7}{8}$	10.25	200 yds 30 lb + 10 line
Model #4	$3\frac{7}{8}$	11.0	450 yds 30 lb + 12 line
Model #4-1/2		12.5	450 yds 30 lb + 12 line
Model #5	$4\frac{1}{2}$	14.5	700 yds 30 lb + 15 line
ISLANDER (can be ordered in direct-drive or antireverse; all have rim control and quick left-to right-hand-wind change) (Note: model with AR is antireverse; model with FR is direct-drive)			
Model #1	3.33	7.8	175 yds 20 pound + 7 line
Model #2	3.73	8.9	250 yds 20 lb + 8 line
Model #3	3.95	11.3	275 yds 30 lb + 11 line
Model #4	3.95	11.8	350 yds 30 lb + 12 line
Model #5	4.50	15.7	425 yds 30 lb + 12 line
Model #6		16.5	500 yds 30 lb + 12 line
Lamson (all models are direct-drive with rim control)			
SW #1	$3\frac{1}{8}$	$8\frac{3}{4}$	150 yds 20 lb + 7 line
SW #2	$3\frac{1}{8}$	$9\frac{1}{4}$	250 yds 20 lb + 8 line
SW #3	$3\frac{9}{16}$	$11\frac{3}{8}$	250 yds 30 lb + 10 line
SW #4	$3\frac{3}{4}$	$11\frac{5}{8}$	300 yds 30 lb + 13 line
SW #5	4	$12\frac{3}{8}$	600 yds 30 lb + 13 line
MARTIN (all reels are direct-drive with disk drag)			
SD910	$3\frac{1}{2}$	8.0	220 yds 20 lb + 9 line
SD1011	$3\frac{1}{2}$	10.0	220 yds 30 lb + 10 line
SD1213	$4\frac{1}{4}$	12.0	350 yds 30 lb + 12 line
MZ78	$3\frac{1}{2}$	7.6	200 yds 20 lb + 8 line
MZ910	$3\frac{1}{2}$	8.5	200 yds 30 lb + 9 line
MZ1011	$3\frac{1}{2}$	9.6	300 yds 30 lb + 10 line
ORVIS			
Odyssey (all models are antireverse with rim control)			
Odyssey III	3.75	9.5	250 yds 20 lb + 9 line
Odyssey IV	3.875	11	350 yds 30 lb + 12 line
ORVIS DXR models (these can be ordered direct-drive or antireverse)			
DXR 7/8	3.375	6.625	200 yds 20 lb + 7 line
DXR 9/10	3.75	7.75	225 yds 20 lb + 10 line
DXR Tarpon	4	12.1	275 yds 30 lb + 10 line
PENN International (all models are direct-drive with rim control)			
International 1.5	$2\frac{5}{8}$	7.0	150 yds 20 lb + 6 line
International 2.5	$2\frac{15}{16}$	10.0	250 yds 20 lb + 9 line
International 4	$3\frac{15}{16}$	13.0	450 yds 30 lb + 12 line
ROSS SALTWATER SERIES (all models are direct-drive with rim control)			
Model SW-III	3.75	7.2	250 yds 30 lb + 10 line
Model SW-IV	4.00	7.9	275 yds 30 lb + 12 line
Model SW-V	4.50	9.5	400 yds 30 lb + 12 line
(Note: Ross offers a number of models useful in saltwater though not especially designed for it; see their Gunnison, R-Series, and Cimarron models.)			
SCIENTIFIC ANGLERS SYSTEM 2 REELS (all models are direct-drive with rim control; convert to left- or right-hand wind)			
Model–78L	$3\frac{1}{2}$	7.8	275 yds 20 lb + 7 line
Model–89	$3\frac{3}{4}$	8.8	375 yds 20 lb + 8 line
Model–1011	$3\frac{3}{4}$	9.5	440 yds 20 lb + 10 line
Model–1213	4	10.4	400 yds 30 lb + 11 line
TIBOR (all reels are direct-drive with rim control)			
Everglades	$3\frac{3}{4}$	$8\frac{1}{2}$	200 yds 20 lb + 8 line
Riptide	4	$9\frac{1}{2}$	200 yds 30 lb + 10 line
Gulfstream	$4\frac{3}{8}$	11	300 yds 30 lb + 12 line

CHAPTER 5

Knots

and

Leaders

There are hundreds of knots, some good, some better, and some very bad. Fortunately, a saltwater fly fisherman need not learn a host of knots. If you master the following, you can go anywhere in the world and know that you will be able to make a connection to backing, line, leader, or fly that will serve you well.

I would like to emphasize the most important factor in building good knots, whether it is tying a two-inch hawser to secure a ship to a dock or knotting a fragile 8X leader tippet to size 22 dry fly. *No knot breaks until it begins to slip.* A poorly designed knot that has been closed firmly will not fail as quickly as a well-designed knot that is not closed securely. Lubricating the monofilament helps secure the knot better. You can use spittle or water. It is not advisable to use silicone or another slippery substance. This certainly helps the coils close easier, but it may also allow the tag end to slither through under strain and lose a good fish. Tying an overhand knot in the tag end to prevent it from slipping through is only an indication that

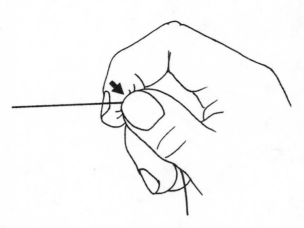

To determine if your monofilament is nicked, conduct this simple test. Place the mono over the inside of your first finger and then firmly press the thumbnail into the mono. Draw the monofilament through while pressing down. Any nicks will be evident as they are drawn over the thumbnail.

the knot was a poor one—or a good one closed poorly. There are some glues on the market that are specially designed to be used with nylon monofilament. These special glues will enhance knot strength. However, most of the cyanoacrylate glues are water soluble—a thing to remember.

It is extremely important when tying a knot to follow instructions carefully. *Especially critical is the number of turns you make around the standing line.* Most recommended knots have had many tests made with machines to determine the proper number of turns that should be made with the tag end. If a knot calls for four turns, and you only make three, there won't be enough turns around the standing line to keep the knot from slipping. If you make five turns (one too many) then you may not be able to close the knot firmly enough to prevent it from slipping.

Another factor in making the strongest knot is how well the coils within the knot are closed. Never overlap a coil. *If the coil overlaps it will break under severe strain.* For example, when building an Albright special, if the coils lie perfectly together the knot remains strong. But, if one coil crosses over another during closure, that is where the knot will break under stress. Too many fishermen are not aware that coils must come together within the knot without crossing over one another.

Laboratory experiments show that when tying monofilament lines of more than fifteen-pound test with bare hands, it is impossible to secure a knot to its full potential. Use gloves, pliers, or some device to ensure proper closure.

Fly fishermen frequently join two sections of monofilament that are of different diameters. This occurs when building tapered leaders and securing bite or shock tippets to the thinner tippet. *The knots will close easier and better if you use monofilaments of the same apparent limpness.* For example, if

Many anglers use 80- or 100-pound monofilament for a bite leader. When it is pulled off the spool, it is in tight coils and unusable. Cut eighteen-inch lengths and stuff them into a length of three-quarter-inch brass or copper tubing. Put the tube in a pot of water and bring the water to a boil. Remove the tube and drop it into cold water. All the strands of mono will be straight. Store them in a section of ½-inch plastic pipe (as shown).

you have hard or stiff monofilament and try to tie it to limper mono, the knot is very difficult to close well.

You may have been using a knot for years that you feel is a good one. Then, someone shows you one that's new to you and claims it to be better. There is a simple test to determine which knot is better. Take two hooks from the same box. Tie your favorite knot to one hook. Then, using the new knot, attach the

To keep eighty-pound (or stronger) monofilament bite leaders straight, and to have the leaders ready-rigged, many anglers use a box like this. The hook is held tight by a rubber band and the leader is stored in a groove on the other side. This particular box is sold by World-Wide Sportsman, but other tackle companies sell similar storage boxes.

second hook to the other end of the same length of mono. Take two pairs of pliers and grip each hook and slowly pull them apart until one knot breaks. Note which one broke. Repeat this test ten times to be sure. You need to conduct one other test. Some knots, such as the spider hitch, are great knots on a slow, steady pull, but fail miserably if a jerk occurs. *To test any knot properly you need to check it for both a steady pull and a quick jerk.* Tie your favorite knot in another strand of mono and the new knot on the other end. Grasp each end with pliers and *jerk* them until one knot fails. Note which failed. Do this ten times. If you have *carefully* tied both knots each time, you will have a conclusive test as to which knot is stronger. I'd like to emphasize that you need to conduct a minimum of ten tests with each method to get an idea of which knot is superior.

Finally, if you want to tie knots well, you need to practice them at home. While few fishermen will do this, tying a knot over and over at home does two things for you. It develops good technique so that the knot is as strong as possible. It also develops speed of operation. This permits you to make a faster connection on the water.

Following are the knots that once mastered will let you go anywhere in saltwater fly fishing and be confident of your connections.

WHIPPED LOOP

This connection has a number of uses. It can be made to connect leaders to fly lines, backing to fly lines, shooting heads to shooting lines, and other areas of rigging fly tackle. I much prefer the whipped loop to any other connection for attaching a leader to a fly line. Loops never hang up in the guides—going in or out. Most important, there are many times when you should change the leader on your line. If you are bonefishing in shallow water on a calm morning, for example, you may need a leader that is twelve feet or longer to prevent frightening the fish. Later, when the wind comes up, you may have trouble straightening that leader on the cast. Since the surface is rippled, you can use a much shorter leader. With a whipped loop, you simply remove one leader and loop on the desired one. Some people use a nail knot to attach a short length of monofilament. Then, they make a nail knot in the tag end of the mono. That has never made sense to me. The heavier monofilament tends to drown the front end of your fly line and it wears out after awhile. Incidentally, with a little practice, you can build a strong whipped loop in less than thirty seconds—less time than it would take to install a section of monofilament with a loop in the end.

Whipping a Loop in a Fly Line

Properly made, this loop will never fail and is stronger than the fly line. Cut the line end to a sharp taper. Use strong fly-tying thread (Kevlar, size A, or similar thread). Place on a fly-tying bobbin and then remove the spool and wrap the thread four times around one leg. Use four—not three or five—turns. This will give you the desired tension to whip the thread. Fold the fly line back so you will get a loop when finished of about a quarter inch. Make several wraps around the two folded loops so that the bobbin will hang free. Then, swing the bobbin to make wraps. The faster you swing the bobbin, the more secure the whipped joint. Make a wrap beyond the tapered end and back to the middle, and then lay a short loop of four- or six-pound-test monofilament on the wraps and make eight to ten more gentle wraps over the whipped section and the mono loop. Cut the thread and insert the end in the loop. Pull on the two ends of the mono loop; this will drag the cut end under the last wraps. Insert a nail or other small object in the loop and pull on the main line to test if you did a good job. If the loop pulls free, you didn't swing the bobbin firmly enough. Coat the wraps with Pliobond, Aqua-Seal, or a similar type of glue.

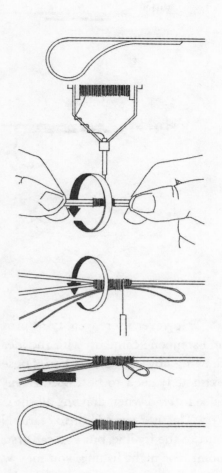

TUBE NAIL KNOT

This is perhaps the most commonly used connection to attach a leader to a fly line. It is easy to do and when properly made, it is a strong connection. It also flows well through the guides if correctly trimmed and if the joint is tapered smoothly with glue.

Joe Brooks, the famed outdoors writer of the 1950s and 1960s, discovered this knot when fishing in Argentina. Natives there used a tapered horseshoe nail to make the knot—hence the name "nail knot." Joe wrote about the knot in *Outdoor Life* and it was a revelation when compared to the various crude knots in use at the time.

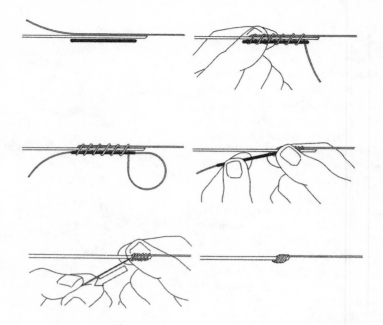

Tube nail knot.

However, there were tying problems encountered when using the nail and someone came up with the idea of using a tube. You can see from the drawing how the knot is tied. These coils (after the nail or tube had been extracted) need to be closed firmly. The smaller the tube, the less slack encountered when drawing all the coils tight.

This is a good knot to learn. Not only is it used to attach the leader butt to the fly line, but you can install this nail knot on your fly line at any point. For night fishing, you may want to place a knot where you would normally make a pickup for a backcast. For clear lines, such as those made from monofilament, it's advisable to place a nail knot where you can best lift the line from the water to backcast.

SURGEON'S KNOT

There are many fly-fishing situations where this knot is used to connect lines of two different diameters. It can also, of course, be used to connect two lines of the same diameter. But, it can also connect braided wire to a monofilament, a fact many fishermen don't realize. For many fly fishermen it is the preferred knot for building tapered leaders. When properly tied it has a knot strength exceeding 90 percent of the weaker of the

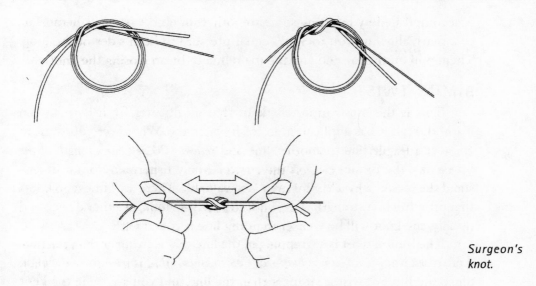

Surgeon's knot.

two lines used in the connection. I consider this one knot *every* fisherman should know.

The most important factor in building this knot so that it retains maximum strength is that after closure, *all four ends of the knot must be firmly pulled tight.*

SURGEON'S LOOP

This knot is made the same way as a surgeon's knot, except you double the end of the line to form a loop. It is vital to tighten all four ends. This

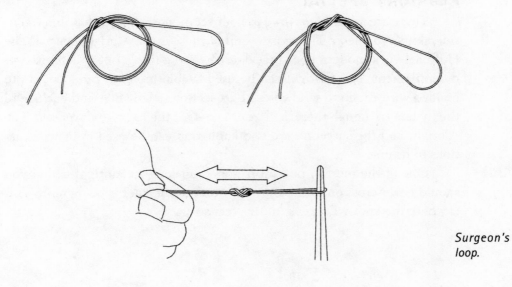

Surgeon's loop.

is accomplished by inserting some smooth, thin object (such as hemostats or a pen), allowing you to apply equal pressure to both sides of the loop. Then, pull on the tag end and the main line to finish closing the knot.

BIMINI TWIST

This is the most important knot that a saltwater fly fisherman can learn, though it has application in fresh water, too. Whenever you want to connect a fragile line to another line and *retain 100 percent strength of the fragile line*, the Bimini twist is the answer. Many fishermen do not understand the reason why a Bimini twist is so valuable. There are almost no knots that offer full line strength. Tie a knot to a swivel, hook, or other device and usually, the knot will be weaker than the line it is tied with.

The Bimini twist is a wrapping in the line that is stronger than the line. And, most important, *it is a loop—or two strands—that is used to tie the knot*. Since the Bimini twist is stronger than the line, and you are tying the knot with two strands of the line, almost any knot you tie will be stronger than the main line. For example, if you connect ten-pound-test line to something, the knot strength will almost always be less than ten pounds. But, if you make a Bimini twist in your ten-pound, you have a loop, or two strands, of ten-pound. *Any knot you now make is constructed with twenty-pound test.* That knot should be stronger than the ten-pound-test line. This is the reason why the Bimini is used throughout the fishing world, from big-game trolling to fishing with a four-pound fly tippet.

ALBRIGHT SPECIAL

There are many knots used to connect monofilaments that differ considerably in diameter. The most useful of these is the Albright special. The Huffnagle is a modern knot that does the same thing, but it is limited to monofilament. The Albright can be used to join mono to mono, mono to braided wire, mono to solid wire, a butt section to a fly line, and backing to the fly line (although there are better knots for the last two purposes). The Albright and the surgeon's are two knots that can be used in many situations in fishing.

One of the most important factors in making an Albright is that you should never cross one wrap over the other as the knot is being built. This is where the knot will break under great stress.

Bimini Twist

This knot is extremely useful in all areas of fishing, but is essential in some situations in fly fishing. Anglers often feel that this knot is too difficult. Follow the steps and you will soon master this knot.

Fold back the line about eighteen inches, insert your hand, and make twenty twists or revolutions with your hand. Bend your knee beyond 90 degrees and place the loop over it. Hold the short line in your right hand and spread your two hands apart (as shown).

Here is where people have trouble—just follow directions. Spread your hands apart while securely gripping the line. This will "pack" the line twist into tight spirals. Be sure to continue pressure until the lower spirals come flush with your leg. Now move the main line to a near vertical position and your right hand at right angles to the spiraled twist. While pulling firmly on the line with your left hand, move your right hand until the line just flips over the twist. Don't go too far—as soon as the line jumps over the twist, move your right hand back so that the line is at right angles to the twists. Insert your finger, as shown, below the twist and while pushing up with it, permit your right hand to feed coils around the twist.

After the coils cover the wraps, work your left hand down to the end of the twist while keeping a grip on the main line. Insert your finger as shown and the loops will remain in position. Place the loop over a nail, cleat, or similar object and make six half hitches, as shown, then carefully tease the loops down to close the knot firmly. Clip the end.

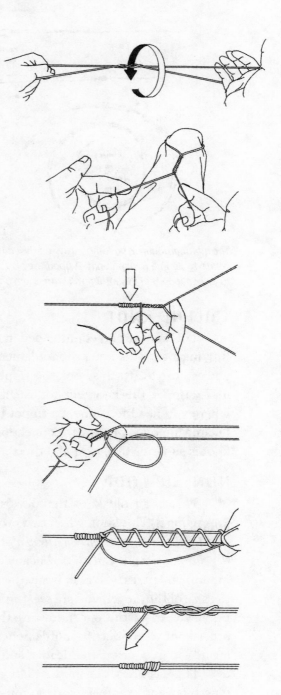

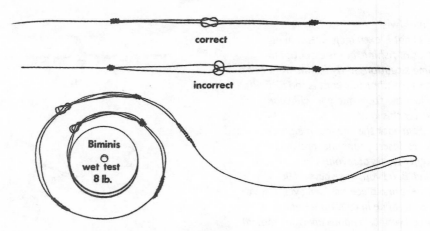

correct

incorrect

Biminis
○
wet test
8 lb.

The major problem in building saltwater fly leaders is making the Bimini Twists. This is especially tough to do in a rocking boat. A good trick is to make a series of Biminis of a specific line test and then loop them together and store them on small labeled spools, as shown in the drawing.

TRILENE KNOT

This knot isn't recommended in lines of more than fifteen-pound test. But, in smaller-diameter monofilament lines it is one of the strongest knots you can use to attach a hook to a tippet. When tied correctly, even in a fragile 7X tippet, this knot will not usually break—the standing line does. Anywhere you need to connect a tippet to a streamer, bonefish fly, or Clouser Deep Minnow—or similar connections—when properly constructed, this knot is superior to almost all others.

NONSLIP LOOP

This is an old knot that I worked with for months before finally improving it. This knot, when tied properly, also will not break. The important factor is that *the correct number of turns be made with the tag end around the standing line.* It can be tied in any diameter line, from 8X to 150-pound monofilament, as well as in braided wire, and you have the liberty to adjust the size of the loop. If you are seeking a loop knot with the greatest strength, I urge you to try this one. I now use the nonslip loop more than almost any other knot to connect monofilament leaders to flies. It is superb for making a loop in your tapered leader, and for looping the tippet to the leader.

There is a host of fishing situations where a loop knot is desirable. Popping bugs, for example, work so much better when attached with a free-swinging loop. Anytime a heavy tippet is connected to a smaller fly, the

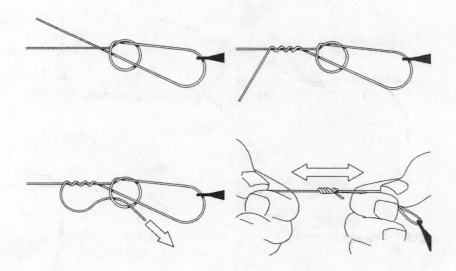

junction between the two can stifle the action of the fly. In this case, a loop knot is best. Some people use the uni-knot for this connection, but the uni-knot is not nearly as strong a knot as the nonslip loop and the uni-knot often slips down and tightens on the eye under fighting pressure. The nonslip loop retains its shape regardless of fishing conditions.

I also much prefer to make a nonslip loop when making a loop in the end of a monofilament line.

GEL-SPUN LINE CONNECTION

Gel-spun lines have poor basic knot strength. When you want to connect gel spun to monofilament do the following: Make a Bimini twist in the gel-spun line end. Then spiral wrap the Bimini doubled line seven times around the monofilament strand. Pass the monofilament end through the loop end of the Bimini. Carefully draw the connection as tight as possible. See pages 59–60 for a thorough description of gel-spun lines.

JOINING BRAIDED LEADER
BUT MATERIAL TO FLY LINE

This is a knot you can use to repair a fly line that has been cut, to join two fly lines together, or, most often, to install a shooting line to the rear of a shooting head. I use Cortland's Braided Mono Leader Butt Material. For lines testing less than seven weight, I use thirty-pound, but the most useful size is the fifty-pound-test line.

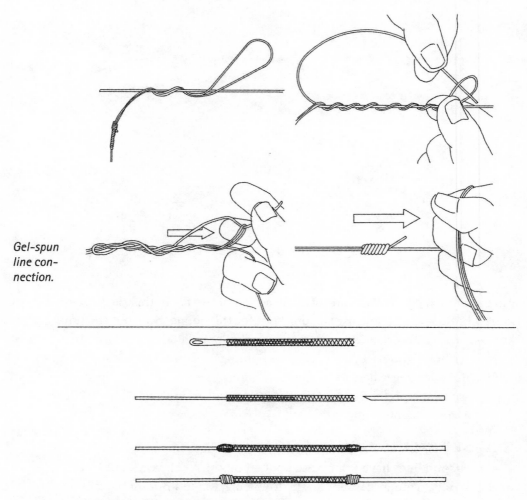

Gel-spun line con-nection.

Connecting Braided Butt Material to Fly Line
Cut approximately a three-inch length of Cortland Braided Mono Leader Butt Material. Insert a large needle or small finishing nail into each end to flex open. Cut the two ends of the fly lines to be joined to a sharp taper and insert in both ends of the braided material.

   Secure only the very ends of the braid. Use a nail knot with six- to eight-pound-test monofilament or a whipped finish with fly-tying thread (see "Whipping a Loop"). Coat the nail knots or whipped finish with Pliobond, Aqua-Seal, or clear nail polish to make a smooth joint. The braided material acts as a Chinese finger trap, gripping the line under tension, so leave all but the ends untouched and supple.

FIGURE-EIGHT KNOT
   This knot is *only* used to attach braided wire to a swivel or hook eye. *It should never be tied using nylon monofilament.* If you do, the knot will slip

or fail miserably. But, it is incredibly simple to tie in braided wire and has excellent knot strength.

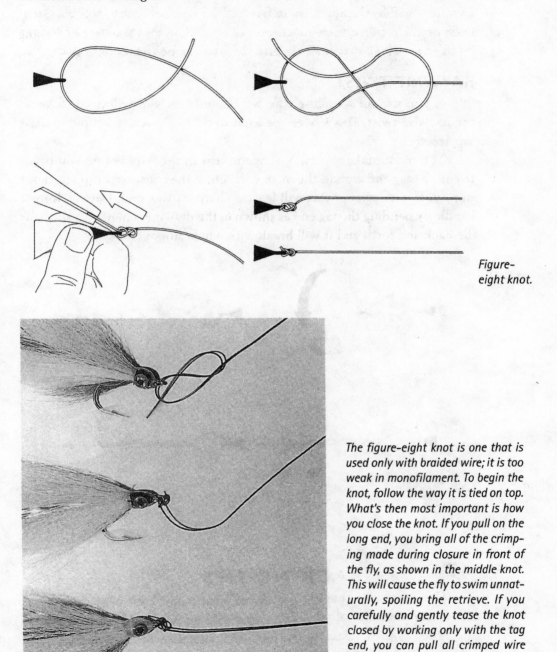

Figure-eight knot.

The figure-eight knot is one that is used only with braided wire; it is too weak in monofilament. To begin the knot, follow the way it is tied on top. What's then most important is how you close the knot. If you pull on the long end, you bring all of the crimping made during closure in front of the fly, as shown in the middle knot. This will cause the fly to swim unnaturally, spoiling the retrieve. If you carefully and gently tease the knot closed by working only with the tag end, you can pull all crimped wire outside the knot, where it can be clipped and discarded.

Aside from tying it correctly, the most important factor when making this knot is how you draw it tight. *Never pull on the standing line to close the knot.* This will feed kinked line in front of the fly, causing it to wobble erratically on the retrieve. Carefully draw out all slack within the knot by pulling on the *tag end*. That way all kinks in the line can be clipped and discarded.

HAYWIRE TWIST

If you use solid trolling wire for bite leaders, you will need to know the haywire twist. This is a simple knot to tie, but it is also simple to tie it incorrectly.

You must make several X-shaped turns in the wire before you begin to coil the tag end around the main wire. Once the coils are complete, don't snip it off with pliers—this will leave a sharp cutting end. Instead, form a handle by bending the tag end as shown in the drawing. Then, rock the handle back and forth and it will break with a nice smooth end.

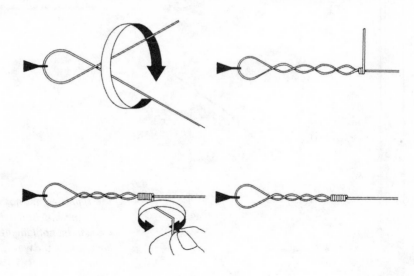

Haywire
twist.

BACKING TIPS

Great fish are often lost because of what might have been considered an unimportant part of your tackle. Probably no piece of fly-fishing gear is so ignored as the backing on the reel. And, this does not apply just to saltwater situations. Steelheaders often watch in dismay as a fish escapes downstream, where they can't follow, only to see the end of the backing, and the fight. Atlantic salmon fishermen are often called upon to give more line than they want to a battling fish. Even on very light gear, a good trout hooked in heavy water may run off more than ninety feet of fly line.

Fly lines are rarely longer than 105 feet—which is a short run for some freshwater, and certainly many saltwater, species. To allow a fish to make long runs and exhaust itself, there has to be enough backing on the reel so that the best fish you hope to hook can be landed. The kind of backing used, how much, sometimes the color, and even the combination of backings, can be important factors in catching fish.

There are a number of types of lines used for backing. Nylon monofilament is rarely used because it stretches when pulled taut. When you are fighting a strong fish with mono backing, you may recover line on the reel that's in a stretched condition. Piling more loose line on top may create a critical problem. The fish makes another long run, comes to the stretched portion (this now thinner mono has dug into the bed of line), and a jerk occurs as the embedded line is encountered—this will often snap your leader.

The most popular backing is **Dacron,** available in most tackle shops, or a very similar material called **Micron,** manufactured by the Cortland Line Company. These two lines owe their popularity to the facts that they stretch very little under stress and that both lie flat on the spool. For many years experienced fly fishermen used squidding line, which worked well, but is now difficult to obtain.

The ultra-thin braided casting lines, called **gel-spun** or **polyethylene,** that appeared on the market in 1993 might appear to be a breakthrough in fly-reel backing—but there are some drawbacks to these lines, as I will explain shortly. Stren manufactures a slightly different line using Kevlar; others use various braiding systems and materials. These lines are unlike any other Dacron, Micron, braided nylon, or nylon lines. They have one outstanding characteristic—a thin diameter for their strength. For example, the average gel-spun line of thirty pounds has the diameter of about a ten-pound nylon monofilament line. Fly fishermen immediately said, "Great— I can put two or three times as much line on a reel as I do now for the same line test." But, I believe that if you use a gel-spun line testing *less* than thirty pounds (for larger fish I recommend fifty-pound test) for backing you will encounter trouble. Lines of less than thirty pounds are so thin that they tend to dig into the backing, causing the same kind of problems associated with nylon monofilament. And many of these lines are round and very slick. If you fail to wind the line *very carefully* back on the reel spool as you recover it while fighting a fish, and it piles higher on one side of the spool, it has a greater tendency to tumble into a disastrous mess. You will also need special knots to tie most of the braided casting lines. *Conventional knots are usually poor performers with these lines.* If you want to connect a monofilament leader to one of these gel-spun lines, you can use the gel-spun line connection knot (see pages 55–56).

If you do use these gel-spun lines for backing on fly reels, the most important factor in getting good performance is the placement of the line on the spool. You must make sure that all the backing is put as firmly as possible on the reel. *I use a glove to put tension on the line as I reel it onto the spool. If you fail to do this, even thirty-pound may dig into the bedding and cause a lost fish.* Many experienced anglers using the gel-spun lines for backing fill at least half the spool with Dacron or Micron and then add the gel-spun.

The gel-spun lines (of approximately thirty-pound test) also have advantages fly fishermen may consider. If you fish offshore, where your fish may run a long distance, a huge belly can develop in the line with Dacron or Micron. This belly causes tremendous drag on the leader and may break it. Because the polyethylene lines have almost no stretch, the line does not belly—it remains in almost a straight line of contact with the fish.

The saltwater angler who carefully installs the gel-spun backing properly on the spool can add about 50 percent more backing than if Dacron or Micron is used. Anglers who prefer smaller saltwater reels (for example, when bonefishing) can now fish with the proper fly line and adequate backing. And, those who seek long-running fish, such as billfish, will be able to put considerably more line than on a reel loaded with Dacron or Micron.

It is worth realizing that when backing is the cause of a lost fish, the reason is usually improper installation of the backing. Regardless of whether you use Dacron, Micron, squidding line, or a gel-spun line, it is extremely important that the backing be placed on the spool under pressure, so that the bedding is firm and won't allow line to dig into it.

The two most often used backing lines are twenty- or thirty-pound-test Dacron or Micron. Factors that determine which test should be used are the size of the reel spool (if it's small you can't get very much thirty-pound-test line on it) and the strength of the leader tippet. Obviously, you don't want to use backing that has less strength than the tippet. If the backing breaks, you may lose leader, line, and fish.

Many fly fishermen who seek seatrout, bonefish, redfish, and other species that don't require a heavy leader tippet—and where light, small reels are comfortable—will select twenty-pound-test Dacron or Micron. However, I use thirty-pound Dacron or Micron for almost all my backing needs on fly reels. If you want to make an illuminating test, take a two-foot strand of twenty- and another of thirty-pound-test Dacron or Micron. Have someone hold a fly rod firmly in front of you. Insert one end of one of the strands in the butt or stripping guide. Grasp the two ends and saw the line rapidly back and forth about thirty or forty times. Then, do this with the other piece. Now, look at both of them (you may need a magnifying glass). It might surprise you that the twenty-pound line will resemble a barbed wire fence. This test indicates to me that Dacron and Micron do abrade. My experience has led me to believe that you will need to check twenty-pound braided Dacron or Micron for wear fairly often—but that thirty-pound will last for years.

Another mistake many longtime fly fishermen make is never to replace backing. It can wear out. Abusive conditions can ruin even new backing. For example, if you are fishing a coral-studded flat and a fish makes a long run, the line will be dragged over the sharp rocks. There is a distinct possibility that the backing will be nicked or frayed. It pays to routinely check your backing.

A major reason for backing on fly reels is to have enough line to allow the fish to make an escape run. Outdoors writers and fly fishermen have for years vastly overrated the distance that many fish will run. Bluefish and stripers will *rarely* run more than 125 yards of backing (plus thirty yards of fly line). I've caught some large stripers, and a number of bluefish weighing up to eighteen pounds, on a fly. None ever hit 100 yards of backing plus fly line.

Bonefish are legendary—running up to 250 yards. I am not sure how many bonefish I have caught weighing more than ten pounds—but it has been quite a few. *None ever ran more than 150 yards of backing.* If you include the fly line and leader, that is nearly two football fields away! Many fly fishermen who seek snook, redfish, seatrout, and similar species routinely carry reels loaded with 250 to 300 yards of backing—this will never be needed.

There are some fishing situations where a lot of backing is demanded. You'll need a lot of line (at least 300 to 400 yards) for billfish and some of the offshore speedsters, such as wahoo, tuna, and mackerels exceeding forty pounds, to mention a few. A giant tarpon can pull a lot of backing from a reel, especially if you are fighting from a staked or anchored boat. *But, with these few exceptions, a fly fisherman who has a reel loaded with 150 yards of backing and a fly line will almost never in his lifetime hook a fish that will run that far.*

SOME BACKING TRICKS

These are several techniques concerning backing that anglers have devised that you may want to consider:

(1) Some anglers have fly line and backing that are almost the same color. This is not a good idea! I prefer to connect a backing that is markedly different in color from the rear of the fly line. It gives an indicator of where the end of the fly line is.

(2) It is often advantageous to know just how much backing has been pulled from your reel. For example, if you are on a saltwater flat and you know there is a marker or channel buoy 200 yards away, knowing how much line the fish has pulled out could have a major bearing on how you fight the fish. Backing comes in many colors, ranging from fluorescent to dull reddish brown. Some anglers will use various lengths of different colors to tip them off. For example, you may connect 100 feet of bright chartreuse backing to the fly line; to that would be connected 100 feet of a much different color, and so forth. Bimini twists can be made in both ends of each color of backing, then looped together. Many fly shops can also build blind-spliced loops in your backing if you don't know how. The loops will flow through the guides, and if at any time you want to add or remove a color link, simply unloop it.

(3) There is one other way of modifying the backing that is a real asset when fighting billfish, or subduing tarpon. Any fish that jumps with great frequency and ferocity lunges against the leader and can break it. Many anglers who fish a great deal for such species scorn any efforts to reduce the shock against the fly or leader. However, for fishermen who only occasionally encounter these jumpers, there is a way of

building a shock absorber into the backing that will reduce the chances of a leaping fish breaking the leader or ripping the fly loose. Connect 100 feet of twenty-five- or thirty-pound brightly colored nylon monofilament with a Bimini twist to the rear of the fly line. Then, connect the other end of the nylon monofilament to your backing with a loop-to-loop system. If you have the fly line and the monofilament outside the rod tip when a fish jumps, the mono will stretch like a giant rubber band. This prevents the leader from snapping. You want brightly colored monofilament, so that a boat operator can see it during the battle and not run it over—which has happened to me.

Backing is often ignored when fly tackle is considered, but it forms a vital link between you and a trophy fish and deserves your attention.

(4)   While modern saltwater fly reels require little maintenance, one area of the reel that almost never receives attention is the backing. If you fight a fish that runs well into the backing, it will soak up a lot of salt water. After the long run, the backing line is recovered. When you get home, the reel surfaces are cleaned. But, the salt-encrusted backing is generally left untouched. What I recommend is that upon returning home, you fill a sink with *warm soapy water* and place the backing in it. Wash the spool sides with the water, too, and wipe them clean. Drain the soapy water, flush the backing line with clear water, and replace it firmly on the spool. You need to securely connect the backing to the reel-spool axle. There are two popular knots that accomplish this: the uni-knot and the arbor knot, which is not as strong, but rarely fails.

Once the backing is securely fastened to the spool axle and the backing is *firmly* installed on the reel, the fly line can be reconnected.

CONNECTING BACKING TO FLY LINE

First, let's examine the criteria for a proper backing/fly line connection. A knot that is easy to disconnect is not a necessity, but it is a plus. This allows the angler to easily exchange one line for another. Any connection should be as strong as the backing, or very close to its strength. Also, it must pass smoothly through the guides and tip. Some knots pass smoothly through the guide when traveling out, but not when traveling in. Two good examples of such a connection are the Albright and the nail knot. With the Albright, the fly line is folded over (in a horseshoe shape) to connect the backing to it. One leg of the Albright is the stub of the fly line. Unless this stub is coated with something to create a smooth joint, it can catch on a guide or the tip-top as the fish pulls the knot through. A nail knot also has a stub, and unless a smooth coating is placed over it, the stub can catch in the guides when returning the line to the reel. Neither of these knots allows you to exchange lines.

My personal choice for a connection to the backing is the whipped loop. *When properly constructed, this loop is stronger than the fly line.* Because there are no protruding ends, and it is rounded as it passes in and out of the guides, it is a trouble-free knot. It allows the angler to change lines quickly. I urge you to try the whipped loop. With a minimal amount of practice it can be made in less than two minutes.

Another connection favored by some experienced anglers is the double nail knot loop. The fly-line end is doubled and two nail knots are used (generally with ten-pound monofilament) to secure the loop. There is a chance that a small protruding stub may be formed when the knot is finished. A smooth joint can be made (also with the Albright knot) by coating it with Goop, Pliobond, Aqua-Seal, or a similar flexible glue. Use enough to form a taper on both sides of the knot that resembles a football shape.

Commercial braided leader loops can be used to connect the backing to the fly line, too. When you buy the loop there are instructions on the packet for joining it. Don't use the small plastic ring to secure it. Instead, make a whipped loop or double nail knot to keep the loop in place.

There are a number of other methods of connecting fly lines to backing, but any of the options mentioned here is sufficient.

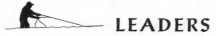 ## LEADERS

The leader has been defined as a nearly invisible connection between the fly and the fly line. A well-designed leader is essential to an accurate presentation. A leader must be supple enough to allow the fly to work properly in the water. This can be accomplished by using a thin, light monofilament tippet (the weakest portion of a leader). A thin strand, however, is often impractical in salt water; fish with either sharp teeth or abrasive mouths will go through it.

In such situations the angler will use what is called a **bite tippet** or **shock tippet,** which is a heavier, protective section of either wire or monofilament that is tied between the tippet and the fly. To get freedom of movement for the fly when using a bite or shock tippet, the angler will often connect the tippet to the fly with a loop knot, although some fine anglers prefer a three-and-a-half-turn clinch knot when mono is used.

Because a leader must be able to turn over and present the fly properly, one that collapses and doesn't turn over well can be disastrous. Equally important is the leader's role in diminishing the line's impact on the water when the fly is presented. *I'm totally convinced that many times it is the impact of the heavy line crashing to the surface near a fish that causes it to refuse your offering.* If you cast well away from the fish and bring the fly to it, the length of the leader has little to do with the fish's inclination to strike. Most of the time the diameter of a monofilament leader tippet with an underwater fly, and the diameter of the bite or shock tippet, seem to be of little importance if the line's impact on the surface doesn't alarm the fish.

Let me give you two instances where line impact and leader length can affect angling success. When it's windy and the water's surface is ruffled, a successful bonefisherman will often use a nine-weight rod and line with an eight- or nine-foot leader. Under these conditions he can effectively fish with a relatively heavy line and short leader. If the wind stops and the surface calms, however, this heavy outfit and short leader will make it difficult to catch a bonefish. It would be wiser to either switch to a lighter line (if that's possible) or lengthen the leader. If you are forced to stay with the nine-weight line, the leader should be lengthened considerably.

The second instance concerns cruising giant tarpon that are easily spooked. They seem to sense that their dark green bodies contrast with the white sand flats, and the slightest disturbance will frighten them. The much shorter eight- or nine-foot leader that worked earlier in the day when the fish were over dark green grass will have to be lengthened to as much as sixteen feet!

Bear in mind that the same fly tied on a bite or shock leader of eighty- to 100-pound monofilament will catch those tarpon on either white sand or green grass. Leader diameter is often ignored by fish, even in clear water. Yet, if you fish a small fly on a heavy leader, the fly cannot work properly unless a loop knot is used to give it freedom of movement.

While it is important to extend the leader to reduce line impact, there are some situations where a short leader is more effective. Where the fly can be dropped into deep water, well away from fish, the shorter leader should be considered. I've caught hundreds of fish of many species by eliminating the butt section of the leader entirely. I use the Bimini twist in the tippet, with it looped to my fly line. More anglers are using the Teeny sinking-head lines, as well as a host of other sinking lines and shooting heads. When using any fast-sinking fly lines, consider using much shorter leaders. The long leader streams above the sunken line and never gets to the desired depth. How short can the leader be? There are many situations when using a sinking line where I use a simple tippet of just two feet to catch fish.

What all of this means is that no saltwater leader is right for all situations, even when you are fishing for a specific species. For example, when water temperatures hit about 67 degrees Fahrenheit in the spring from North Carolina to New England, big bluefish move into the shallows. But, these voracious blues can be easily frightened when in calm water less than four feet deep. A long leader is required to keep the line impact away from the fish. But, a week or so later when these fish retreat to deeper water and are being lured to a chum line, a two- or three-foot leader is fine. The saltwater fly rodder must be able to ascertain the situation and adjust the leader accordingly. That's why it's important to learn the knots suggested in this chapter.

Four variations of the saltwater leader are used frequently. These four variations are shown in the illustration. I suggest using Leader A in the shallows for fish that do not have an abrasive mouth. It is perhaps the leader most utilized in saltwater fly fishing. You can build this leader in lengths from eight to as much as sixteen feet, if you keep the same proportions. (Generally a tippet of eighteen to twenty-four inches is ideal. To connect the various diameters of line you can use either the surgeon's or the blood knot. I recommend the nonslip loop for attaching flies with a loop knot.

LEADER A

Leader A is used for striped bass, bluefish, redfish, snappers, seatrout, barramundi, threadfin salmon, and a host of other species. Sometimes, you may add a bite or shock tippet if conditions demand a small amount of protection. For example, snook have a cutter on the gill cover, so I generally recommend a short section of thirty- or forty-pound mono in front of the tippet.

One of the great myths in fly fishing is that you need a stiff butt section to turn over a leader. As the forward cast begins, the line is relatively straight. The rod sweeps forward and stops. At this moment the line begins unrolling toward the target. The line continues to unroll until it reaches the leader. If the leader has a stiff butt, it will resist unrolling. But, if the butt section is flexible and heavy enough to maintain the energy of the cast, the leader straightens well. A stiff butt actually restricts the ability of the leader to unroll properly. The best leader materials are premium spinning or plug-casting lines. It does help to get spinning line that is relatively limp. *When you make a basic*

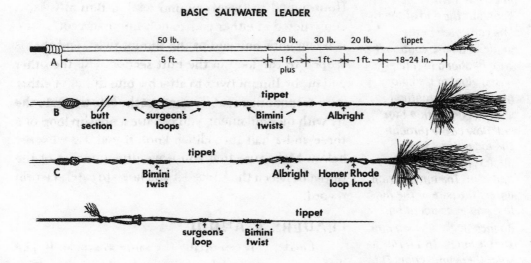

BASIC SALTWATER LEADER

tapered leader (Leader A), you should make the leader with all the same material. This is important in getting a tapered leader to unroll well.

Here are my recommendations for making the basic saltwater tapered leader (Leader A). *All suggested lengths are approximate.* The butt section should be about 50 percent of the total leader's length. I know this sounds like a departure from all conventional leaders, but give it a try. Let's use an example of what is the most popular tapered leader in salt water—one of about 9½ to ten feet in length. If you want a ten-foot leader, begin with a five-foot butt section of fifty-pound mono. Add a little more than a foot of forty-pound test. Connect to that about a foot of thirty-pound-test mono and then a foot of twenty-five-pound test. Add a little less than a foot of twenty-pound and then tie on your tippet. Or, just connect enough twenty-pound to make a tippet about two feet in length. This will give you a leader that is approximately ten feet long. Suppose you want a sixteen-foot leader. Start off with eight feet of fifty-pound butt section and then, using the various tests above, make them proportionally longer. *Don't worry if you don't get each length exactly right—the leader will still turn over well if you make a good cast.*

Connecting the Leader to a Fly Line

Several methods are used to connect a leader to a fly line. One is with a nail knot, but the end of the fly line can catch in the guides. I advise coating it with Pliobond (a rubber-based glue) or a similar glue to form a football-shaped connection that will flow easily through the rod guides. Some anglers prefer a needle nail knot. The butt section enters the core of the fly line and exits about half an inch back, where a nail knot is made. This forms a smoother connection. The fourth method of connecting the fly line to the butt section is my favorite—one I have been using for more than twenty-five years without a single failure. This is the whipped loop, which is well described on pages 48–49. The loop in the fly line enables you to quickly switch from one leader to another—a definite asset in successful fishing. And, if the loop is properly made, it is stronger than the fly line.

LEADER B

Leader B is what many consider to be a standard for much of inshore fishing. A surgeon's or nonslip loop is made in the butt section, which is generally about four feet in length. If you are using a class leader tippet (four-pound to twenty-pound test), a Bimini twist is constructed in either end. A nonslip or surgeon's loop is made with one end of the Bimini twist, and that is looped to the loop in the butt section. Use the other end of the Bimini twist to attach a bite tippet of either wire or monofilament. To connect the bite tippet to the fly with monofilament, you can use a nonslip loop or a three-and-a-half-turn clinch knot. If you use wire, see below. Make sure that you leave fifteen inches of the tippet between the knots—if you hope to catch a world record.

LEADERS C AND D

Leader C is essentially the same as Leader B. The difference is that no butt section has been used. This shortens the leader and is often used best when you need to get the fly down deep. Remember, the shorter the leader used with a sinking line, the more likely the fly is to ride at the same depth as the line.

The bottom drawing on page 67—Leader D—shows how you can connect the butt section of a leader to a lead-core line. Many people make a surgeon's loop in the end of the line after the lead core has been removed. I prefer to make a whipped loop. The rest of the leader is connected similar to Leader C.

CONNECTIONS WITH WIRE

Assuming that you have constructed the proper leader, you will, when fishing for certain species, want to attach a bite or shock tippet. Wire is difficult to turn over at the end of the cast, especially if you are throwing long line into the wind. There are also occasions in very clear water when a wire leader might result in refusals—so you want to use the thinnest wire practical and keep it as short as possible. Rarely do you need more than five inches of wire.

The upper drawing in the illustration for connecting *solid wire* and the fly shows a haywire twist—explained on page 58. Attach the wire with the haywire to the fly. Then use an Albright knot to connect the wire to the leader. After you have made the Albright, use a haywire twist to ensure that the monofilament never sneaks through the connection.

If you are using braided wire, a haywire twist won't work. You can use either a figure-eight knot or a nonslip loop with only one turn on the wire around the main section. How to tie both of these knots is explained on pages 54–55 and 56–57.

Connecting *braided* wire to the tippet is also explained in the third drawing. An Albright is used to attach the braided wire to the Bimini and then a figure-eight knot is used to connect the wire to the fly. You can also use a nonslip loop.

The bottom drawing shows the figure-eight knot; to the right demonstrates slack in the knot being pulled from the tag end.

CONNECTING WIRE TO THE LEADER AND FLY

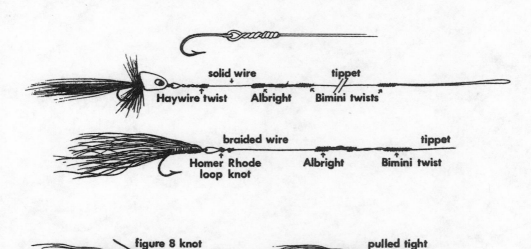

 # Flies

The fly is the heart of your tackle. No matter how well the rod casts, the line flows out, the leader and knots are tied, and the reel performs, if the fish doesn't hit the fly the battle is never joined.

The most important yet rarely discussed design feature of a fly is its castability. Several factors influence castability: hook size and length, amount of dressing, whether the fly is weighted or not, and silhouette or shape. No matter how correct the pattern, if you can't throw it to the fish, you'd better select something else. Two people may use two different sizes, shapes, or weights of a fly, depending upon their casting skill. All this indicates that the better you cast, the wider the range of effective fly patterns you will be able to use in your fishing.

The sea hatches few insects as we know them in fresh water. Mayflies, caddis, and stone flies, or their counterparts, just don't exist. Pioneers in saltwater fly fishing pretty much ignored exact imitations of the various prey species, and they were successful enough to believe that imitation isn't necessary. Modern fly rodders know that while many fish can be caught on some really wild patterns, reasonably good imitations of local foods can be very effective. Certainly, there's no harm in first offering an imitation of the food source. If that doesn't work, try one of the wild attractor patterns.

Fortunately, the major sources of food for most of the saltwater species we fish for are baitfish. Various types of streamers do a good job of imitating them. Streamer flies can range from tiny one-inch glass minnow imita-tions for snook, redfish, tarpon, albacore, bonito, tuna, rainbow runners, and similar game fish to the huge sailfish patterns that may be nearly a foot long. There are so many small fish of a multitude of colorations that trying to imitate specific baitfish is often difficult. But, anywhere you fish you will find some baitfish that has a dark green or blue back and silvery sides and belly. Never be without a few patterns in various sizes that imitate such baitfish—it's your insurance.

Imitations of local squid can be deadly also. In the shallows there are many types of crustaceans (shrimp, crabs, and lobsters are some), sea worms, small eels, and other incidental foods. Bear in mind that most fish are opportunistic and will take what they can find to eat. But, they also home in on things that look familiar. Thus, if you know that the flats you are fishing have a lot of ghost crabs, clam worms, or snapping shrimp, you increase your chances for a hookup by using a fly that resembles one of them.

Before you ever tie a fly, you need to know the best size for drawing strikes. Bonito and albacore (little tunny) often feed on tiny, almost invisi-ble baitfish, so a huge fly won't draw interest. Conversely, a sailfish isn't going to eat the fly that was so deadly on that bonito. A meal for a mouse is a tidbit for a lion. To a large degree you have to offer something to the fish that's worth chasing. A major reason that big popping bugs are used on offshore species, such as amberjacks and cobia, is that the bug, when worked, creates the illusion of being much larger than it actually is. A bone-fish has a small mouth, and it simply isn't going to eat a huge prey. Many times just looking at the mouth of a fish indicates the general size of the fly pattern that should be used.

The sink rate of a fly is vital, too. *Remember that almost all fish will strike better if a fly is at the same depth as the fish, and that while the fish may rise a bit to take a fly, very few species (except bottom-feeding types, such as bone-fish and permit) will take a fly that swims beneath them.* When trying to dredge a striper from the bottom of San Francisco Bay, or a tarpon lying on the bottom of a jungle river, you need to get the fly down to the bottom before the retrieve is started. When fishing for tarpon on the flats, the fish is first sighted—and then the cast is made far enough ahead so that it does-n't frighten the fish and so that the fly can sink to the same depth as the swimming fish. A striped bass cruising a quiet, shallow flat generally requires a fly that sinks slowly. You need to consider the sink rate as an important factor in fly selection.

The sink rate of any fly can be determined in several ways. The style or type of hook has some effect. Those with stout or long, heavy shanks will obviously sink faster. Adding lead to the hook shank will also make it sink quicker. A good trick is to add various sizes of bead chain or other metallic eyes at the head of the fly. If the fly is tied sparsely, it will sink faster than one with a bulky wing. *Remember, you're not always trying to control how fast the fly sinks—often it's controlling how slowly it sinks.* For very shallow flats cruisers such as bonefish, redfish, and sharks, you may construct the fly with a bulky wing and palmered hackle to slow its sink rate. My favorite fly when redfish are located in less than a foot of water is the Seaducer. This is an all-hackle fly (see photo) that almost hangs motionlessly in the water. It can be teased up to a redfish and then manipulated ever so slowly, keeping the fly in front of the red until it finally sees it with its poor eyesight. Yet, I also weight the Seaducer fairly heavily when I want to sink it quickly and fish it deep. The point is that the same pattern can be dressed so that it sinks at different rates to match existing fishing conditions.

The silhouette of a fly is important, and I'm not just talking about making it bigger. A streamer that is too lightly dressed becomes almost invisible when it is retrieved (and in some conditions that may be good). But, a look at a favorite saltwater fly will illustrate what I'm trying to say. When fishing at night or in dirty or roiled water, getting the fish to locate the fly is a problem. We know that they can sense its presence by the vibrations the fly makes as it moves through the water. At Casa Mar Tarpon Camp in Costa Rica, the Rio Colorado runs dirty all the time as it carries its silt load from the jungle to the sea. The huge number of tarpon that live here can feed well in this water. But, to fish effectively here, flies with bulky heads are a must. Successful anglers use a very bulky wing (hair creates more bulk than feathers), building an extra-large head and then adding a pair of bead chain eyes. It's called a Whistler and was created by top-notch West Coast fly rodder Dan Blanton. When this fly is drawn through the water, it "pushes" shock waves that help the tarpon and snook find it. A sleek Florida Keys–style tarpon fly is virtually useless under such conditions. The same fly used at Casa Mar would probably catch some tarpon in the Florida Keys, but in the clear shallows of the Keys, the heavy splash and fast sink rate of the Whistler would make it a poor choice.

The color of a fly is important, too. Paul Johnson, in his book *The Scientific Angler*, proves that color can often be important in drawing strikes from fish. *For bottom-feeding fish, such as bonefish, it is almost always best to have flies that closely match the color of the bottom*. It should be obvious that if fish are cruising over white sand, any dark creature would have been eaten eons ago. Thus, on white sand a light-colored fly would be best. Where the bottom is carpeted in olive-tinted turtle grass, a tan or olive fly would be a good first choice. Certainly imitation of local fish foods can mean a difference. Either check with local successful anglers to determine their color preferences in flies or take along a variety in your fly box. Exact imitation isn't necessary, but the closer you imitate—as long as the fly has realistic motion in the water—the better are your chances.

Hooks are important. They must be strong enough but not so large or heavy that the fish can't handle them. Large hooks with protruding barbs are difficult to drive home on the strike, and they create a large hole that may lose the fish during the fight. I suggest sharpening all hooks before you tie flies—it's easier. Sharpening stones can't give you the fine cutting edges of a triangulated or diamond-shaped hook point—you need a file. There are two files available that do a great job. The Nichelson Smooth File is available from large hardware stores, or it can be ordered for you. I like the eight-inch size for saltwater use, the six-inch for fresh. Another good file is sold by Luhr-Jensen & Sons, Hood River, OR 97031. It offers the Hook File in four- and five-inch models. It is inexpensive and should be available from many tackle stores. This file has fairly fine teeth (but not as fine as the Nichelson Smooth File). To keep a file from rusting, I make a holster of leather and cover it with tape. Take an old leather belt and cut two sections from it nearly as long as the file. Lay the leather on a piece of waxed paper or aluminum foil, rough side up. Saturate the two pieces of leather with WD-40 or a similar rust inhibitor. When you can't get the leather to accept any more inhibitor, lay the file on one side, and place the other rough side against the file. Then, wrap the leather and file with duct tape. You have created a leather holster that is saturated with the inhibitor. I have been able to keep a file in good condition in this holster for almost a year of hard fishing in the salt. Another fact overlooked by many is that a file will give several years of good service if you clean the teeth with a suede brush occasionally.

There has been a trend lately to complicate fly patterns for saltwater fishing. For decades now, trout fishing techniques have become more involved each season. New anglers to trout fishing must believe that they are going to have to master Latin, learn a mass of intricate jargon and a bewildering selection of flies, as well as get a degree in entomology. All of these items can make the sport more interesting—but they certainly aren't necessary to catch trout.

This same trend seems to be creeping into saltwater fly fishing. It can be fun to learn all about the creatures that crawl around the bottom and swim in the water. I am not knocking anyone who wants to get seriously involved in fly fishing and master all areas—that's part of the pleasure of the sport. But, saltwater fly fishing is not complicated when it comes to selecting the flies that you will need.

You can make a bare-bones selection of eight patterns that will be successful most of the time, almost anywhere you fish. You may need to vary the lengths and color combinations, but *with these eight patterns you can be comfortable in knowing that there are few saltwater fly-fishing situations that you are not prepared for.* This selection will let you fish for striped bass, barramundi, Pacific sailfish, bluefish, bonefish, albacore, threadfin salmon, dogtooth tuna, tarpon, redfish, snook—need I go on? You will be able to fish in weed-filled waters, on top, or down deep.

 ## POPPING BUG

The popping bug is an essential fly for many reasons. Larger cobia and amberjacks, for example, rarely take a streamer fly—they want something big! A large popping bug creates an illusion of something much larger than it actually is. Poppers can draw strikes from larger fish, and also from those that have a hard time noticing your offering. A streamer is a silent offering. A popper attracts attention by its noise. It resembles something that is helpless and unable to escape—something few predators can ignore.

You can use a host of popping bugs. I really don't have any one favorite. But, there are some criteria that govern how you select a popping bug. First, if you have difficulty casting it, you won't be able to fish it properly. It should pop when you want it to, making the noise you want it to. It should lift from the water easily on the backcast. Some popping bugs dive if any appreciable amount of fly line is on the water, requiring the angler to strip the line too close for easy casting.

After years of fishing popping bugs I am convinced that color of the popper is unimportant. What is vital is how the bug is manipulated.

CRAB FLY

Crabs exist in every sea and represent a substantial meal to most predatory fish. They are one of the finest baits for permit, tarpon, and striped bass. You don't need exact replicas of local crabs. Just use a Del Brown Crab Fly of the color combination that roughly matches most of the crabs in the area. It is easy to cast, has a rather soft impact, and looks enough like a crab to fool the wary permit and a host of other species. It is a great fly that I now carry for fooling many species of fish. It is easy to tie—it takes only a few minutes to produce a pattern. I have learned from fishing experience that you never have to make this fly any larger than a twenty-five-cent coin. Rubber bands are generally used to imitate the crab's legs. They work fine, but I prefer to use the strands of a skirt found on a largemouth bass spinnerbait. These inexpensive skirts can be purchased in many shops and through many catalogs. You should carry crab flies that float, sink slowly, and sink quickly. Sink rate is determined by the weight of the metallic eyes on the fly. I usually tie the pattern with either $\frac{1}{36}$- or $\frac{1}{24}$-ounce lead eyes. (I never paint eyes on a crab fly.) To float a crab fly well, add a dry-fly paste float to an unweighted pattern. Since a crab fly is rarely retrieved any distance, I don't use weed guards on mine. If you are forced to fish where there are a lot of weeds or hook-snagging coral, then a monofilament guard is called for. Most of the time the best presentation is to let the crab dead drift with the tide. Few fly rodders realize how effective this fly is in all salt waters.

SURF CANDY

This terrific fly is generally tied in small sizes, not exceeding four inches. It is one of the best imitations of small local baitfish. It casts beautifully and is very durable. The original Surf Candy had a coating of epoxy over the hook-shank area of the fly. But, Bob Popovics, who developed the fly, now uses clear bathroom silicone sealer instead of epoxy. The body looks the same but is softer, and fish seem to take it better on the strike. It is also lighter than the epoxy model, making it easier to cast.

 ## CLOUSER MINNOW

This is an essential fly that any saltwater angler should carry. Originally conceived for smallmouth bass, the pattern has been developed into a host of variations and can range from one inch to a foot in length. At this writing, I have caught seventy-nine species of fish around the world in salt and fresh water with the Clouser Minnow. I introduced this pattern of Bob Clouser's to the fly-fishing public through *Fly Fisherman* magazine. I predicted that within a year or two it would be embraced by thousands of fly fishermen. It has been even more successful.

The most effective color combination for me in a host of situations and locations has been a white underwing, a good bit of pearl Krystal Flash, and a top wing of chartreuse. The fly can be tied sparsely (to imitate a needlefish or sand eel) or bulkily. It can be lightly weighted to run high in the water column, or it can carry heavy eyes, which make it one of the best patterns to get deep on a sinking line. If you are not currently using this pattern I urge you to try it. One of the great advantages of the Clouser Minnow is that it is rather sleek and has lead or metallic eyes. The Lefty's Deceiver and many other flies, when cast into a stiff breeze, often fold back at the end of the cast. If you have enough line speed, a Clouser Minnow will turn over in all but the stiffest of breezes.

 ## LEFTY'S DECEIVER

This is perhaps the most-used fly around the world today. I began to develop this pattern in the late 1950s—and perhaps more saltwater fish have been caught on it than any other fly. There are many variations on the fly. It can be as short as an inch or as long as fourteen inches. As with the Clouser Minnow, you can vary length of the total fly, hook size, and sink rate; tie it sleek or fat; and vary the color combinations. The Lefty's Deceiver lifts from the water and travels through the air during casting with a minimum of resistance. Because the wing is attached at the tail and the collar surrounds the spot where the wing joins the hook, the wing almost never fouls or wraps under the hook in flight. *What many fishermen don't realize is that this fly can be tied in a number of ways to match local fishing conditions.* It can be tied very sparsely, using only one or two hackles in the wing and with a meager amount of bucktail collar. This makes a good sand eel imitation. It can also be tied to push water—with a number of saddle hackles (ten or more) and with a dense bucktail collar, dressed on a light wire hook. This fly is so buoyant that it can be fished in inches of water or just under the surface, imitating mullets. Finally, it can be tied with a stout hook that has lead wrapped around its entire length. Add a tail of eight to ten saddle hackles, and finish by putting a dense collar of bucktail at the front. This fly can be fished deep in the water column. The important point is to remember that the Lefty's Deceiver can be tied to match the conditions of the moment.

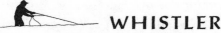

WHISTLER

This great fly, originated by Dan Blanton, is another superior pattern for a host of saltwater species. It is one of the best flies for fishing deep or in dirty water. The bulky head and large bead chain eyes "push" water, sending out sound vibrations that help fish locate the fly. The original fly was tied very bulkily and with some weight, usually lead wire, added to the hook shank. But, Dan also ties it unweighted so that it swims high in the water column. It has produced for me in many waters.

SEADUCER

This is a very old pattern, dating back to the last century, and was first developed as a bass fly. It has one characteristic few other patterns do: it can sink so slowly in the water column that it seems to be suspended. The long, fluffy hackles that form the tail or wing, and the palmered hackles at the front, act like outriggers so that the fly can be fished slowly in inches of water without snagging bottom. Because the fly is essentially nothing more than a hook with some feathers on it, it falls to the surface like a thistle. It can be dropped close to wary fish without frightening them. Like the Clouser Minnow and Lefty's Deceiver, this fly can be made short, long, and in a variety of color combinations.

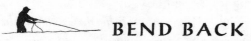

BEND BACK

This is another pattern that was developed decades ago for bass fishing in the mid-South. The hook is bent, and the pattern is tied so that the hook rides up and is protected by the wing. The original Bend Back flies had a body dressing on the hook shank. *But, I find that if you leave the shank bare and just incorporate a wing, the fly fishes better.* This is by far the best fly to fish when the water is filled with weeds, or against a mangrove shoreline with its spiderlike roots. You can cast almost worry-free with a Bend Back pattern. As with the Clouser Minnow, Lefty's Deceiver, and Whistler, you can vary size, length, shape, and color of the wing.

 ## SAR-MUL-MAC

This is a superb baitfish imitation. Like the Clouser Minnow and Lefty's Deceiver, it can be tied in various lengths and in color combinations to match local baitfish. It is a great fly all over the world.

 ## BACKCOUNTRY FLIES

One of the most exciting places to fish is what is referred to by many anglers as the backcountry. **Backcountry** usually means an area where an ocean or other salty waters mingle with fresh water. It is often a place where red, black, and white mangrove are found—indicating different degrees of salinity. These are wonderful waters for fly rodders. There are many challenges—sometimes just finding your way in and out of a place. Target casting along fly-grabbing mangroves, and the variety of fish found in such locations, make it a favorite of many of us. Snook, baby tarpon (sometimes big ones, too), redfish, ladyfish, barramundi, threadfin salmon, and a host of other fish can be found there. Backcountry waters exist in far-flung places, such as the Ten Thousand Islands of southern Florida, many areas of Central America, and much of the north coast of Australia, to mention a few.

Fortunately, five fly patterns will allow a fly fisherman to catch almost any fish he seeks in the backcountry—providing he varies the size and/or color combination of each pattern: a popping bug, small Lefty's Deceiver (sometimes called a Glades Deceiver), Seaducer, Clouser Minnow, and Bend Back.

In closing, if you want to further reduce the number of patterns you carry, you would be well prepared for most fly-fishing situations if you had in different sizes, lengths, and color combinations the following three patterns: Clouser Minnow, Lefty's Deceiver, and popping bugs. While it's fun to learn more about the sea and all its creatures, just a few patterns will let you catch most of the fish you seek. Instead of spending huge amounts of time on all sorts of patterns, it will be more rewarding if you spend that time working on casting and presentation—which are the real keys to catching fish on a fly.

PART TWO

Techniques

CHAPTER 7

 Saltwater

Fly Casting

The freshwater fisherman new to saltwater fly casting will have to alter his approach, learn a few new techniques, adapt himself to slightly heavier tackle, and work in many ways—if he is really to succeed to become a better fly caster. Saltwater fly fishermen must almost always deal with a wind factor. Flies are usually larger; one dressed on a 5/0 hook is not considered really big. The materials on the flies are more intricate; as many as fifteen to twenty saddle hackles adorn some hooks. An additional factor not often considered by the freshwater man is the difficulty of casting with a shock-leader tippet. A shock-leader tippet is a heavy wire or monofilament leader (never longer than twelve inches) placed in front of the weakest section in the total leader. Its purpose is to prevent a sharp-toothed or raspy-mouthed fish from biting through the connection to the fly. The shock leader radically increases air resistance, especially if the angler must cast against a breeze.

All of these elements, unfamiliar to freshwater fly fishermen, create casting problems that must be overcome. One solution is to use heavier lines, which will develop more line speed for the angler. Heavier lines, of course, demand stouter rods. Freshwater fly-fishing rods take an average line size of from 4 to 8; saltwater lines will average from 8 to 11.

Newcomers to saltwater fly fishing have often been misled by articles playing down the necessity for making long casts. There is an oft-repeated story that most saltwater fish are caught on a fly at a distance of less than fifty feet. Writers have assured readers that they are well armed if they can operate efficiently at that distance.

It's not true!

Most fish are caught at fifty feet simply because most fishermen can't cast any farther.

When I was a year-round resident of Florida, I frequently guided northern anglers; generally, we would go fishing, then call a halt for a casting lesson. Then we resumed fishing.

A recent incident is a perfect example of what occurs all too frequently. A close friend of mine, a bass fisherman, came down to fish with me for three days. He was extremely anxious to take a snook on his favorite fly rod. I knew that a few snook nestled under the mangrove bushes at high tide among certain Florida Bay keys near Flamingo, so we made the forty-eight-mile drive through Everglades Park before dawn, arriving at the dock to be greeted by mosquitoes big enough to romance turkeys. Slapping at them, we quickly slipped the boat into the dark brown waters at the ramp, leaped aboard, and headed for the fishing grounds. I think we lost a pint of blood between us before we got the engine started. I jumped two flats so shallow that the motor prop left a yellow-stained mud trail. We stopped a quarter mile from a key that showed deep black in the predawn light. I poled into the key, while my buddy stripped line from his reel and made ready to cast.

Big snook lying under the mangroves are the best lure inspectors I know. In fact, I used to think the fish had lockjaw and received nourishment through their scales. But in early morning a quiet approach, and a long cast with a fly that drops silently under the overhanging limbs of the mangroves, will sucker them into striking.

Knowing well where the snook were lying, I pushed the boat within eighty feet of a little ditch with overhanging bushes. I softly stuck the pole in the bottom and tied the bow rope fast to it. I whispered, "Throw the fly under the bush and don't slam the fly line down on the water. Do what I say and you'll get a snook."

He nodded again, gritted his teeth, and after five false casts he shot out the line. The fly landed fifteen feet short of the bush. He stripped the fly back and made another cast. "That's no good," I whispered. "The fly has to drop *under* the bush—that snook ain't gonna move out to get it. And do it quietly!"

He nodded again, gritted his teeth, and after five false casts, he shot out the line. The fly fell within inches of the previous casts, no more than seventy feet away and ten to fifteen short of the bushes.

"Throw the damn thing *under* the bush," I whispered hoarsely.

"What the hell do you think I'm trying to do?" he grunted as he made another cast that also fell short.

"Push the boat over a little so I can reach it," he urged.

I shook my head. "No use; if we get closer the fish will move out."

After ten minutes of futile casting, and because he became so insistent, I pulled the pole from the soft bottom and shoved the boat within sixty feet of the bushes. Out shot four green fish at least eight pounds apiece. They bolted right by the boat and we could plainly see the black stripe that identified them as snook.

I moved to another key and we repeated the entire operation with the same results. No luck.

I pushed the pole into the muddy bottom at the third key and turned to look at my friend. He shoved the rod toward me. "Here, damn it, I don't think you need to cast from way out here. Prove it to me."

I shrugged my shoulders, quietly moved to the casting platform, and stripped out enough line. I made a long cast, with the loop tilted slightly to the side. The yellow fly came over and rolled under the limb, dropping into the water with hardly a ripple. The hackles came alive as I made three slow strips with my right hand.

I never saw the fish take, but I felt the line tug, and I struck.

A ten-pound snook came out of the water, gills rattling. It took a few minutes to bring the fish to boatside, where I slipped the fly from its mouth and released it.

"I'll be damned," was all my friend could say.

We drank a cold soft drink and talked about what had happened. My friend explained that he had never used a fly as heavy as a 3/0 with a shock leader tied to it. He figured he could make the necessary cast, since his bass poppers had offered him little trouble up to eighty feet or so.

We had a fifteen-minute casting session and he mastered the technique well enough to gain ten feet over his previous cast. We didn't take a snook at the next key, but he got a seven-pounder at the last place we tried, and I think he was as proud of the cast as he was of the fish.

Long casts have *no* disadvantages. Some anglers have told me that you cannot set a hook beyond sixty feet. Perhaps that is true for big tarpon, which have a mouth resembling the interior of a cinder block. But experienced tarpon fishermen will tell you that it's tough to set the hook at any distance.

Providing you have sharpened the hook, and you strip retrieve by pointing the rod toward the fish and stripping with your hand to impart fly action, the fish will hook itself. Distance has little to do with driving that hook into the flesh. Hooks that are properly sharpened will penetrate bone.

I have never lost a fish because I struck it at sixty or even over 100 feet away. Some saltwater fly-fishing groups used to practice making a long cast in deep water, then stripping all additional line and considerable backing from the reel, allowing the fly to sink deep in the ocean, then retrieving slowly. This method is deadly, but it takes patience, and in fact is so effective that it has been outlawed by many fishing clubs as not really being fly-casting technique. The point is that no one ever noticed that a long length of line interfered with properly setting the hook. Indeed, it was *too* effective.

There is another vital reason for learning to cast a long line. A fisherman who can throw 100 feet of line downwind can do his casting effortlessly. And, since many, many casts have to be made either into or across the wind, the ability to throw a long line becomes vital; a 100-foot downwind cast might only go thirty-five feet into a stiff breeze.

I hate to belabor the point, but learning to cast a long distance is the major problem for most freshwater fly fishermen who make the transition to salt water. If you cannot cast well to at least eighty feet, you should always be striving to reach that point—and I consider 100 feet the desirable distance. When you can cast that far, you will be able to meet the demands of most saltwater fly-fishing situations.

The reason most people cannot cast to 100 feet is that they have not *thoroughly* understood good casting techniques.

There are several basic rules to fly casting. If they are understood and mastered you can fish anywhere in salt or fresh water and cope with any practical casting situation.

Rule One: You can't make any cast until you get the end of the line moving.

A good example to understanding this principle is to use a garden hose. Let's assume that it is lying on the lawn in snakelike curves; the sprinkler is at the far end. If you want to move the sprinkler, you can grab the other end of the hose and start walking—but, the sprinkler is not going to move until you straighten the hose. So it is with fly casting. Before you can move the fly in either direction, you must eliminate all slack. It is vital to make the backcast as straight as possible and with no slack. If that occurs, all forward motion of the rod contributes toward driving the fly to the target.

Rule Two: The longer the distance the rod moves during the back- and forward casts, the more the rod contributes to the cast and the less effort is required by the angler.

The lower you start with the rod on the backcast (I recommend that most of the time the tip be within a foot of the surface of the water) the more the rod can assist you. As the lowered rod is raised, it eliminates slack and starts the line moving. You can make a cast anytime *after* the line is moving, but not before. Many instructors and articles tell you to make the backcast between ten and eleven o'clock. I don't care what time it is, you can't make a cast to the rear or front until you have the line in motion.

The rod should be stopped as low as possible on the backcast as is practical for existing fishing conditions. This allows the rod to move through a greater arc on the forward cast. God rarely lets you throw a perfect backcast, and any slack in the line can only be removed by forward motion. The lower the rod is held before the forward cast is begun, the more it contributes to the cast.

Rule Three: The direction in which the rod stops at the end of the cast totally determines where the fly goes.

This is a badly misunderstood principle, but once it is realized, the angler can perform all sorts of casts and his accuracy improves. Not being aware of this principle results in poor backcasts for perhaps 80 percent of all anglers.

The most common fault among anglers is that they begin the backcast with the rod held too high above the surface. Here is what happens: there is always some slack in the line that must be removed before the cast can be made (Rule One). With a rod held high at the beginning of the backcast, it has to be moved to remove slack, load the rod, and finally make the cast.

By the time all of this is accomplished, the rod is usually past twelve o'clock. That means that the cast will be directed behind the angler, but the tip will be moving in a downward direction. Rule Three tells you that the cast will be thrown back and downward, creating a dip in the line or excessive slack. That slack must be eliminated before the angler can begin moving the fly forward.

Even if all slack is eliminated before the rod is moved, when the rod is stopped at the end of the backcast, the butt section halts, but the tip continues to move a short distance back and slightly downward. Rule Three tells you that if the tip stops in a slightly downward thrust, then the line will have a resultant dip in it.

To obtain a straight backcast is simple—you have to *stop the rod in the direction you want the cast to go.* I believe that the conventional method of snapping the wrist at the end of the backcast causes serious casting problems for most anglers. At the end of the wrist motion the butt stops, but the rod tip doesn't, causing an unwanted dip (slack) in the backcast.

I get incredibly good results with students by asking them never to move the wrist on the backcast. Instead, I ask them to start with a low rod and to remove all slack before the tip is raised. They bring the rod up smoothly, quickly freeing the line from the surface, and anytime *after* they get the line end in motion, they *stab the entire rod in the direction they want the cast to go—without moving the wrist. The stab is made with the forearm.*

If the stab, or the jab, is made with the entire rod stopping say at 45 degrees to the rear, the line will go back straight and at 45 degrees. Since the stab or jab causes the forearm to be extended in the direction of the backcast, the entire arm can now be moved forward along with the rod, which will travel through a long and efficient arc. The rod loads through considerable distance coming forward, assisting the angler in making a long and effortless cast.

Rule Four: The size of your loop is determined by the distance the wrist moves at the end of the cast.

In most fishing situations the tighter or smaller the loop, the easier you can throw into the wind, underneath something, or a long distance. Therefore, we generally want to throw the tightest loop possible.

Try something that will teach you an important factor in casting. Lay a long line out behind you on the grass with the rod parallel to the ground. Hold the wrist stiff and sweep the entire arm forward and over. The long,

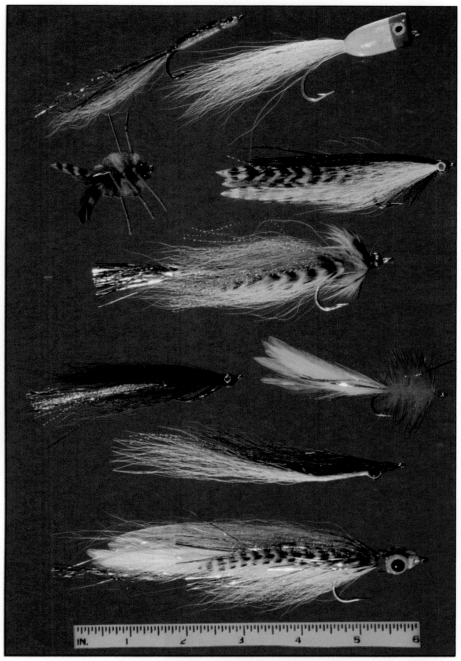

Equipped with these patterns in different sizes and color combinations, you can effectively saltwater fly fish almost anywhere in the world.

Top row: Surf Candy, Popping Bug
Second row: Crab fly, Lefty's Deceiver
Third row: Whistler

Fourth row: Bend Back and Sea Ducer
Fifth row: Clouser Minnow
Bottom Row: Sar-Mul-Mac

Basic Bonefish Fly Selection

Top row: all four are Tailing Bonefish Flies
Middle row: Gotcha, Crazy Charley Tan, Crazy
    Charley White, Snapping Shrimp
Bottom row: chartreuse-and-white Clouser
    Minnow, tan-and-white Clouser Minnow,
    Del Brown Crab Fly

A good choice of Florida Keys-style tarpon flies.

Top row: Cockroach, Stu Apte Tarpon Fly
Middle row: red-and-white Tarpon Fly,
    Blue Death
Bottom row: Chinese Claw

Basic Crab Flies

Top row: Jan Isley Wool Crab
Bottom row: Various examples of
    Del Brown's Crab Fly

A basic selection of backcountry flies.

Top row: Popping Bug
Middle row: Glades Deceiver, Sea Ducer
Bottom row: Clouser Minnow, Bend Back

Shark and Barracuda Flies

Top row: Popping Bug
Middle row: Lefty's White-and-Chartreuse
    Shark/Cuda Fly
Bottom row: Lefty's Yellow-Orange
    Shark/Cuda Fly

Lefty's Deceiver in different size and color variations.

The Clouser Minnow in different size and color variations

Striped Bass Basic Fly
Selection

Top row: Popping Bug, Crab
　　Fly, Surf Candy
Middle row: Clouser Minnow,
　　Snake Fly
Bottom row: Lefty's Deceiver,
　　Whistler

sweeping arc of the rod will easily throw all the line in front of you. But—and this is important—it will throw the line in a huge and inefficient loop.

Next time, lay the line behind you, rod parallel to the ground, and when you sweep it forward, *keep the wrist locked* until the final moment of the cast. Up to this point the rod will throw the line in front of you. Following Rule Four, at the last moment in the forward cast, make the shortest, quickest wrist motion you can, bringing the wrist to a dead stop. The sweeping rod will throw the line and if you will mentally think, "I'm not using the wrist to throw the line—but to create the size of the loop," you'll be amazed as the line sizzles in front of you in a tight loop—if the wrist motion was very brief.

The common mistake in the past, I believe, was to try to create a "power stroke" with the wrist. All but the experts make the wrist motion too long. Many casters exert excessive power with the wrist, causing standing waves in the line. Sweeping the rod forward through a long arc *will* generate the power to throw long line. If you don't try to power cast with the wrist, but move it in a very short, quick motion, it will throw a tight loop and a long cast free of air-resistant humps or waves. It is impossible to make the wrist motion too short. On the backcast the stab or jab creates an incredibly tight loop.

This style of casting is a radical departure from the conventional system, but I believe that in the future it will become the standard method.

One important factor was not mentioned. After the brief wrist motion at the end of the forward cast, all of the fly line is behind you and the loop is being formed right at the rod tip. If you drop the tip immediately after you stop, you literally pull your loop apart. Instead, allow the loop to roll forward and away from the tip at least a rod length in front before you drop the rod. Letting the loop escape the tip before the rod is lowered prevents the loop from opening.

This system of casting is really simple and once mastered can be applied to any type of fishing in either fresh or salt water.

CHAPTER **8**

Angling
Techniques

The mechanics of catching saltwater fish on a fly rod start with a thorough understanding of the role of the boat. It serves two purposes: it gets you within range of the quarry, and, once there, it becomes your casting platform.

Your boat should be considered fundamental, too, in your angling, and should be used as efficiently as your other equipment. Loose gear, including anchors and ropes, should be stored away from the range of your casts; windshields should be eliminated or folded down to offer more area for casting; and the cockpit or casting platform should be completely free of line-entangling items. Dropping loose coils of fly line on a deck that is filled with tackle boxes, gas tanks, loose rope, and other things could mean failure at a critical moment. Saltwater game fish usually don't give you a second chance.

Since a crucial part of saltwater by fishing is spotting the fish, communications between people in the same boat are important. When one angler spots a fish, he must be able to alert his companion as to the exact position of the moving target. Experienced Florida Keys guides have worked out a system that allows one angler to help his companion quickly determine the direction of an incoming fish.

Imagine that you are standing in the center of a giant clock face—the boat. The front end of the boat, where the angler stands, is always considered to be twelve o'clock; the rear, where the guide stands, is always considered at six o'clock. To the immediate left of the angler who is facing the bow is nine o'clock, and to his right is three o'clock. Look at the drawing to get a clearer explanation. No matter how the boat is turned, the bow always points at twelve o'clock and the motor end at six o'clock. *What is important, however, is to realize that what is eleven o'clock for the guide will probably be about eleven-thirty to you.* By studying the drawing you can see that this is true. However, it does give you a darn good idea where to look. Almost all guides are unaware of this, and sometimes get emotional (if that's the right word) if you don't look where they say. It's best when you first get into the boat to ask the guide to point to several clock positions. Using the clock technique is absolutely vital in sight fishing to incoming fish.

Let's examine how this works in actual practice. You're motoring slowly across a shallow bar and a fish swirls in the water, or the guide, standing on the elevated rear poling platform, spots a bonefish tipping its silvery tail into the air as it feeds. "Quick, ten o'clock, fifty feet away," the guide whispers urgently. You know immediately that fifty feet away to your left oblique is a fish; it's that simple. Without having to look at the guide, you can turn to ten o'clock and start making the cast, knowing full well that you will be able to see the fish very soon.

Much of the best saltwater fishing is done in shallow water where spotting the fish becomes the primary task. The fisherman should wear polarized glasses to help eliminate surface glare. Under different light conditions various shades of polarized lenses do better. The best all-around color for me and many of the people I fish with is an amber or brownish shade. This builds contrast, and yet is not too bright. Two other shades I like to use under certain light conditions are blue-green (I especially like this shade offshore) and a rather light yellow. The latter is good on overcast days. On days when the sky is very overcast I have found that a pair of bright amber (unfortunately, not polarized) shooting glasses aid me in seeing fish. What I'm suggesting is that the angler should have not only a spare pair, but several shades for various light conditions. Salt spray gets on glasses constantly and must be wiped from them, which often results in scratching the soft plastic lenses.

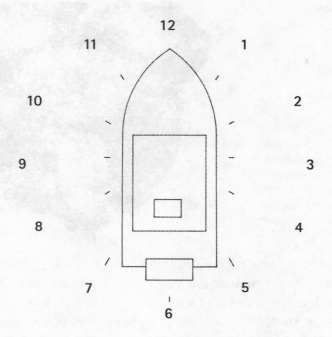

Fishing the Clock System
It is often vital when fishing tropical flats to get a cast off quickly. The guide will use the clock system to help the angler find a fish. The guide stands at six o'clock, and the bow of the boat is at noon or twelve o'clock. If the guide suddenly shouts that there is a fish at eleven o'clock, the angler can immediately begin looking to his left front.

Today, there are several companies that offer polarized glasses with a protective sheet of optical glass on either side of the polarized filter—this is really the only thing to have, and they are inexpensive.

When banks of white clouds are lying in the foreground putting a snowy reflection in the surface even polarized lenses often won't eliminate the glare. At such times, if it's possible, the boat should be maneuvered so that the clouds are at the side or to the rear.

The most important consideration in maneuvering the boat is that the fly caster should always be in a position to cast downwind if at all possible. A fish fifty feet away in a twenty-miles-per-hour upwind breeze is safe from nearly all fly casters, but is an easy downwind target. Your course is also important when chasing schools of deepwater fish feeding on the surface. It's vital that the boat approach the school from an upwind position.

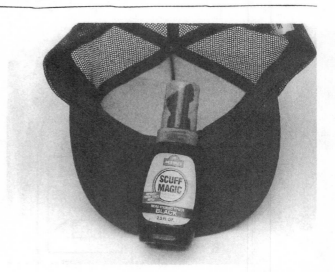

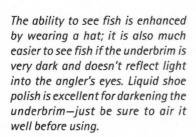

The ability to see fish is enhanced by wearing a hat; it is also much easier to see fish if the underbrim is very dark and doesn't reflect light into the angler's eyes. Liquid shoe polish is excellent for darkening the underbrim—just be sure to air it well before using.

If your boat doesn't have a casting platform you may have problems handling the yards of running line that develop during casting. Jim Green, superb rod designer and expert angler, told me of a technique that works better than anything I've tried. Buy a seven- or eight-foot square of one-inch mesh netting from a marine hardware or commercial fishing outlet (a minnow seine available in many tackle stores also works well). Attach half-ounce pinch-on sinkers along the sides and the corners—usually a well-spaced dozen is about right. Drape the netting over tackle boxes, gasoline cans, and whatever lies in the boat. The sinkers hold the netting firmly in place—even on windy days. Strip your line and drop it on the netting. This netting trick also works if you are casting from a jetty or wherever the running line snags on things underfoot. The netting can be carried in a small plastic bag and goes with me on trips where I don't know what kind of boat I'll be fishing from.

A large garbage can can also be placed beside the stripping hand and can be used to deposit the line as it is retrieved. Be sure the line is dropped into the can. The disadvantage to this system is that it does require a rather large can.

Several decades ago Florida Keys guides became aware, as more fly fishermen came to them, that the standard type of boat was not designed with the fly caster's needs in mind. Thus was born the casting platform. The forward end of the inner hull was built up so that the angler was elevated for visibility and had a clean deck on which to drop his fly line. It was a vast improvement. But, you can talk to a thousand anglers who spotted a fish

Many boats have line-entangling gadgets that grab your fly line and ruin a cast. A small mesh net or common minnow seine works well to prevent this. With a few sinkers spread around the edge of the net, it remains in place and permits tangle-free casts.

and made what they thought was a perfect cast, only to find that they were standing on the running line and lost their chance. For a long time I have been convinced that almost all the casting platforms in flats-type boats could be improved. What should be done is to construct a mini-platform large enough for the angler to stand comfortably on, and then behind it to make the normal casting platform. This would allow the angler better visibility, but more important, he wouldn't be standing on his line.

 ## MAKING READY TO CAST

Once the angler has solved his boating problems, he can begin his actual fishing procedure. It starts with stripping the line from the reel. Floating fly lines are made with a braided nylon core over which a specially prepared softer plastic is coated to the desired thickness. The braided core, like all nylon line, has a quality called "memory." This refers to the fact that nylon tends to stay in the position it was last stored—which was in tight coils on your fly reel.

You can remove the memory by a steady, firm pull—letting a companion help you speed up the process. Or you can do it yourself by placing your foot in the center of a long coil and pulling firmly on both ends.

After the line has been stripped from the spool, and the coils have been removed, let it fall to the deck. When you first pulled the line from the reel, you dropped the forward portion of the line on the deck, then placed the rear part of the line on top of that: if you don't make a practice throw and reverse the order of the coils, you are certain to get a tangled mess when you cast to a fish. *The fly must be cast one time and the line retrieved, and dropped to the deck in the correct casting position.*

Be sure that you are using the right line for your particular fishing conditions. There are situations for which a floating line is most efficient, and others where a sinking-tip, slow-sinker, or very fast-sinking line is best. Many anglers now carry several rods in the boat rigged either with different lines or different types of flies to be able to accommodate various situations.

It's worth mentioning again that before any cast is made, proper drag tension should be set on the reel.

Prior to the first cast, double-check for casting hazards. Boat poles being used as anchors by sticking them into the bottom and tied to the boat should be set at a very low angle so that they won't interfere with the back-cast. If there is a possibility that you may have to follow the fish after it has been hooked, rig a quick-release anchor. This is simply a float attached to a snap at the boat end of the anchor rope. If you suddenly have to follow a fish, your companion simply opens the snap and frees the anchor. Later you can return and pick up the anchor rope, which will be buoyed by the float. A crab pot trap float works well and is inexpensive.

If you are blind casting along the edge of a bar, for example, and you hook a big striper or blue, the anchor must be instantly available. Your partner may also get a strike and may not be able to operate the motor; tossing the anchor overboard will enable both of you to fight fish.

The purpose of the short belly section of a fly line is to enable the angler to hold as much of this line as possible outside the guides prior to the firm cast. The more belly he holds outside, the faster he can deliver the fly over a satisfactory distance. There are a half-dozen methods for holding the line in the ready position, but the simplest is to hold the rod in your right hand—if that is your favored hand—and to hold the feathers of the fly clasped between the first finger and the thumb of the same hand. The

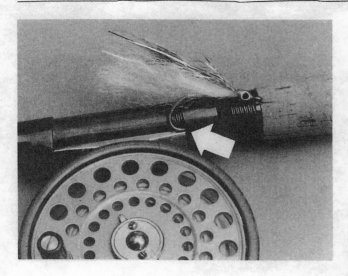

One of the safest ways to store a sharp hook on a ready-rigged fly rod is with the point hidden under the reel seat.

left hand holds the line coming back through the guides.

When a spot cast is to be made, rock the rod back sharply, allowing the ten to fifteen feet of line and leader hanging outside the rod tip to pull free the fly clenched in your fingers; two or three false casts and you can usually shoot the required line. Don't throw the fly loose; allow the line to pull it from the clenched fingers. This is an important factor for it causes the rod to load better for the backcast. If the fly is tossed free, poor loading results. *If you are going to fish the flats you must master the speed cast.*

The name of the game when you see a saltwater fish is speed and accuracy—something many anglers have a great deal of initial trouble with.

In shallow water the angler and his companion search until they see a fish. At that moment a decision has to be made—one has to decide immediately how far in front of the fish to direct the cast. Several factors affect that decision: how fast is the fish moving, what is the closing rate of the boat, how deep is the fish running, and from what direction is the wind blowing?

Most saltwater fly casters feel it's unethical to cast from a boat under power, or to troll a fly; the motor should be out of gear when the cast is made. The species of fish to which the angler is casting must also be considered in determining where the fly is to be dropped in front of the fish. Redfish (channel bass), for example, possess very poor eyesight; most of the time a fly slapped on the water near a redfish's eye will draw its attention. Amberjacks and cobia often slash savagely at a loud, burping popper, and jack crevalles love to hit a lure that falls with a plop beside them.

Much of shoreline fishing is seeing fish. Here Bob Marriott of Fullerton, California, stalks a bonefish on a Christmas Island flat; he is properly equipped with polarized glasses and the right kind of hat.

Other fish—permit, bonefish, mutton snappers, and sometimes stripers, if they are in calm water—demand a silent entry of the fly into the water. In this case the fly should be cast rather far ahead of the fish so as not to spook it. Few anglers would believe, until they witness it, that a 150-pound tarpon cruising over a white sand flat is spooked by a tiny, three-inch fly presented closer than four or five feet.

Learn the habits of your quarry, but assume that a noisy entry will scare the fish, and that you should cast far enough ahead of the fish to prevent frightening it.

The angle at which the fish is approaching you is important. A fish coming toward the boat at a very slight angle is in the best position for a good presentation. The worst angle from which to present a fly is when a fish is going away from the boat, and the fly line must fall over the fish; this almost always scares the fish.

Two anglers fishing the same flat may score differently even though they have the same tackle, flies, and casting ability. One realizes the importance of the approach of the fly to the fish—the unsuccessful angler does not. A bonefish, for example is easily spooked. A fly that comes charging toward it is considered by the fish to be a threat and it bolts away. *Try always to have your fly approach the fish in a natural manner.* For example, if a fish is facing into the tide, throw the fly up-tide of the quarry and slowly strip in the fly as it drifts *naturally* toward the fish. A fly that comes from behind and suddenly appears, or one that rushes at the fish head-on, usually results in a refusal, and the fish often flees.

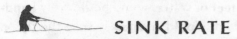 ## SINK RATE

Closely linked to how far ahead of the fish you should cast and the natural direction approach is the sink rate of the fly. A few bottom feeders (flounders, bonefish, and permit are examples) will dive below them to grab a fly. But most species will not. Generally, the best cast is one where the fly and the fish meet at the same depth. Few fish will descend to grab a lure, but they will often rise a bit to take one—keep that in mind when making your presentation.

The sink rate of the fly is obviously important in deepwater fishing, where the fly must get down to the fish's feeding level. Spotted seatrout, for example, usually live in grassy basins and bays, and a fly that runs just above the grassy carpet will appeal to them most.

It's just as important to consider the sink rate of a fly in shallow water—maybe even more so. Bonefish often feed in water so shallow that their backs partially protrude above the surface. A fast-sinking fly that dives into entangling grass is for all practical purposes useless under these conditions. The fly must sink slowly, giving the angler time to manipulate it and allow the fish to notice it.

How do you control sink rate? There are several methods. The most basic way is to change the hook size; naturally, a fly tied on a 3/0 hook is going to sink faster than one dressed on a 1/0. Many times the fly's overall size can remain the same, and a much larger or smaller hook can be substituted to control the sink rate.

Another way to control sink rate is to add thin lead wire to the hook shank, or add bead chain eyes at the head of the fly. By having a very sparse or bulky wing, a fly can be made to sink quickly or slowly. Adding palmered hackle will slow the descent of a fly. Buoyant materials can also be used in the fly body to make it resist sinking.

In summary, you must decide the type of fly pattern you need to control the sink rate, and then be able to judge how far in front of a moving fish to throw the cast in order to make a successful presentation.

LINE SELECTION

The various kinds of lines and their uses have already been discussed, but it bears repeating here that the angler must consider the best type of line suited for his specific fishing conditions (and the kind of line can also influence sink rate). For example, the angler wading in shallow water casting to fish in two to four feet of water would be severely handicapped with a fast-sinking line, which would constantly snag the fly on the bottom. Here, the angler needs a floating line with a sinking tip. If long casts must be made, a shooting head might be an asset in covering more water. When waters are very choppy, or the surface is littered with strands of floating grass, a floating line, even though you are only fishing a few inches under the surface, might not be the best choice. A slow-sinking line would be better. There are two reasons for this. A floating line would bob up and down on the waves. These undulations would give extra action to the fly, which may be undesirable. The other reason is that a floating line on the retrieve will "funnel" grass so that it is fed down the line to either the leader or fly, spoiling the presentation. The slow-sinking line would settle through the grass, and as it sinks the strands would slip free.

Faced with extra-strong currents and fish lying deep, such as at Casa Mar, the famed tarpon camp in Costa Rica, you need at best a heavy and very fast-sinking line. Most people choose a lead-core shooting head for this, although it's not always necessary. When bonefish are in the shallows, tossing flies on a weight-forward eight or nine line may spook them from the line's impact. Under such condition if there is little or no breeze a weight-forward five or six line would be ideal.

The point to be made is that there are no absolute rod-line combinations in salt water. One or two outfits won't do it. The angler will need a range of fly lines in different sizes from floaters to sinking-tips, slow-sinkers, fast-sinkers, extra-fast-sinkers, and lead-cores if he is to be able to adjust to various situations.

THE RETRIEVE

If the fly is improperly retrieved the game will usually be lost. Most freshwater anglers manipulate the rod tip to impart action to the fly. That technique should almost never be used in salt water—the same could be said for fishing in fresh, too!

They flip the rod tip in an upward motion, then strip in accumulated slack. Then they repeat the process, often failing to hook the fish on the strike. Here's why: when the rod tip is snapped upward, the line jumps forward and falls on the water in front of the rod in loose coils; should a fish strike before this slack is removed, the chances of setting the hook are poor since there is no tension on the line.

Proper technique is actually simpler—almost foolproof, in fact—guaranteeing a slack-free line from angler to fish at all times. With the correct stripping retrieve the fish always strikes against a tight line; so if the hook is sharp the fish will usually impale itself on the fly. Proper stripping technique demands that the tip be placed either just under the water or within inches of it with the rod pointed toward the fly and the butt at your belt buckle. The action is imparted to the fly by the manner in which you strip with your line hand. You can vary the fly's movements by varying the strip.

One of the most important factors in retrieving an underwater fly is to keep the tip near the surface and pointed at the fish. Use the line hand to manipulate the fly. Never use the rod tip—this would develop unwanted slack that would make striking difficult.

A series of short strips causes the fly to dart forward accordingly; long pulls will swim the fly forward in graceful strokes. Virtually no slack occurs with this stripping technique, and when the fish hits the fly the angler can instantly strike.

When retrieving the fly, the angler can frequently see the fish and how it is reacting. If the fish is just following the fly, or showing little interest, changing the retrieve—quick little strokes or several long pulls—may cause the fish to think the quarry is escaping, and the fish will strike.

Since there are only a few cases where you should deviate from the basic retrieve described above, they are worth mentioning. If you are fishing deep with your fly where strong current exist, often the best retrieve is almost none. In jungle river mouths, and in deep channels with a fast-flowing tide, tarpon and other species will lie on the bottom behind small uprisings, just as trout will lie in a riffle in the quiet flow behind a rock. You have to get the fly to them, and the current will cause the feathers to pulse in a lifelike manner if you can bomb the line and fly to the bottom and bring the fly back at a snail's pace.

When chumming fish to the boat, particularly in deep water, the fish move in and slowly "sip" the morsels being fed to them. A fly that is dropped into the chum slick and zipped back to the angler at high speed is usually ignored. The trick here is to cast the fly alongside of the drifting chum and allow the fly to flow naturally back to the sipping fish. In this case a reverse stripping is sometimes used, where line is paid out instead of brought in.

Joe Brooks taught me another retrieve method that turns on some species that are notoriously difficult to coax into striking, like the wary barjack. Barjacks ride the warm seas, often feeding on the many small fish that gather and hide in the floating weed lines that may string out for miles in the current. I love to cruise these weed lines looking for barjacks as well as a number of other species. But when I find the jacks they sometimes refuse to strike. Joe taught me this trick and it often saves the day.

Drop the popping bug down on the water in front of the jack, pop it once, then lift it immediately. The jack will spin on its fins to see what happened. Then drop the bug back again, just in front of its nose, and lift it immediately. Repeat this several times and the jack will be frantic as it tries to locate this noisy, disappearing thing. Then sit the bug down softly, make one or two slight popping sounds, and the fish will usually tear into it. I've worked this trick on cobia, dolphins, barracudas, amberjacks, bluefish, and many other species.

One other retrieve is worth knowing, especially if you need to bring the fly back over a considerable distance at a high speed. Make the longest cast you possibly can. Slip the rod high up under one arm, clenching it so that both hands are free. Then, begin a hand-over-hand retrieve, bringing the line back as quickly as you can.

Wrong Way to Retrieve
If the fly fisherman manipulates an underwater fly with the rod tip, the chance of a hookup is reduced. Each upward motion of the rod tip causes the fly to jump too fast across the bottom, and worse, creates line slack as the tip is lowered for another flip. Make it a rule not to manipulate the fly with your rod.

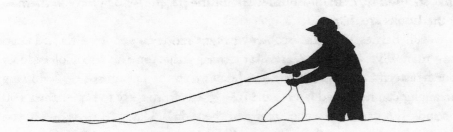

Right Way to Retrieve
The right way to retrieve an underwater fly is to point the rod low and toward the fish, then manipulate the fly by how you strip in line. The low rod is especially effective when the wind is blowing. A rod held high allows the wind to push against the line dangling between the rod tip and the surface. By keeping the rod tip low (as shown) and using the line hand to work the fly, the line stays tight and better hookups result.

I have been frequently criticized for advocating that saltwater fly fishermen try to learn to cast ninety or 100 feet. The two arguments used against this philosophy are that few fish are ever 100 feet away when you cast; and you can't set the hook at that distance. Remember that in saltwater fly fishing God very seldom lets you cast downwind, and a 100-footer when it's calm may only be a thirty-foot cast when throwing into a twenty-miles-per-hour breeze. As for striking at that distance: if the hook is sharp and the line taut on a proper retrieve, I have hooked many fish at seventy to eighty feet. And so will anyone else, if they use a retrieve where the line is always tight between the fly and the angler.

And, if you are teasing the fish with different types and speeds of retrieve without success, vary the size of the fly. If that fails, switch to a totally different type of fly. *But, first vary the retrieve!*

 ## WHEN THE FISH TAKES THE FLY

When the retrieve is successful, the angler must learn what to do with various fish. Tarpon, despite fabled stories to the contrary, strike so softly that many anglers are not aware that the fish has taken the fly. Tarpon give themselves away, however, in other ways. They will usually move up deliberately, slowly suck in the fly, then roll to one side. When the fish rolls, or you see a silvery flash, that's the time to set the hook. There are two methods of hook setting on tarpon and many other big fish (including billfish) that are used successfully. Both work for the people who believe in them— if the hooks are sharp.

Bill Barnes, who has probably caught more tarpon on a fly rod than any man alive, operates Casa Mar fishing lodge on the Rio Colorado in northeastern Costa Rica. On a good day when the tarpon are really hitting an angler can hook and land two dozen giants from sixty to better than 100 pounds. Bill has experienced many of these days. Harry Kime is one of the finest saltwater fly rodders who ever lived. For years he has visited Casa Mar annually, staying for several months and fishing daily. Between Bill and Harry, they have caught more tarpon with a fly than I'm sure any other pair of anglers. These two men began experimenting years ago on striking techniques, and after years of testing them on tarpon, they feel that the best technique is a very simple one. With the rod pointed at the fish and the line tight, when the fish strikes, they simply grasp the line firmly and pull straight back with a sharp, one-foot jab. This drives the hook home solidly, and they have instant control of the line as the fish races away.

A totally different technique was worked out by Flip Pallot and Bill Hegley, in the early 1970s, who first tested the idea that tarpon don't quickly reject a fly when they take it—if the hook is sharp. They would make the cast, the tarpon would accept the fly, and then they would throw slack, allowing the tarpon to swim away with the fly. Some tarpon held the fly for as long as nine seconds before expelling it.

From these experiments they tested a new striking technique. As the fish took the fly they would lower the rod to the side and at right angles to the fish. The line would be clenched in the left hand (if the angler held the rod in the right), and as the fish moved away with the fly, the line was held tightly, allowing the fish to pull the hook into its flesh. This technique resulted in many fish being hooked. The only flaw in this system is that when the fish suddenly realizes that it's hooked it's going to bolt away and the clenched line must be released—if not, the leader breaks.

Bob Stearns and I fished for Pacific sailfish in Costa Rica once. We used their striking technique on more than a dozen sailfish—all but one were hooked solidly.

Each system works, and also doesn't. Try both and choose the one you prefer. What doesn't work, and it is a mistake commonly made by freshwater anglers, is to have a big fish take a fly on a heavy rod and line, and then the angler snaps his wrist upward to drive the hook home. The fish's mouth is tough, and the heavy hooks can't be driven home with a wrist snap. Either jab backward with the whole rod arm, use the Barnes/Kime method, or hold the rod firmly at right angles on big fish to strike well.

Many smaller fish require only a lifting of the rod to drive the hook home. Bonefish will pick up a lure with a very subtle take and move off. When you realize that the fish has the fly, you need only lift the rod slowly or pull back gently on the line in your hand.

One area where missed strikes result and a longer than normal sweep of the rod is needed is when using popping bugs. Since the popper rides on the surface and is often pushed away by the fish on the strike, more slack can occur. Because of this slack, the angler needs to make an extended rod sweep to ensure hooking the fish.

Many freshwater anglers use monofilament shooting line on their shooting heads. If you fish for larger quarries in the salt do not use monofilament. During the fight you can cut your hands badly with the super-thin monofilament, and it's very difficult to handle as well as the ever-constant wind that blows the light, thin stuff all over the place. If you use the ultra-thin fly line available from Cortland and Scientific Anglers, make sure that the core strength of the line will test more than the leader you are using. Several types of such shooting lines in strengths to thirty pounds are now available and are vastly superior to monofilament for fighting big fish.

Unlike freshwater fish, most saltwater fish seem to go crazy when they feel the steel of the hook driven into their mouth. The line lying at your feet is going to come up through the guides like a striking snake, and unless you enter some controls at this point, you'll surely get a tangle. As soon as you have struck a fast-running fish, forget it and concentrate on the loose line—your immediate problem is to get *that* under control. Your fish is going to make a blazing run, and you should curl the first finger and thumb around the line to form a large ring guide. Hold the rod high! Ignore the fish and look at the line below, making sure it flows freely as the fish runs. Don't hold the rod low, and if the reel is rotated away from the line hand you reduce the chances of the line catching the reel handle or the butt of the rod. Allow the line to flow through the "ring guide" made by the fingers until it comes tight against the reel spool. Now you can play the fish normally.

PLAYING A FISH

Most freshwater fishermen who make the transition to salt water discover for the first time that many of the fish they hook cannot be brought to the boat at will. All of a sudden a new set of problems arises: there is a need for backing on the reel, for some sort of mechanical drag, and for learning the technique for give-and-take battle tactics. In most freshwater situations the angler plays the fish because it's fun—actually, he could have landed the fish anytime he chose. In salt water it is often very different. Of course, small fish can be boated easily and quickly, but others may take an hour—or five hours. Strain on both angler and tackle can be severe.

The most important rule in fighting any big fish, in salt or fresh water, is *never allow a sudden lurch or sharp jerk against the line.* As long as a steady pull is exerted by the fish the line generally won't break.

To prove this, hold a piece of six- to ten-pound monofilament in your hands, each one grasping an end. Snap your hands apart and the line breaks easily. Now, holding the line in the same manner, snap your right hand to the right, and your left in the same direction. Because the left hand follows the path of the force, no strain occurs on the line, so it doesn't break.

The same principle applies when you're fishing. When a fish makes a sudden surge away, the angler should thrust the rod *toward* the fish, to reduce the jolting impact on the line.

It is difficult to appreciate how much steady pressure can be applied to a line before it will break—as long as the pressure is even and steady. To test how much power you can get from a twelve-pound-test tippet, tie the line to a doorknob, then back off and begin to raise your fly rod, holding the line taut so no tension is released. The rod will take on a deep strain, your arms will begin to quiver, and you'll find it actually impossible with some rods, and tough with all rods, to break the twelve-pound line with a steady pull. Remember—it's the sharp jolt on the line that breaks it.

Drag is essential for fighting many saltwater fish, so knowing how drag works—and how it can be used to your advantage—is vital. If the drag is set too light, the fish will strip the line from the reel; if it's too tight, the fish will break the line. Proper adjustment will allow the line to slip when needed, enabling you to keep control, so you can return line to the reel spool. Drag adjustment is really a complicated matter, but some simple rules will allow you to fish effectively—and experience will take over.

How does a drag work on a fly rod and line? You may think that if you run the line through the guides and adjust the drag until it slips with a one-pound pull, the drag will slip any time a fish exerts a one-pound pull against it. Not true! After such a setting, raise the rod to about a 45-degree angle; then have someone attach a scale to the line and pull a deep bend in the rod. At 45 degrees you will discover that the drag doesn't slip until maybe two pounds of pull is exerted. Now, hold the rod so that the butt points vertically. Repeat the process. As the rod forms a deeper bend the drag pressure will increase to three or four pounds—depending upon the rod's action and guide placement—before the drag will slip.

If you watch the scale reading closely it will also be apparent that while the 45-degree angle allowed the drag to slip when two pounds of pressure was applied, it also took twice that pressure to get the drag started. In other words, starting drag for most reels is almost twice that of the force needed to keep it slipping. The angle at which the rod is held, how many guides are on the rod (there is line friction against each one), and the starting drag all affect how the drag slips under a strain from the fish. While a fish is pulling the heavy fly line through the guides, the drag will increase; then it drops off for awhile when the thinner backing line begins running through the guides.

However, as the diameter of the backing line on the reel spool gets smaller, the ratio of resistance increases radically. A Fin-Nor Model #3 fly reel (which holds about 200 yards of thirty-pound-test Dacron) set at a running drag that slips when two pounds is exerted will, when only 100 yards of line remains on the spool, have an increase in drag pressure to nearly seven pounds. Add the curvature of the rod, the guides, and any force exerted by the current, and you can see that you could quickly lose a fish on a twelve-pound-test tippet.

The problems seem immense. But, by applying a simple technique, even an inexperienced angler can land a fairly large fish with confidence.

When the fish has struck, the hook has been set, and the line is taut from its mouth to the reel, the actual battle begins. Most fish will make their fastest run the moment they feel the strike. Saltwater fish roam freely in their domain, and they experience terrible panic when they first feel the steel of the hook and the tightness of the line. A saltwater fish will try to escape with every instinct and fiber of its being. During that first frantic run try to keep the fish from getting too far away from you. But, do so with gentle pressure—your immediate purpose is to restrain the fish as much as possible without putting too much strain on your tackle. And you must prevent any jolting pulls against the line!

Once the fish has settled down from its first run, you should do everything in your power to take command—either you or the fish should be getting line. There should be very few times when either the line is not coming toward you or you're not losing line to the fish. Many anglers put a deep bend in the rod, then merely hold it; the fish can actually *rest* in such a condition, and this eventually prolongs the fight.

There is only one way to move a large fish against its will toward the angler—by pumping. Pumping is simply raising the rod from a horizontal position to nearly vertical. This draws the fish several feet toward the angler. As the rod is lowered to the horizontal position, the angler winds in the accumulated slack. *The only time the angler should wind in the line is while the rod is being lowered*. Pumping ensures a smooth flow of power exerted against the fish as the angler draws his quarry toward him. Not generally known is that once the rod butt nears the vertical position pressure lessens on the fish. If the rod continues to move away from the fish, pressure continues to drop off. You can check this by attaching the line end to a spring scale then have someone begin raising the rod. At first the scale will indicate an increase in pressure, but as the rod nears and passes vertically by the angler, pressure begins dropping off. The best method of pumping is to move the rod from a near horizontal position until the rod butt points at about 75 degrees. Then, lower the rod and wind in, repeating the operation over and over.

Very important during the pumping operation is that the angler must be aware of the fish. Should it suddenly surge away from the angler, the rod must be dropped instantly toward the fish to reduce the shock. This is the most vital point in taking big fish on a fly rod and light leader.

Jumping fish present special problems. As a child you must have waded into a stream and lifted a large stone from the bottom with surprising ease, yet found when you got the rock into the air that you could hardly hold it. When a fish rises above the surface its weight on the rod increased several times. Let's take an example: a big fish with a fly dives for the bottom, shaking its head to rid itself of the fly. These jolts, while dangerous to the tackle, can usually be controlled. Suddenly, the fish leaps high above the surface, shaking its head. The fish can now throw several times as much force against the leader and what little purchase the hook has in the fish's flesh (experienced tarpon fishermen have noticed that frequently a tarpon has been hooked and rehooked several times during a fight).

What do you do about it? When any fish jumps, you need to take the pressure off the line. That way the only thing the fish can rip and tear against is the fly stuck in its mouth. For years a technique called bowing to the fish has been practiced that creates controlled slack. With this technique thousands of leaping fish have been taken. When the fish jumps, bow toward the fish with your rod and shove it toward the leaping fighter. Enough slack is given to prevent the fish from raring against a taut line and pulling the hook free or breaking the tippet. It also eliminates the chance that the fish may fall on the fragile leader.

But, there are hazards in bowing to a fish. A common one is that too much slack is given. Sometimes the line actually wraps around the rod tip or the hook falls free.

Harry Kime, one of the greatest saltwater fly rodders who ever lived, pioneered much of the fishing in Baja and has caught uncounted numbers of tarpon; he has developed a technique for leaping fish that I believe is vastly superior to the bowing method.

"When a fish leaps," Harry explained, "all I do is dip the rod tip to the water in the direction of the fish. I've found that it works much better than the bowing technique, which I used for many years."

I've tried it, too, and agree with Harry. If the rod tip is simply lowered to the water the required slack occurs. But, the line remains straight, in a gentle bow from tip to fish, with enough slack to prevent the fish from gaining enough leverage to dislodge the fly or break the leader. Try Harry's technique by having someone simulate the leaping fish as you drop the rod tip—you'll be amazed at how easy it is to do, and how well it works. With either bowing or tip dropping, as soon as the fish falls back into the water you begin placing pressure on the fish again.

Many good anglers know about fighting fish with only side pressure. If the fish is more than fifteen yards from the boat it matters little at what angle the rod is held so long as you are applying pressure against the fish when you want. But, when the fish gets fairly close to the boat the angler should be very aware that side pressure will shorten the battle.

Whenever possible, *hold the rod at right angles to the direction the fish is swimming.* This forces the fish to be turned to the side, constantly off balance, using up its energy quicker and ineffectively. If the angler applies pressure exactly opposite of the swimming direction of the fish, it's like holding the reins on a mule pulling a wagon—the animal is in the best position to pull when directly in front of the wagon. But if you pull to one side with one rein, the mule (or the fish) is levered sideways as it struggles. *Side pressure only works when the fish is close enough to the boat so that a pull to the side can move the fish.* But, make it a rule that whenever you can, use side pressure when fighting a fish. It will mean tiring the trophy much faster.

So, the basic strategy is this: allow the fish to make its first run against a lightly established drag. Then, begin to fight the fish as hard as you feel the tackle will bear. Apply side pressure whenever you can to shorten the battle. Be on the alert at all times to compensate for a sudden lurch against the line, or if the fish leaps, either bow or drop the rod tip to prevent line shock. And, keep the boat to one side while fighting the fish.

If you begin the fight with a lightly established drag of about 1½ pounds, then you will have to apply additional pressure against the fish during the battle. As the line diminishes you can slip the fingertips inside the spool and apply more pressure by pressing against the smooth inner side. The fingers can apply a delicate or a strong application of pressure. Naturally, anytime the fish needs to be given line, a quick release of the fingertips will put the fish against a light drag again.

Even more drag can be obtained by trapping the line against the rod with the fingers. It is surprising how much pressure can be applied this way. It can be especially handy when, the battle at an end, you raise the fish to the surface so it can be netted, gaffed, or released, and the fish bolts away. Simply lifting the fingers from the line as the rod tip is dropped puts the fish pulling against only the light drag. The better you become at fish fighting, the lighter the mechanical drag you'll be using and the more you will rely on finger pressure.

Real familiarity with your rod—how it bends under stress and the particular curve it takes—is vital in fighting big fish. You can learn about each rod's curves through a simple technique. Run the line through the guides and attach the end to a spring scale held by a companion. Have a friend call out the various scale readings as you vary the curve of the rod under pressure. Later, place various amounts of strain on the rod and call out to your friend what you think the scale readings are. Your friend will surprise you at how far you are off at first.

One other point: lifting a series of weights up to seven pounds off the floor with the rod and leader will make you appreciate that it takes enormous pressure and a very stout rod to lift even three pounds. Few saltwater rods can do that and have any reserve power.

Let's take a typical fish-fighting example: we'll assume that you've hooked a jumping fish of respectable size. The column on the left lists the effects of the drag and the reaction of the fish. The right column gives correct responses to the fish's action and the accumulated drag.

You're using twelve-pound-test tippet. The aim of a top-flight angler is to apply ten to eleven pounds of pressure at all times against the fish; this is one of the major secrets of light-tackle fishing—*apply maximum pressure all the time.* The angler must observe and judge the pressures that accumulate in the left column, and respond with the proper measures to build the resistance to ten or eleven pounds—leaving a few ounces for a safety margin. Naturally, inexperienced anglers would strive for about seven or eight pounds, leaving a larger safety factor. The following table describes top-efficiency fish fighting:

Accumulated Resistance at Fish's End	Angler's Responses
Running drag is adjusted to slip with 1½ lbs. of straight pull; it takes twice that much pressure (3 lbs.) to get the drag moving. When fish strikes, rod bends and resistance is actually about 5 lbs.	At the strike, angler drives hook home with several sharp but very short jabs with rod. He allows fish to run, feeding the loose coils through his hand until line comes up on reel spool. He lets fish pull line as it speeds away. Drag safety margin is 7 lbs.
Fish has run off from boat 100 yards (30-yard fly line and 70 yards of backing). (Many anglers clip 10 to 15 feet of fly line from rear end, to reduce water resistance against the line and obtain more backing.) Drag resistance accumulated by pull of fish, water resistance against line, bend in rod, and mechanical drag is now 7 lbs.	Angler begins applying pressure as fish slows; 3 to 4 lbs. is a safe maximum.
Fish at 100 yards leaps—if line comes tight against fish with all drag resistances, coupled with the fish's weight, the leader will part.	Angler sees fish rising from water, realizes that total pull against his 12-lb.-test leader will exceed leader strength. Angler lowers rod and shoves it toward fish to create as much controlled slack line as possible.
Fish falls back into water.	As soon as fish descends from its jump and hits water, angler raises his rod and rapidly reels in all slack.
Fish swims slowly to one side, pulling line from reel. Resistance it creates against tackle is 8 lbs.	Angler applies 2 to 3 lbs. more pressure by holding his fingertips against the inside of the reel spool, or by using his fingertips against the line between the rod grip and butt guide. Angler attempts to pump fish and draw the fish toward him. He succeeds in bringing fish a little closer. He places line back on spool by reeling each time rod tip is dropped down toward fish.
Fish is brought slowly to boat against its will by pumping strokes. As fish is drawn closer, pressure at fish's end due to rod bend, adjusted mechanical drag, line resistance, and swimming motions of fish is 4 lbs.	Angler now increases pressure trying at all times to keep 10 to 11 lbs. of force against fish. He applies 6 to 7 lbs. of pressure using fingertip controls, always bringing fish closer by pumping motions.
Fish refuses to come closer and begins to swim around boat, slowly beating its tail. Resistance is 9 lbs.	Angler keeps a good bend in rod and applies 1 to 2 pounds of pressure. At this time, angler is extremely alert in case fish bolts quickly, placing shock on leader.

Accumulated Resistance at Fish's End	Angler's Responses
Fish sees boat and swims under it.	Angler races to end where fish swam under boat, pushes several feet of the rod underwater, and keeps it there, so line won't foul on boat (motor should be raised by companion if fish may catch line on sharp edges of propeller). Rod is manipulated so that the line under the boat is kept free and rod moved to side of boat where fish is, then rod can be brought back to fighting position.
Fish suddenly bolts away from boat.	Angler drops rod tip and shoves rod and reel toward fish to reduce shock on leader.
Fish continues to move away at a slower pace, creating 8 lbs. drag.	After initial surge by fish, angler should apply—with fingers to line and inside of reel spool—2 or 3 lbs. of pressure.
While fish is swimming away, the line picks up floating grass—increasing drag resistance to 10 lbs.	Angler should immediately shake grass from line or have companion move boat forward to angler can remove grass by hand. Light pressure should be kept against fish during this event. Angler should guide line away from floating grass when he can.
Fish swims slowly away, creating 7 lbs. of resistance.	Angler applies 3 to 4 lbs. of force. It is very important that the boatman keep the craft to the side of the fish—*not* directly behind it—at all times. With the boat behind fish, the line falls across fish and leader or line could be cut by tail, or sharp portions of the fish.
Fish finally tires and nears boat. Resistance at fish's end, from all factors, is about 3 lbs.	Angler now increases pressure to 7 or 8 lbs., always looking for a sudden surge by the fish.
Fish tires and angler can now move fish at will. Companion is ready with gaff or net.	Angler steps back in boat, while companion moves in front of him. This places the companion nearer the fish but angler should always have fish in sight. Boats with high freeboard can create visibility problems.
Fish is moved to boatside.	Companion is ready to gaff. Angler backs off on mechanical drag and alertly watches his companion.
Terrified, fish bolts away from the boat.	Companion strikes at fish with gaff, misses getting good hookup, and scares fish. Angler, with drag lightened and ready, drops rod tip toward fish. Then, after initial burst of speed by fish, angler draws fish near again, and his companion gaffs fish and places it in boat.

If you are in a small boat and a tarpon jumps, never pull on the fish. You might pull the fish toward you and "slide" the boat under it; several people have been hurt doing this. Either bow to the fish or use the dipping rod technique (see page 234) while the fish is in the air.

During the battle your fishing companion is part of a team that is trying to subdue the fish. Without his help you are severely handicapped—and a poor boatman can often cause the angler to lose his prize.

Immediately after the fish has been struck the boatman must assay the situation. Is the fish going to strip all the line? Is the fish heading for an obstruction? Are sharks near?

If it appears that the fish will surely run all the line off the angler's reel, he must up-anchor, or get rid of the release anchor, start the motor, and head for the fish. During the entire fight the angler should be off to one side of the fish—not directly behind it. If the boat is directly behind the fish, it can exert the full pressure of its swimming ability against the tackle. The tail, rough back, or fins can often slice through the leader or even a fly line. A tarpon, in particular, often wears right through a fly line with its strong, beating tail. Sharks are even worse: their skin is like sandpaper. Keeping the boat to the side of the fish allows the angler greater control over his quarry.

The biggest mistake a boatman can make is overrunning the fish—that is, approaching so fast that the angler can't keep pace retrieving slack, and the hook falls free. The angler must constantly communicate with his companion: the boatman should watch the rod to make sure he is going slow

One of the major tricks in fighting big fish, or any fish where the tippet is fragile, is to apply side pressure when the fish is close to the boat. Here the author applies side pressure in the direction opposite from which the tarpon is swimming. Side pressure makes the fish burn up energy and keeps it off balance.

enough to keep a bend in it. And, he must keep a course that is to the side of the fish.

Should the fish be near an obstruction that could cut the fly line, the boatman must race ahead and place the boat between the fish and the obstruction. Sometimes putting the boat in neutral and racing the engine will frighten the fish into changing direction.

Many times, particularly near the end of the battle, the fish will suddenly turn and swim rapidly under the boat. Since most propellers are razor sharp and will easily slice a line or leader, the boatman should shut off the motor, lift the lower unit from the water, and get everything out of the way that would prevent the fisherman from moving to the back of the boat.

Should the fish dart under the boat, the most effective thing you can do is plunge the rod tip deep underwater and allow the line to flow without striking the boat or motor. Then you can walk the rod past the end of the boat and then safely raise the rod and continue the battle.

The angler should always be warned before any sudden moves are made with the boat. The fisherman, intent on battling the fish, has his hands full; a sudden surge of power from the motor could knock him down, breaking the line and possibly resulting in injury. *Warn the man fighting the fish before you apply motor power or make any sudden moves with the boat.*

If, during the fight, the boat is moved over a long distance, or often, if you are fishing an area carpeted with thick grass, floating grass can accumulate on the line, and if too much collects on it, the increased drag will break the leader. Usually, you can rid the line of grass by a series of short shakes of the rod tip. If not, step back and bring the grass near enough to the boat so your companion can remove it. But, remember, for many tournaments and for world records, no one may touch the line or tackle but the angler fighting the fish.

GAFFING OR LANDING FISH

Most fish are either lost on the strike or at the boat. It has been my experience that more are lost near the end of the fight than at the beginning.

The landing net has to be larger than the fish you intend to catch. That may sound obvious, but on a number of occasions, I have been forced to land a fish with a net entirely too small. In such cases all you can do is get the head of the fish in the net—and then pray. Two or three pinch-on sinkers attached to the bottom of the net will help it fall open when it's picked up.

Many landing nets have bright nylon twine that will spook fish. You can dye them easily with household dyes, eliminating much of the problem. Be sure the net has a handle long enough to reach the fish easily from the boat.

Never chase a fish with a net. Hold the net motionless at roughly a 75-degree angle and lead the fish toward the net. Once the head of the fish is in the mouth of the net, sweep forward with a swift, upward motion. Never approach a fish from the rear with a net. If you touch the tail of most fish, unless it is exhausted, it will surely bolt away. And, that sudden jerk may break the line.

Nets should be stored out of the way in a boat but where they can be reached quickly. Nylon or plastic nets are better than cotton ones, since they don't rot.

Gaffing a fish requires greater skill than netting. There are two basic types of gaffs: flying gaffs and hand gaffs. The flying gaff is a hook that is detachable from the handle. It has a ring on the shank to which a line or cable is attached. When the fish is stuck, the hook slips free of the handle, and the fish is battled on the line. The end of the gaff line is usually tied to a boat cleat. Flying gaffs are often used for dangerous big-game fish such as sharks and marlin. But for general use the hand gaff (a hook permanently attached to a handle) is more desirable.

Hand gaffs come in many shapes and sizes. Most well-equipped boats carry at least two, and many experienced anglers will have as many as five different ones on board. The handle length of a gaff depends upon its purpose, and whether the boat has a high or low freeboard. For general fishing in most inshore waters I'd recommend two gaffs: one with a handle from four to seven feet long for reaching out to get fish, and a short hand gaff,

Albacore are some of the fastest-running targets for inshore fly fishermen.

with a handle approximately a foot long. Both usually have a three- to four-inch bite. The short gaff is perfect for reaching down beside the boat to lift exhausted fish; it is also great for assisting in bringing in a large fish. The longer gaff can be used to hook a fish several feet away from the boat. When the fish is struck, the gaffer often doesn't get the point to penetrate just where he intended, resulting in an insecure hold on the fish. The angler can lay down his rod and use the smaller gaff (which has no barb and is referred to often as a release gaff). With these two gaffs in a fish, even respectable-sized trophies can be hauled aboard easily.

I think it is important to emphasize that no fish should be gaffed unless you have to. Many people gaff barracudas, inflicting a serious or fatal wound. Then, after removing the hook, they toss the fish back to die. This should never happen. Many fish can be immobilized by slipping the release gaff point inside the mouth and lifting the fish into the boat so that the lure can be removed and the fish released relatively unharmed.

There seem to be two schools of thought regarding gaffing giant tarpon—fish weighing more than sixty-five pounds. In the Florida Keys, where certainly the best-informed saltwater guides in the world practice their skills, the common agreement is to use an eight-foot gaff. This gaff carries a huge hook, usually eight inches across, of one-half-inch-diameter stainless steel with a razor-sharp point. It is a formidable weapon. Many experienced Keys guides carry two such gaffs in case one is lost during the battle. I personally know several top-flight guides who, when a giant tarpon was brought alongside, struck the fish and were pulled overboard.

The small, but strong, Indians who live in Costa Rica and spend about six months of the year guiding anglers for tarpon in the jungle rivers use a tiny three-inch gaff, with a rather dull point. Often the handle is a broomstick, or is fashioned from a straight limb. I have witnessed these small Indians gaff many 100-pound tarpon and can't honestly recall ever seeing a fish lost because the gaff was inadequate.

Instead of driving a sharp, large gaff into the flanks of the tarpon as guides in the Keys often do, they slip the tiny three-inch hook inside the mouth, and then pin the point against the side of the boat where they can hold the fish until it stops thrashing. Then they remove the fly or lure and let the fish go. If the fish is to be kept, they take a stout club and strike hard, once or twice, across the tarpon's head, which permanently ends the fight.

I like a gaff with a sharp triangulated point. To protect the point I slip a short section of automobile radiator hose over it. This can be pulled free when needed. There are a number of spring wire protectors, but I know of several fish that were lost when the leader entangled in the spring. Gaffs should always be stored where they can't hurt anyone in the boat.

I prefer a release gaff with a loop of cord on the rear of the handle through which the wrist can be slipped. But, it's very important that the loop be attached to the handle with a stout swivel. I remember watching one guide sticking a shark with a release gaff. The shark began twisting and spinning and wrapped the loop so tightly that we had to cut it free from the guide's wrist, which required hospital treatment. A good swivel would have prevented the problem.

Let's assume that the proper gaff is at hand and that the angler has tired the fish. The angler should always stand *behind* the gaffer, but still be able to see the fish. If the gaffer stands behind the angler he can't reach the fish easily. Both people should be able to see the fish at all times.

The first and most important rule is to keep the gaff behind the leader at all times. If the fish should surge forward, the leader won't touch the sharp gaff. The second basic rule of good gaffing is that once you have struck the fish with the gaff you must keep coming until the fish has been lifted into the boat. Naturally, all loose tackle and equipment should be cleared away before the gaffing operation.

If the fish is heavy you can gaff it near the head. As the fish is struck it will violently vibrate its tail, assisting the angler in lifting the fish into the boat. If the fish is still "green" (not tired), you may want to hit the fish near the tail. This lifts the tail out of the water, which is where the fish gets its propelling power.

Thin fish are more difficult to gaff than wide fish, and those with hard scales, like tarpon, are tougher to sink a gaff into than, for example, tuna. In a survey I once conducted among some top gaffers, all agreed that barracudas, king mackerels, and wahoo were among the toughest fish to gaff simply because the thin body offered such a poor target.

The gaffer can place the gaff in the water with the hook up and wait for a fish to swim over it (never chase a fish with a gaff—you only make it more frantic) or poise above the fish waiting to sweep downward with the point at the right moment. Most good gaffers prefer to strike down rather than up. They sweep down, the handle riding against the back of the fish as the point is forced into the flesh. The moment the hook is sunk the fish is swept in a continuous motion into the boat.

Don't rush, and strike only when you feel that you're able to do it properly. Too many fish are lost by gaffing at a poor opportunity.

If you make a bad strike with the gaff the fish becomes gaff-shy. Often sharks move in, attracted by the blood.

Fish react in all sorts of ways when gaffed. Cobia twist violently— stand clear. Bluefish will often snap at anything close and some nasty wounds have resulted when one was dropped onto the deck. Big tarpon, amberjacks, and many other tough species can wreck the inside of a boat if gaffed and dropped inside. If you have a large fish box, try to gaff the fish and, as it is lifted from the water, drop it immediately into the box. *Never gaff a shark and put it in a boat. In fact, don't put an apparently dead shark in your boat—often they aren't dead.* Their skin is like a sharp file and they can peel the hide from an angler. I've seen a "dead" shark come back to life and bite a section out of a boat seat; and I know of one case where everyone abandoned the boat to a shark they thought was long gone. Tow sharks to port, but don't put them in your boat. Towing is a quick method of drowning a shark.

Billfish should be neither gaffed nor netted when taken on a fly. The mate should wear gloves because the bill is very abrasive. As the tired fish is brought alongside, the mate should grab the bill and lift it up to be released or brought into the boat. It is very important that the bill be grasped with both hands and the point held away from the body. That way if the fish surges forward the deadly bill point can be pushed away from the body. Several mates have been hurt badly when the fish was held so that the bill was pointed toward their stomachs, and the fish bolted forward. Any billfish put in a boat should be first dispatched.

If you're fishing in the surf, you're in luck. After the fish has been thoroughly beaten, back up slowly toward the beach. Wait for an incoming roller, and carefully lift the fish with the wave and run up on the beach while the wave carries the fish forward. As the wave recedes the fish will be deposited on the sand, but you must quickly grab it and carry it farther up the shore to prevent the next incoming wave from towing it seaward. Never attempt to kick a fish; the spines can cause a painful injury.

HANDLING FISH THAT HAVE BEEN CAPTURED

Nearly all freshwater fish can be handled safely. The catfish has spines that can give you trouble and the pike and pickerel have pointed teeth, but, in the main, freshwater fish are relatively safe to pick up. Saltwater fish are a different matter; almost all species can be hazardous to handle.

Many fish in fresh and salt water held belly up (as the author is doing with this bonefish) will lie perfectly motionless, allowing the hook to be removed without injuring the fish.

Nearly all saltwater species have coarser and stronger gill covers than freshwater varieties. You should not put your hands inside the gill flaps of *any* saltwater fish unless you know exactly what you are doing. The channel bass and many bottom species have extremely rough gills, and can inflict nasty cuts if the fish flops around while your fingers are inside those gill covers. Snappers have earned that name, so respect them.

Bluefish have sharp teeth. As with barracudas, mackerels, wahoo, and others, not only are its teeth sharp at the ends, but the sides are honed to razor edges. If you see teeth in the mouth of a saltwater fish, assume that those teeth will be dangerous.

Other saltwater fish crush their food. Any fish with soft, rubbery lips must do something to its prey so it can swallow it; such fish have strong

An alternate method of handling fish is one the Australians call the "comfort lift." Here Ted Juracsik shows how it's done. Position the hand under the fish on the belly side in the center of the fish's weight (not length) and simply lift the fish from the water. The fish will lie perfectly still.

crushers in their mouths. The fish grabs its victim, flips it back between the crushers, which close quickly with the force of a steel vise, and the prey is reduced to pulp. I have seen a permit pick up a hard-shelled crab, crush it with a gulp, and spit out the shell as easily as you would a peanut. Any angler who sticks his hands inside the mouth of a fish with smooth or leathery lips is taking a good chance of losing fingers.

Some fish present hazards that are not really apparent to the angler with little saltwater experience. The jack family, which has many sub-species, usually have soft rays in the dorsal fin. However, some jacks carry a small pair of stiff, sharp spines on the belly near the anus that can cause a painful stab. You can immobilize a jack by gripping the fish across the back of the head and clamping the fingers at the junction of the gill covers. For some reason the fish will be immobilized.

The snook is another fish that can hurt you. In the middle of the outer area of the gill covers is a transparent cutter blade that is as sharp as a knife. About the size of a nickel, it can slice your finger if you carelessly grab the fish. This cutter is why most snook fishermen use a thirty- or forty-pound monofilament shock leader. Most guides when holding a snook place their thumb inside the mouth and curl their first finger inside the gill at the point where the gills meet the throat.

Barracudas, mackerels, king mackerels, and other thin, hard-to-hold fish are best grabbed with either a glove or a towel.

 ## RELEASING FISH

Many fly-caught fish are inedible; if not kept for a trophy mount, you should return these to the sea without harm. Some fish are so exhausted when captured that they require special handling if they are to survive. Bonefish fight so valiantly that they often arrive at the boat in a state of collapse; if released immediately they will usually sink to the bottom and die. Tarpon often meet the same fate, as do many other species.

The general technique for reviving distressed fish is to hold the fish underwater in its normal swimming position, then swish it back and forth rapidly. Many anglers simply hold the fish by the tail when doing this. But I've determined that I can revive fish faster and better if I slip my thumb inside the mouth to hold it open. Apparently, when the fish is swished back and forth in this manner, much more life-giving water is passed over the gills. Try to release the fish in shallow water, so that if it is still in distress you can recapture it. And, put it back gently in its normal swimming position. Sometimes the fish will start to roll over or be unable to swim well. Touching it with the boat pole or gaff handle will often stimulate the fish so that it begins swimming away in a normal manner.

The number of fish in the sea may seem to be unlimited, but it is not, and any fish not kept for food or mounting should be carefully returned to the water in as good a condition as possible.

Guide to Dangers of Handling Fish

Species	Specific Dangers	Special Problems	How to Hold and Remove Fly
Barracuda (Great and Pacific)	Very sharp teeth, leap a great deal.	Be aware of leaping fish near the boat.	Hold fish firmly and use pliers or similar tool to remove fly.
Channel Bass or Redfish	Has strong crushers in mouth and gill rakers are very sharp.	Never put fingers inside mouth or gill covers.	Grasp fish behind head and pinch gill covers together. Large fish should be placed on deck or ground, and held firmly.
Striped Bass	Gill rakers can cut.	Keep fingers outside gill covers.	Hold fish firmly with a rag; smaller fish can be grasped by lower lip.
Bluefish	Extremely sharp teeth.	Use special tool for removing fly.	Hold fish with a rag to keep it from slipping, and use metal tool to remove fly.
Bonefish	No dangers, but fish is considered inedible and should be released unharmed.	"Crushers" deep inside throat can mangle fingers.	Gently.
Cobia	Extremely strong and muscular.	Fish should be tired before attempting to land.	Don't try removing fly from fish until it is tired; place fish in fish box until it calms.
Dolphin	Thrashes about violently and bleeds profusely.	Same as cobia.	Same as cobia.
Black Drum	Same as redfish.	Same as redfish.	Same as redfish.
Jack Crevalle	Small cutting projection next to anus; very strong fish.		You can paralyze fish by holding behind head and pinching behind head.
Mackerel (all kinds)	Extremely sharp teeth.	Fish thin, a little slippery, and hard to hold.	If possible, hold with a rag or towel.

Species	Specific Dangers	Special Problems	How to Hold and Remove Fly
Marlin (Blue, White, Striped) and Sailfish	Bill can inflict serious wounds.	Fish are powerful and the leader cannot be grasped to control fish.	Fish should be completely exhausted, then handled first by lifting by the bill. Gaffing not recommended on larger fish.
Permit	Crushers in throat.		Can be lifted by tail, netted, or gaffed.
Pollack	Crushers in throat.		Should be netted or gaffed; fly can be removed by hand.
Roosterfish	Extremely strong and could inflict damage by thrashing.		Hold with a rag.
Shark	Terrible teeth, very strong, can thrash or chop the angler.	Fish is often alive and dangerous when it appears dead. Has no bones, can curl around and bite person holding it.	Don't hold. Cut leader and let in fish.
Snapper	Have caninelike teeth that can snap closed like a steel trap. Spines on back are sharp and can cut.		Hold fish across belly to avoid spines. Keep handle away from mouth; use a tool to remove fly.
Grouper	Crushers in throat, stout spines on back, gills raspy.		Fish should be tired before fly is removed, and should be held firmly.
Snook	Cutter blade on side of gill covers.		Grasp fish with thumb over lip and first finger through lower opening of gill cover.
Tarpon	Big ones are powerful, and can thrash and hurt angler.	When being gaffed, giant tarpon can pull angler into water, so fish should be exhausted before being gaffed.	Small fish to 35 lbs. can be held by lower lip. Larger fish: leave fly in until fish is very tired.

Species	Specific Dangers	Special Problems	How to Hold and Remove Fly
Tuna (all kinds)	No specific dangers, except that fish are extremely strong.		Fish should be tired before fly is removed.
Wahoo	Very sharp teeth.		Use tool to remove fly; teeth are very sharp.
Weakfish (Seatrout)	Some sharp canine-like teeth.		Teeth are not danger-ous, but can hurt.
Yellowtail	Same as tuna.		Same as tuna.

If our sport is to survive, we need to release most of the fish we catch. Here the author gently revives a tarpon before freeing.

PART THREE

Inshore and Deepwater Species and Strategies

CHAPTER 9

Inshore Fishing

The sea holds a lot of fish, and they live, breed, and eat under a variety of conditions. Some, like the spotted seatrout, or weakfish, prefer areas with a grassy bottom, for that protective cover holds much of their food. Roosterfish like surf piling against the rocky projections of a shoreline, where they can voraciously slash into baitfish. Tarpon like to live under the mangroves in the quiet shade when they are young, then move into channels adjoining the flats when they grow larger. Striped bass move around so much that they confuse even biologists. So, it's a good idea to specialize, if you really want to become a successful saltwater fisherman.

Blind casting—casting into what you assume are fruitful waters and retrieving your fly with the hope that a fish will see and strike it—is one type of inshore fishing. Striped bass, seatrout, flounders, bluefish, and other species that either lie deep on the bottom or swim well beneath the surface are often caught by blind casting. If you locate a school of such fish, or you know your area well enough to predict your catch, this kind of fishing can be very exciting and rewarding.

But, *sight* fishing just has to be the most exciting kind of fishing. You can anchor a boat in shallow water and wait for fish to approach. Or, you can wade or boat across these shallows, looking for the fish. In any case the fish is usually sighted before it is time to cast. This is a combination of hunting and fishing, and for many who have practiced it, no other kind of fish-

Fly fishermen are so lucky. There is a profusion of flats boats that are designed to meet a variety of fishing situations.

ing can quite compare. Bonefishing is the best-known kind of sight fishing, but many other species can also be taken by this method. Barramundi, cobia, tarpon, striped bass, permit, threadfin salmon, snappers, sharks, jewfish, channel bass, and snook—all can be successfully sight fished.

A third kind of saltwater fishing not widely practiced but highly successful for some species is called chumming. The angler picks out a choice location, anchors, then puts out the sort of food that will attract the species he is interested in catching. This technique works well with barracudas, tuna, snappers, bonefish, permit, bluefish, striped bass, mackerels, bonito, and numerous other species.

Chumming is not really a haphazard technique; it requires knowledge of the traffic patterns of the fish (chumming in an area where the fish do not pass would be futile), understanding the tides, and the selection of the type of chum most likely to attract these species.

The well-equipped angler will have at least two tackle outfits to fish the shallows. One will be with a floating line and, depending upon the species sought, the second reel will be loaded with one of the weight-forward taper designs. This will be the line that will see the most use. Many U.S. West Coast fishermen prefer a floating shooting taper instead of a full-length line; that is simply a matter of choice—both will accomplish the same purpose. This floating line (ranging from sizes 8 through 12, again depending upon the size of the flies) will be the workhorse line that will catch most of the fish.

The angler will also have with him either a spare shooting taper, or another reel loaded with a sinking line—in most cases an extra-fast-sinking line (such as one of the Teeny saltwater lines), which will enable him to position the fly deeper, or on the bottom when necessary.

Other lines may be called for by specific conditions. For example, an intermediate sinking line is very helpful in fishing for giant tarpon. Some anglers prefer a sinking-tip line for fishing permit, when they want the fly to bomb to the bottom but prefer the remainder of the line to float. But, first equip yourself with a floating and a fast-sinking line. As you gain experience, you'll probably find plenty of reasons for using other types of lines.

An inshore reel should be just as good as the one selected for offshore. If you fish for many inshore species, a reel with a small line capacity and little or no drag will do—but it may not suit for that trophy you are always seeking. Certainly, if you fight bonefish or permit—both long-running, fast-moving fish—you will need some sort of drag device, whether it's a hand or a mechanical one. If you pursue giant tarpon, albacore, tuna, many of the faster offshore species, or any of the billfish, you'll need a stout reel with plenty of backing and a good drag. For flounders, channel bass on the flats, weakfish, striped bass, bluefish, jack crevalles, snappers, and other fish that will slug it out over a short distance, an inexpensive reel that can resist the ravages of salt water will usually suffice.

HOW TO LOOK FOR INSHORE FISH

Learning to spot inshore fish is an acquired skill. The ability to see what others do *not* often means the difference between success and failure. It really is like stalking; there are many "signs" that will help you determine where the fish are.

Almost any fisherman knows that hovering birds indicate baitfish beneath. The *action* of the gulls will tell you if larger fish are disturbing the bait: when the bait is lying near the surface, unconcerned about predators, the gulls will often wheel in slow spirals, watching and waiting. But, when the gulls drop down in quick, tight circles, or dart to the water and obvi-

The circling birds and rippling water surface indicate that baitfish are desperately trying to avoid the predator fish below them.

ously pick up something as they tower upward—that's the time to head full bore for the birds. Field glasses are often a help; some of the newer ones are made with a sealed, plastic, or fiberglass housing and are completely waterproof, even if dropped overboard.

If you can see baitfish showering above the surface, that's the best time of all. A cast into that spray of fish can draw an immediate strike. Sometimes, while running and looking, you'll come across a huge flock of gulls sitting on the surface. Unless you have an urgent destination, hang around for a few minutes; break out a sandwich and wait. The gulls are there because, from aloft, they have located a large school of baitfish and they are simply resting until a school of larger fish finds the food.

You'll scatter a feeding school of fish by racing your boat through it. When you see a school of surface fish tearing into baitfish, work the boat from the outside edges—never run it through the school. The fly rodder is aided immeasurably if the captain manning the boat will also approach the school from the *upwind* side, allowing him to toss his fly with the wind into the feeding fish. If you are the only boat—and if you stay on the edges of

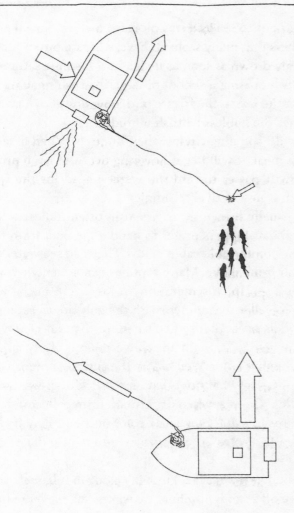

Approaching a School of Fish
When a school of fish is near or breaking the surface, they fear predators. A boat that runs over the school or gets too close will often cause them to dive deep. A fly fisherman can cast better downwind. As quietly as possible, approach a school of fish on the upwind side, far enough away to avoid frightening them, and slightly in front of the direction they are traveling. That way you can stop the motor for best results, or at least stay in front of them while casting.

Drifting and Blind Casting
There are many situations where no fish are evident but are believed to be in the area. By drifting with the tide or current, the angler can cover a lot of water. The best way to do this is to cast downwind and to the side of the boat's drifting direction. This prevents the boat from running over your fly and reducing the efficiency of your retrieve.

the school—you can often catch a number of fish before the school moves on or is frightened and sounds. The best approach, if the fish are wary, is to come in on the school from the up-tide or upwind side, cut the motor, and drift to them before making your cast.

Another bird that aids in spotting fish is the man-o'-war bird, or frigate bird, easily identified by the peculiar W shape of the wings and its seven-foot wingspan. Seen only in the warmer seas, the frigate bird usually follows a single large fish, rather than a school of fish. It will drop to the surface, grab a tidbit from the water, and lift again into the sky in a display of incredible flying skill. The huge bird, which has the lightest wing bones for its size of any bird, will often go out to sea and stay aloft for a week. Lacking the oily coating on the feathers that many seabirds have, a frigate bird that falls to the water will probably drown as soon as its feathers become saturated. I have frequently seen fish chasing a school of larger baitfish, making the bait leap frantically from the water; the frigate bird, hovering above, swiftly darts seaward and catches the hapless baitfish in midair.

This bird flies in wide, spiraling circles when hunting. When it sees a fish that may produce a meal, it will begin hovering over the large predator. If the bird makes swift passes toward the water—head for the spot; chances are the large fish is now actively feeding.

Discolored water, usually brownish or greenish, often indicates fish. That's why good charterboat skippers prefer to handle the boat from topside, rather than from the comfortable cabin below. They can see water discoloration or moving fish from above. Many captains can actually tell you what kind of fish causes a specific discoloration. In Key West, in the wintertime, schools of jack crevalles sometimes roam the gulf side, feasting on tiny sardines. These schools of jacks often cover more than an acre, with individual fish ranging in size from eight to twelve pounds. They appear under water as a yellow-amber color. Well below the surface, bluefish will chop so many menhaden (an oily baitfish) that an oil slick of green can be seen on the surface. In New Guinea, when fingermark brim collect in feeding schools, the water turns to a dull pink—the color of their many bodies. Dark spots or intense small ripples on the surface often are indicators of densely packed baitfish.

School fish (and bait near the surface) moving along in relatively shallow waters will often give off a series of miniature waves. Whenever you see wave patterns that do not appear normal, it will pay to check them out.

Fishermen spend much of their time cruising and looking over the surface for feeding fish, or birds. But, not many know that on days when there's a chop on the surface, splashes from feeding fish can best be spotted from a *downwind angle*. Unless the splashes are so pronounced as to disturb the top of the waves, they are often hidden under the waves' curl. With the wind in your face, looking toward the breeze, you are better able to see the telltale white splashes on the downwind side of the curler.

High-rolling waves will often reveal hordes of baitfish, frightened right up to the shore by larger fish lying just seaward. Maneuver your boat close to the shore and cast right into the surf. Fishing this way along the North

Carolina coast in November and December produces some fantastic catches. Experienced striped bass fishermen know that waves crashing into heavy rocks along a shoreline traps bait in the backwash, giving the fly rodder a wonderful opportunity.

Barracudas and big mackerels often give away their presence by spectacular thirty-foot leaps. One of these mighty fish skyrocketing out of the water in a curving arc is a sight to remember. When fish are skyrocketing they are actively feeding, and a well-placed fly will often draw strikes. Smaller mackerels also skyrocket, although their leaps usually carry them only a foot or two above the surface. Albacore and bonito are also located by their leaps just above the surface as they chase bait.

When fishing from rocky jetties or an offshore bar, you will often see fish chasing bait right against the obstructions. Cast to any boils or swirls you think may be fish. Striped bass fishermen recognize that pilings, sunken or abandoned piers, and other underwater structures can produce great fishing. Where a jetty or rock bar extends out into the water, an eddy forms on the down-tide side, trapping bait. This is always a good place to prospect with your fly.

The long arrow indicates the rocky bar projecting out into the bay. The smaller area indicates a down-tide eddy that collects baitfish. This is a good place to cast.

At night in warmer salt waters the angler often can locate feeding fish, especially snook and tarpon, around bridges. They almost always lie on the up-tide side of a bridge, but inside the shadow line cast by the lights on the bridge. However, their dark shapes, lying near the surface awaiting drifting shrimp, crabs, and other food, give them away.

Sharks and billfish often betray themselves as they bask near the surface with their dorsal fins protruding. Laid-up tarpon do the same, especially on calm mornings. A careful approach must be made to basking fish, for they're easily alarmed and will dive at the slightest noise.

Big blacktip sharks, and sometimes lemon sharks, cruise the shallow flats looking for food. Often the upper part of a shark's body sticks above the surface. In shallow bays along the East Coast, sharks feed for crabs right up along the sod banks. It's hard to intercept them, but they do betray their presence occasionally as the dorsal fin protrudes above the surface. Usually, for such specific fishing, it is best to locate the sharks by their movements, then set up chum lines in anticipation of the fish reappearing in the area.

The dorsal and tailfins clearly show this is a large shark cruising a flat.

Tarpon are able to breathe air from the atmosphere and are frequently seen as they roll to the surface, exhale and inhale, then slowly submerge. In calm water you can spot a rolling tarpon at several hundred yards—a standard method of locating fish. In quiet bays you can often determine whether tarpon are in the area by watching for bubbles floating on the calm surface.

Where there is little current, the air bubbles exhaled by tarpon will linger for several minutes.

Tarpon can often be found asleep near the water's surface, their dorsal fins clearly showing in the air, early mornings in calm, protected areas. Years ago, my son's favorite fishing place was the inside of the Marquesas, west of Key West. If we arrived there right after dawn we would often see both permit and tarpon sleeping contentedly side by side in the dim light, their sharp-pointed fins protruding above the surface like a poorly installed picket fence. These fish are extremely difficult to approach; silence is essential if you want to score. Of course, heavy traffic in the Marquesas has disturbed these fish so they no longer rest there by the scores. However, there are other such wonderful places still to be found.

The depth of water also determines how you must look for fish. If you are searching for fish on the flats in water less than a foot deep, *do not look at the bottom;* it's the surface that will give you clues. The fins or tail will often stick out of the water as the fish swims, or tips up on its head to root

Rolling tarpon are easy to locate, and it's also easy to determine their swimming direction.

out a morsel. Redfish, bonefish, permit, and mutton snappers are all tailing species. Clearly defined V wakes indicate moving fish. Remember that the fish will be a foot or more in front of the wake it creates.

There is another phenomenon called "nervous water" that is simply tiny ripples that form no real pattern on the surface, which tell you that fish

One of the most exciting of all sights on the flats is a tailing permit.

are swimming directly below. It's important to keep in mind that in extremely shallow water if you look at the bottom instead of the surface, you will miss many of these fish indicators.

However, when striped bass, bonefish, barramundi, threadfin salmon, permit, baby tarpon, redfish (channel bass), and similar species are swimming in clear water *deeper than a foot*, it's vital to search the bottom. You may miss a fish ghosting over a changing bottom if you are looking at the surface. And it pays to know your fish, of course. Bonefish, permit, and snappers move constantly. When you see a long green object suspended motionless on a Florida flat, you can bet that it's probably a barracuda or tarpon.

You should know the depth of water that the fish you seek prefers. Permit, for example, like at least eighteen inches of water on a flat, while bonefish will feed in water just deep enough to allow them to maneuver. Mackerels will be in six or more feet of water, and bonito and albacore will prowl the beaches, but generally are found in depths exceeding six feet. Striped bass seem to go wherever they can find food—a storm-battered jetty, an outside sandbar boiling with heavy water, or the quiet shallows of mud flats.

Polarized glasses are the single most valuable aid to spotting fish. There are a number of different tints, ranging from a bright tan or yellow through green, blue, and gray. Brown-yellow (it was once called Cosmotan) is the most popular with experienced anglers; smoke-colored glass seems to be the second choice. Yellow or tan is preferable on overcast days. Regardless of color, these glasses are designed to polarize the light waves usually

If you see a long, green, indistinct, and motionless object on the flats, it just may be a big barracuda.

encountered in fishing, and you may find that under certain light conditions, by tilting your head a little to one side or the other, you'll be able to remove even more glare. Newer models have optical glass on either side of the polarized lenses to prevent scratching. And, one model carries a small magnifier at the base of each lens to help in tying knots. Side shields are important, for they cut down additional glare reflected on the back side of the lenses.

Even the type of hat you wear can help you spot fish. The brim should be long enough to shade your eyes. The "Florida-style" hat has become very popular; it shields the eyes and protects the neck and ears

Experienced fly fishermen will use three different tints of polarized glasses for different light conditions: gray-blue, brown-yellow, and yellow.

from sunburn. The underside of the brim of any hat you wear should be a dark color. Test this theory for yourself: put on a hat that has a light-colored brim on the underside and look at an object under water in the bright sun. Then exchange the hat for one that has a dark underside. Baseball players who range the outfield have been darkening the areas around their eyes for years to obtain this same effect. Many fly fishermen don't realize that they really do monitor the line during the forward cast. A long-brimmed hat prevents seeing the unrolling line until the cast nears the end. This can affect accuracy. You can prove this to yourself by casting a number of times at a distant object and measuring how far each cast missed the target while wearing a long- and a short-brimmed hat. Total the distance you missed while wearing each hat and you'll quickly determine that you did better with a hat brim about the length of the one on a baseball cap.

When fishing shallows, always approach the fish with the sun over your shoulder. Even polarized glasses are of little help when you approach into the sunlight and peer into a water surface filled with glare.

The background sky affects your spotting fish. Large banks of white clouds lying on the horizon act in much the same way as the sun, reflecting light off the water into your eyes. It's obviously much easier to see fish in flat, calm water than in water that's wind rippled. Water in the shadows of cliffs or shore vegetation appears to be transparent.

Wading is another great way to fish inshore waters with a fly rod. But, one immediate word of caution: *never wade potentially dangerous water alone*. It may make the difference if help is only a few yards away.

Wading at night, a specialty of many northern striped bass fishermen, can be especially dangerous if you're not familiar with the terrain. You should be aware of every drop-off, tide rip, boulder-studded area, or other local hazard. If you're trying out a new area, be sure to explore it carefully before wading after dark.

Rock jetties can be extremely dangerous, since there's usually treacherous water at their base. Many anglers wear shoes with golf cleats embedded in them when fishing from jetties. Other soft aluminum "cleats" make walking on slick surfaces safer—most trout fishing catalogs carry these models. Certainly, you should avoid rubber-soled sneakers for such work. Even felt-soled wading shoes are inadequate.

Do all wading on jetties with great caution and never alone!

The angler who is dressed correctly can fish the surf, even in cold weather, and not fear the elements.

Regardless of your location, your wading pace should always be slow. Carefully place one foot forward and ascertain your footing before you move on. If you're ever caught in a stiff tide, turn sideways so your body presents less resistance to the water; this will also brace your feet better for a return to shore.

If you wade in colder climates, protect yourself with neoprene chest-high waders; a belt around the top will prevent you from shipping water on a fall. Your waders should have rubber soles. Felt soles simply wear out too quickly on raspy sand and gravel beaches. The felt also traps bacteria. Unless you wash and clean the felt soles thoroughly after each trip, you will have waders that can really be smelly.

If you're fishing where surf may at times flood over you, a raincoat with a hood is good insurance. The raincoat should drape down over your waders so that a crashing wave can't get inside them. If you want to fly fish and wade in colder weather, there is specially designed waterproof surf-fishing clothing that does a great job of protecting you from cold water.

Cold weather and high surf are not usually problems in tropical areas. But stingrays and sea urchins are. Proper wading techniques and equipment will allow you to fish free of concern. Three types of shoes work well wad-

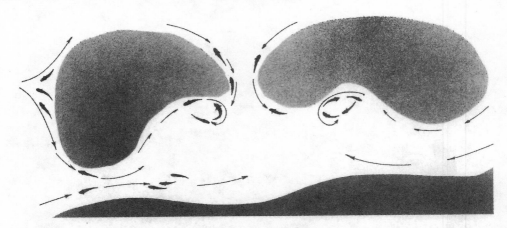

When fly fishing a beach there are often sandbars just off the shore. Tidal currents flow around and over these bars. This forms eddies that trap bait. Study the arrows (indicating tidal flow) and you will be able to pinpoint where the fish you seek may be holding.

Coastal Waters

Predatory fish are smart enough to let the tidal current bring food to them. They will lie at the mouth of a funnel where food is concentrated. When the tide is incoming they will hold where water enters (indicated by the white fish). When the tide is ebbing or falling, they will lie where the black fish are indicated.

ing the flats. Divers' soft neoprene shoes, which carry a tough rubber sole, are perhaps best—they cling comfortably tight to the leg, preventing almost anything from irritating the leg or getting into the sole. Wading shoes with felt soles are okay, but, again, they can trap bacteria. Unless they are scrupulously cleaned when you return home, they will smell to high heaven. Conventional freshwater wading shoes with gravel guards to keep grit out are okay. Sneakers work, too, but allow irritating grit to seep into the shoe.

A sea urchin looks like a tennis ball that's turned into a porcupine. The sharp, brittle spines that stick out from the ball at every angle will penetrate your foot. Then, they break off, and usually have to be removed by surgery. Avoid contact with them.

A stingray that you can see, and that sees you, will present no problem. Like most snakes, all it wants to do is get away. But, the stingray has a habit of hiding from its natural enemies by settling its body into the soft mud. It flaps its wings a number of times and the descending mud completely covers the ray, camouflaging it perfectly. The stingray has a protective device in the form of a sharp, rough stinger on the tail. Should you step on a hidden stingray, in self-defense the ray will try to drive the stinger into you. This is extremely painful, and people have been hospitalized for treatment from stingray attacks. However, it's important to realize that the ray doesn't want to get into a fight. It will leave if only you warn it of your presence. This you can do easily. Instead of picking your foot up in a normal walking manner as you wade a flat, allowing the foot to descend onto the ray, *slide* your foot along the bottom to your next position. If your sliding foot contacts a ray, it will flee in panic and leave you unharmed.

I have not heard of a single attack on a wader from a shark or a barracuda. Obviously, if a large shark is acting aggressively, the proper thing is to retreat, although my experience has been that in shallow water, the larger the fish, the more easily it's frightened. Apparently, a large fish feels out of its element there, and the slightest unusual sound or movement will generally cause it to run. If you are wading in clear water and you feel threatened by a nearby shark, slap your rod tip near the fish and it will be gone. The same can be said of barracudas. In fact, the unusually large fish, when on the flats, are often the most difficult to catch, simply because they're so difficult to approach. It's my belief that *you can safely ignore sharks and barracudas on clear-water flats*. If a flat is murky, however, and a shark cannot see you clearly, then it may strike. I've often fished the lower west coast of

Florida in Everglades Park at Cape Sable. On a number of occasions I've battled a snook, jack, or tarpon in those murky waters right to the beach. Just before I landed the fish, a large shark inhaled the prey. Wading in such a place would indeed be a dangerous stunt. But, where waters are clear, sharks and barracudas offer no threat to a wader.

Unlike the companion in a boat, the wading fisherman is severely restricted in his movements. He can only search as much water as he can cast a fly over. The fisherman who wades a great deal should seriously consider using a shooting, or stripping, basket and a shooting-taper line. The shooting basket keeps running line out of the drifting tide and away from entangling feet. And, the angler can reach at least 50 percent more water because he can cast so much farther. (See page 154 for more information on shooting baskets.)

The one drawback to using a shooting taper (the more popular name is shooting head) while wading is that correcting a faulty cast is harder. If you've cast to a cruising fish, and the fish turns in a direction not on course with the fly, you must quickly make another cast. A shooting head requires that you strip in all the running or shooting line, then pick up the head, and *then* shoot it. Sometimes this procedure takes so long that the fish escapes. But, it is perhaps the shooting head's only liability for the wader.

Since angling for different species of inshore fish varies in so many details, it may be best to treat each major species separately, even though basic technique for many will overlap.

 ## STRIPED BASS

TACKLE AND GEAR REQUIREMENTS

Striped bass fishing is practiced from the beach, casting from boats, and wading shallow flats, as well as during both day and night. Because of the variety of conditions, anglers need some specialized gear.

Let's start with boats, perhaps the most popular way striper fishermen seek their quarry. On the shallow flats of Florida, Louisiana, and Texas, specially designed boats are used to pole for permit, tarpon, redfish, and bonefish. In most cases this type of boat is not the best design for striped bass from Virginia to Maine. Tropical flats boats are designed with low sides, so that in the breeze there isn't much "sail area" on them. A boat with higher sides would be much more difficult to pole. Striper fishermen from Virginia to New England often have to traverse choppy waters, and, with the low sides of a tropical flats boat, you can get very wet. I think an ideal boat for most striper fishing would be one from about eighteen to twenty feet that was relatively light and had fairly high sides to protect you from the waves. The inside of the boat would be as devoid as possible of line-grabbing devices. Captain Greg Weatherby charters out of Newport, Rhode Island. One feature I really like on his boat is a bow rail constructed similarly to the rail on a pulpit. The fly caster can position himself inside this railing and lean against it. Then, Greg can work a boat in close to the rocks, where waves cause the boat to rise and fall. The railing offers full support while fishing this white water. With his hands free, the angler can lean against the rail and cast in very rough water. One of the keys to this idea, I believe, is to keep the railing design very narrow, just enough for the angler to slip in. A wider railing allows the angler's body to sway, and it can catch line when shooting to the target.

If your boat has cleats, try to get those that flush with the boat's surface when pushed down. If that's not possible, use a block of Ethafoam and cut a slot on the underside so that it can be jammed over the cleat. Taper

Greg Weatherby, using a highly maneuverable boat with a pulpit in the front for his client, is able to get the angler right into the white water slashing against the rocks.

the outer edges. If you make the slot small enough on the underside, the block will remain on the cleat even on a high-speed run. Captain Norm Bartlett and I once fished all day in the Chesapeake and his foam blocks never caught our fly lines.

A tremendous advantage for anyone in a boat is the use of a depth finder. After two years of using a depth finder equipped with both vertical and side readings. I am convinced this is the way to go. On a number of occasions, the side transducer looking horizontally through the water showed us fish we never would have known about with only a vertical finder.

For more information on boats, see chapter 11.

The fishing tackle needed for any kind of striper fishing is pretty simple. The best rods are either size 9 or 10. Because you will be called upon to sometimes throw rather large flies, Clouser Minnows, or other patterns that carry weight, a smaller rod is often a handicap. There are those who persist in using lighter or heavier rods and lines. But, for those who want to operate most efficiently, 9 and 10 rods are best.

Two-Handed Rods

I believe that the two-handed fly rods—somewhat similar to those that have been used in Europe for generations—are going to become very popular for striper, albacore, and other fishing where fly fishermen practice their sport from the beach. There are several reasons why.

For many years two-handed rods were heavy, cumbersome to use, and difficult to obtain. But, I have been fishing with a Sage Model 9140-3 (it's a three-piece rod, which makes it easy to transport). Because this rod is constructed from modern graphite materials, it weights only 8½ ounces. A 12½-footer (Sage Model 9126-3, a three-piece) weighs only 7⅜ ounces, but I prefer the longer fourteen-footer. Both rods will cast a 9- or 10-weight line, but I use a size 11 or 12 shooting head on either of these models with great results. Both of these rods cost only about $100 more than a standard one-handed rod. The European rods were designed mainly for roll casting. They have a long, relatively slow action. Two-handed rods that are needed in the surf for fly fishing are of a modern design and were developed for *overhead casting*—not roll casting. These rods are much stiffer and faster, and allow the angler to develop a high-line-speed cast.

Many people comment that they don't know how to use a two-handed rod. You use it just the way you would a single-handed rod. The difference is that the line hand is positioned on the bottom of the rod. *If you use your line hand on the bottom of the rod in the same way you would double haul, you can quickly get incredible results with a long two-handed rod.*

When casting, trap the line under the second finger of the hand holding the rod. Grip the butt of the rod with the other hand. Near the end of the backcast, when you are making the speed-up-and-stop, move the butt of the rod rapidly forward and then stop as the other hand finishes the motion. The lower hand makes a *short, swift* motion, just as if you were double hauling on the line with a one-handed rod. On the forward cast, bring the line hand back in a short, swift motion toward the body, simulating the second phase of a double haul.

I have been teaching for years that the longer you move a rod through the air, the more the lever (rod) helps you with the cast. Rods of twelve feet (or better—fourteen feet) move the rod tip through an incredibly long arc, making distance casting so much easier. If you can cast fifty feet with a one-handed rod, I assure you that for the same effort, you'll hit nearly 100 feet with a fourteen-footer—and with considerably less effort.

Two-handed rods make casts in excess of 100 feet easy—especially if you are using a shooting head. Both Cortland and Scientific Anglers now make lines designed especially for these overhead-casting, two-handed rods that have long weight-forward heads and thin shooting lines. I prefer to make my own heads from double-taper lines. I make two heads between forty and forty-five feet long from the two ends of a double-taper line. I find that the best shooting line to put behind the head is not monofilament, but the special shooting lines designed by Cortland and Scientific Anglers. These lines are floating level lines, and should test at about thirty pounds for saltwater use. There are some shooting lines that will test at only twelve to eighteen pounds (usually they are less than .028 inch in diameter). Some anglers prefer the braided monofilament lines similar to the type used in braided butt leaders.

Whether you use the special weight-forward fly lines or shooting heads, there are some advantages to using a two-handed rod rather than a one-handed model when fishing from shore. One of the problems fishing the surf is that the rolling waves near the angler often swirl the line around and make it difficult to get a good pickup for a backcast. With a fourteen-foot rod you can raise the line just in front of you so that it is above the waves, allowing you to make an easy pickup and backcast. Women, children, and those who do not have great strength can use a two-handed rod with ease, and it will allow them to make longer casts.

Wind is a constant enemy of surf fishermen. It almost always blows directly in your face. The short arc that a single-handed rod travels makes casting into a stiff breeze more difficult. You may be stunned at how easy it is to drive a line into the breeze with a longer two-handed rod.

There are times when fish are close to you and you make a cast. But, suddenly the fish are not where you cast. A single-handed rod makes it difficult to get a fast pickup and to make a forward cast to a new location. With the added length of a two-handed rod, however, this is easy to accomplish.

Once a cast is made, use the rod as you would a one-handed model. Retrieved line should be dropped into a stripping basket and allowed to flow easily out on the forward cast.

I believe that progressive fly fishermen along the northeastern coast, as well as others who fish the surf in other parts of the world, will come to realize that a two-handed rod offers them considerable advantages. We'll soon see them in more use.

Fly Lines

I have caught more than a thousand striped bass with a fly rod since I first started fishing for them in the early 1960s. While I have not caught any larger than thirty-five pounds, I have battled many stronger fish in the sea. I am convinced that if you have a reel that carries 150 yards of backing plus the fly line, you have *more than enough* line to fight just about any striped bass you will ever hook. Stand at one end of a football field and look at the other end. That's 100 yards; few stripers—or almost any other saltwater fish—will ever run more than 100 yards plus the fly line.

Fly lines are important in striper fishing, and proper selection can often make the difference between catching fish and getting no strikes. I think you should seriously consider four kinds: a weight-forward floater, a weight-forward intermediate (slow-sinking), and a fast-sinking line such as a lead-core shooting head or a line similar to the Teeny 300, 350, 400, or 450. Finally, if you need to search a lot of water or cast long distances, you may want to use a floating and a sinking shooting head. If I had to choose only one line for striped bass fishing (and thank God I don't), I would choose one of the Teeny sinking lines. See chapter 4 for full descriptions of these various lines.

Striped bass are generally not leader-shy, so generally, you need not use extra-long or -thin leaders. A tippet of fifteen pounds will work most of the time. For floating, intermediate, and Wet Cel II sinking lines, a leader of eight to ten feet long is fine. For fast-sinking fly lines, I rarely use a leader that is more than five feet in length.

Reels

Reels for striper fishing need not be the heavy-duty ones associated with giant tarpon, bluefin tuna, or billfish. Obviously, if you can afford to buy a Tibor, Lamson, Abel, Islander, Billy Pate, L. L. Bean Tidemaster, Orvis, or one of the many other types of such superb reels, do so. Not only will it do more than it is ever called upon to perform, but there is also a certain satisfaction in owning one of these fabulous tools. But, thousands of striped bass are caught on reels that are used mainly for catching freshwater large-mouth and smallmouth bass. If the reel will hold 100 yards of backing and a fly line, you will rarely—and I mean almost never—have to worry about lack of backing. The reel needs a little drag. If you can get a pound of drag on a straight pull, that's enough. By using your fingers to control drag on the rim of the reel or your fingertips on the inside of the spool, you can control any striper of up to fifty pounds on such an outfit. There has always been a tendency for fly fishermen to overgun themselves when they go to salt water.

Rods

Rods are so good today that we old-timers wonder how we ever fished with the tools we used several decades ago. The best length is a nine-footer. If you have to buy one rod, I'd get a 9-weight. It may be a little light for throwing very large striper flies, but it certainly will do a commendable job in almost all striper fishing situations. Here again, there is a tendency for some anglers to be overgunned and to use 11- to 13-weight fly rods for stripers. If you are a great caster that's fine. But, the average guy is going to feel like dying after two hours of slinging a 12-weight line on a heavy rod. For almost all heavy-duty striped bass fishing I rarely use anything larger than a 10-weight. But, remember, salt-water fly rods should have the stripping guide enlarged to twenty to twenty-five millimeters, because a lot more line is shot through it than when freshwater fishing.

Flies

There are a host of flies that will catch striped bass. One thing is important to consider when seeking striped bass: often the size of the fly is vital to success. Altering the same pattern to be shorter or longer can mean a difference in the number of strikes. Always carry the same pattern in several lengths. There will also always be some specialized situations where a particular pattern is most effective for catching striped bass.

I mentioned earlier that Lyons & Burford has produced a book that I wrote with several dozen striped bass flies pictured. Along with each color photograph are the instructions for tying it. I am not mentioning this to sell books; rather, if you are interested in tying many of the striped bass patterns you hear mentioned, most of them are included in those pages. The book is available from many fly shops around the country. Again, the title is *Saltwater Fly Patterns*.

It is fun to tie new flies and to believe that if you find that "secret" pattern, you'll catch more fish. However, you need only a few patterns to catch striped bass under most fly-fishing conditions—that is, if you are willing to vary the length and sometimes the color combination. If you use these patterns in various sizes and fish with the correct fly line to get you to the fish, you will score. As more and more trout fishermen enter the sport, they will bring with them the idea of exact imitation. Forget it! There are rare situations—and these are *very* rare—when a very close imitation will outfish other patterns. For example, in New England waters there are sand eels, a favorite food of stripers. Several dozen effective patterns have been developed that work well when bass are feeding on sand eels. But a properly dressed Clouser Minnow or Lefty's Deceiver would do just as well. I urge you not to get caught in the belief that you have to carry a host of flies. And, I will say that of the list of flies I am recommending, you could remove one and substitute another. Just realize that if you carry a few basic patterns in a variety of lengths and sizes, you will be well armed.

Anglers should consider one point when fishing flies to striped bass. Large stripers will often hit a large fly more readily. There have been some flies developed that I consider laughable. These flies look like undressed chickens and it would take someone with the arm of a wrestler to throw them. They are unnecessary and I urge you to avoid using them. Bob Popovics has developed several flies that present a huge profile (for squid or baitfish, such as bunker or menhaden) that are light, easy to cast, and have a realistic appeal in the water. I urge you to try some of Bob's flies instead of these ridiculous patterns that the average person could never cast. Bob's Siliclone Mullet and his Baby Squid are two of the best patterns I have ever used and they are realistic, easy to cast even on a ten-weight rod, and will fool big striped bass.

Lefty's Deceiver

I believe that the Lefty's Deceiver is the most effective fly pattern to date for striped bass, and most other saltwater species—and not because I developed the pattern. This fly resembles a baitfish in shape, and it is a favorite fly of saltwater fly fishermen in Africa, Australia, and other areas of the fly-fishing world. You can make it as long as you wish—from two inches to fourteen inches—and the combination of colors is your choice.

To attract big striped bass, which may be feeding on ten-inch-long bunker or other large baitfish, you need a large fly. You can easily modify a Lefty's Deceiver to get a fly at least ten to twelve inches in length that is easy to cast. Place the hook in the vise and at the rear of the hook tie some long, synthetic Ultra Hair, Super Hair (similar to but a finer diameter than Ultra Hair), or FisHair as the beginning of a wing. This can be as long as you wish. On each side of this wing, tie in six to eight wide saddle or neck hackles. Then add a dozen strands of either Flashabou or Krystal Flash to each side. Carry the thread forward and build a collar of bucktail, making sure that the bucktail extends beyond the hook bend. Finish the fly. You now have a pattern from ten to twelve inches in length that will cast easily—and stripers will hit it.

Bob Popovics's Big One

Bob Popovics's Big One is another good way to attract big striped bass. It weighs less than the average Whistler pattern. Yet, it can be as long as twelve inches, with a huge, round profile. It better represents a large baitfish than any other fly I have seen. And, it casts infinitely easier than some of the patterns that resemble a headless chicken. It has caught big stripers, even sailfish. If you want to tie it, here are the easy-to-follow instructions: put a large hook in the vise and tie in, at the back of the hook, the desired amount of Big Fly Fiber (available in many fly shops). Tie fairly long sheep fleece in front of the Big Fly Fiber so that it encircles the hook and runs all the way to the hook eye. Tie off and press on Witchcraft Mylar glue-on eyes. Another advantage to this super-big and super-light fly is that on the first backcast, almost all water is flushed from the fly. This makes it an easy fly to cast, even with a nine-weight fly rod.

Clouser Minnow

If I were to have only two flies to fish all salt waters, including for striped bass, I would instantly select the Lefty's Deceiver and the Clouser Minnow. Neither of these flies is what you would consider an exact pattern. Both are a method of tying the fly. The length of the fly, how much weight is added, the color combination, and whether the fly is bulky or sleek are the angler's choice. These two flies are what I call "fly designs."

Striped bass fishermen on both the East and West Coasts have found the Clouser Minnow to be one of the best of all striped bass patterns. Two color combinations for tying it are favored by many striped bass fishermen. The most popular is a white underwing, with some flash in the middle combination, and a top wing of chartreuse. The other is a white underwing, pearl flash in the middle, and a green, gray, or blue black or topping.

Whistler

This versatile fly was developed by Dan Blanton for catching striped bass on the West Coast of the United States. It is deadly effective on striped bass anywhere—including freshwater reservoirs. If you have not tried this pattern I urge you to do so. Like the Deceiver and Clouser Minnow it can be tied in many color variations and sizes—and with heads of different weights.

Surf Candy

If you are seeking a streamer fly that is a realistic imitation of the smaller baitfish, this one fits the bill. It is a great imitation of juvenile baitfish, sand eels, bay anchovies, and glass minnows. See page 76 for more information on this fly. Instructions for tying it are simple and are explained in my book *Saltwater Fly Patterns*.

Snake Fly

This fly was developed by that great striped bass angler Lou Tabory, who regards it as perhaps the best striper fly he has designed. It certainly is an effective fly. With long, soft, and fluffy emu plumes, a wide-profile head of spun and trimmed deer hair, and large metallic eyes, this fly really has an action in the water that stripers find attractive. It can be tied in many color combinations. If you haven't tried this fly, it's worth looking into.

Del Brown's Crab Fly (Merkin)

Originally developed by Del Brown for permit fishing, this fly is also a standard pattern for about any fish that eats crabs—including striped bass.

Let me give you three brief examples of how the Crab Fly can produce more striped bass for you. Where waves crash into the rocks and there are eddies, swirls, and turbulent water that trap crabs and baitfish, the Del Brown Crab Fly is ideal. Use one that is unweighted, or lightly weighted, and throw it close to the rocks. Just let the backwash and swirling currents carry it around. Don't try manipulating the fly. Try to keep in touch with it by keeping as much slack out of the line as possible. Most of the time the stripers will simply suck the Crab in and there is no heavy strike.

Another example where the Crab Fly is terrific is during daylight hours when stripers are cruising on shallow flats. The wading fisherman will often see the wake or the fish as it moves along in search of food. Usually the striper is not there to chase baitfish, but is working over the bottom. Determine the direction the striper is swimming, throw the Crab Fly well in front of the fish, and allow it to sink to the bottom. As the fish approaches, *gently twitch the line so the Crab barely moves*. You will know this strike when it happens.

Here is just one other example of the variety of ways Crab patterns can be effective. During late June or early July, along much of the coast of New England, there is a hatch of what fisherman call calico crabs. These crabs are about the size of a nickel. They float in the surface film by the millions, and when they are hatching, stripers gorge on them. The trick here is to fish the proper-sized Crab, so that it is on or near the surface and so that it is drifting naturally with the tide. Locate some stripers working these calico crabs. Use an *unweighted* Del Brown Crab Fly pattern about the size of a nickel and grease it with the paste flotant used on deer hair flies to make it stay on or near the surface. Cast the fly out and then place enough slack in the line so that the fly drifts naturally with the tide. If too much drag occurs, the Crab swims unnaturally and the striped bass will ignore it. I use a reach cast that places much of the line up-current from the fish. This allows the fly to drift a long distance as nature would carry it.

I have mentioned only three examples of how Crab Flies will produce for you. But, as you experiment with this great fly you will come to love it.

Popping Bug

Popping bugs offer three advantages that help you take large stripers. First, they make noise, which will often attract striped bass that would not see an underwater fly. Second, a popper that is worked on the surface gives the impression to an observing fish of a helpless creature that can't get away. Few predatory fish can ignore a food morsel that is easy to catch. Third, keeping the bug in motion on the surface disguises its actual size, and many times larger striped bass will attack it simply because they think it is a much bigger creature than it actually is.

There is a modification to the basic popping bug design that will sometimes outfish the conventional one. This is called a slider. It is simply a popping bug with a bullet-shaped body and the pointed portion of the bug body at the hook eye. Such bugs make almost no noise, but create a disturbance on the surface. When stripers are easily frightened or the water is very calm, a slider that is worked slowly can often outproduce any other fly. This is especially true on calm flats.

Using the above seven fly patterns in different sizes and color combinations, you really have what you need for 90 percent (or more) of the striped bass fishing conditions you will encounter.

Stripping Baskets

Perhaps the best tool a striped bass fishermen can own, once he has assembled the proper rod, reel, line, and fly, is a stripping basket. The first thing a fly caster learns when fishing from the beach or any shoreline is that the fly line can be a major problem. If it drops into the surf it becomes a hopeless tangle. On a jetty or rock pile the stones frequently grab the line and halt it in midflight. A stripping basket solves both problems. Stripping baskets used in a boat can alleviate casting problems, too. Unless there is a strong breeze blowing the line around, I prefer not to use a stripping basket when casting from the bow of a boat designed for fly fishing. I prefer to drop the line to the deck. But, and this is an important but, if you have to cast from the back end of a boat, there are always little things that grab your fly line and spoil the cast. For the angler who must fish from the rear of a boat, a stripping basket is a Godsend! And, when there is a stiff breeze, a stripping basket virtually eliminates line-tangling problems for the man in the bow.

A stripping basket is usually a plastic container that is attached to the angler. During the retrieve the line is dropped into the basket. Properly designed baskets will usually have either heavy monofilament stubs protruding upward, or, better, monofilament in the shape of miniature horseshoes. The curved portion sticks up from the bottom of the basket. The stubs or the tiny horseshoes hold the line in place. When the cast is made the line almost always flows smoothly from such a container. Orvis makes a stripping basket that replaces the stubs with inverted cones that are an integral part of the basket bottom.

There are two basic stripping basket designs. The most popular stripping basket is made from a rectangular container approximately fourteen inches long, ten inches wide, and about six inches deep. This plastic container is often used by housewives to wash dishes in. Plastic stubs are inserted in the bottom. The stubs are best made from the heavy-duty nylon that is used in weed-cutting garden tools, although 100-pound monofilament works fine. To install in the bottom of the container, use a drill or a heated nail of the correct size. Pierce one hole for a stub, or two holes for the horseshoe-shaped kind. Insert the stubs and hold them in place with hot glue; or, you can use Goop or another glue to keep them in position.

This basket is secured by a belt (sometimes with an elastic cord) around the waist and is situated against the belly of the angler. The cast is made, the rod tucked under the arm, and a hand-over-hand retrieve begins. This basket is small and fairly portable. The disadvantages are that it requires you to place the rod under your arm (not so handy when you want to strike) and to use a hand-over-hand retrieve (which restricts your retrieve movement). Finally, because it is so shallow, line will often fall from the basket at the wrong time.

A stripping basket I much prefer is one that is larger, deeper, and hangs on

Larry Kreh using the typical washbasin belly stripping basket.

your side. This basket is a standard plastic wastebasket approximately eighteen inches high. The opening in the container is about eight inches by fifteen inches. The plastic stubs are installed in the bottom. Several fairly large holes are also cut in the bottom, to permit any water falling inside to drain quickly. Captain Norm Bartlett, who plies his trade on the Chesapeake Bay, showed me an improvement in this stripping basket. He has one with a large number of rectangular holes, or ports, in all four sides. This reduces the basket's weight and allows any water that may get in to drain away. This stripping basket is secured to the angler by two straps. One is a shoulder harness, and the other is a leg strap. The leg strap is made with a Velcro closure and fits above the knee. If you need to run down the beach, this basket offers no hindrance. This stripping basket offers several advantages for me over the belly-type stripping basket. First, the line never falls out once dropped inside. Second, the hip basket allows the fly fisherman to retrieve line in a normal manner. I find that while I can strip strike with a rod tucked under my arm, I am more efficient when striking if I am using a basket that is located on my side. The one time in fishing where I think the belly basket is better than the hip basket is when you are fishing where the surf is heavy. This is because the hip basket is lower on the body and larger, therefore more prone to fill when waves break at your feet. If you haven't used a hip-type stripping basket I urge you to try it.

The author using a side-mounted stripping basket, which he believes is better in most situations. Note the profusion of holes in the basket.

Portable stripping baskets (usually made with mesh) without the monofilament stubs are okay, but have never worked well for me. In my view, the perfect stripping basket (and it would be easy for someone to manufacture it) is a basket with light plastic sides and bottom that could be folded flat when not in use. It could be taken with you on near or distant trips and could quickly be put together at the fishing scene. The base would hold the cones, stubs, or horseshoes, and the straps would be wide, comfortable, and secure.

Finally, while it seems that few fly fishermen use a stripping basket, other than those in the New England area, I believe that wise saltwater fly fishermen will begin using them all over the world.

STRIPED BASS: WEST COAST

No other fish is as popular with fly fishermen throughout the country as the striped bass. While other fish may be stronger, jump higher, run faster, fight longer—even be better to eat—the striped bass is where the people are. And, for that reason alone, it is highly prized and sought after. The major concentrations of people in this country—along the coast from North Carolina to New England, and along the California coast to the Oregon shores—duplicate exactly the concentrations of the striped bass.

Striped bass are not native to the West Coast. They were transplanted there in 1879 from East Coast stocks, but they have fared well until recently. San Francisco Bay used to be a super place for stripers. There are still a good number of them there—but it's not like it used to be. However, the Sacramento River delta area of California, which is the outlet end of the Sacramento and San Joaquin Rivers, is a hot spot for striped bass on the West Coast. While fishing at Frank's Tract not long ago with Dan Blanton, we had fish on throughout the day. The Sacramento River delta is a unique fishery. It is composed of many canals and some lakes, of which Frank's Tract is the largest lake, with a shoreline of about 100 miles. Stripers, along with freshwater largemouth bass, can be caught by fly fishermen who throw their flies at the canal banks (the ones lined with stone seem the most productive). The canals entering and leaving the lakes are also great places to catch stripers.

San Francisco Bay is huge, with much of it covered by mud flats separated by channels. The mud is too soft for wading, so shallow-draft skiffs are used to get around on the flats. The prime foods for the bay stripers are jack smelt, herring, and anchovies. As tides rise on the flats the anchovies and other baitfish will move with it, and the striped bass sometimes work in water barely deep enough for them to swim in, in an effort to get at this tasty food. Anglers who fish these flats in shallow-draft boats do so in a manner similar to that used for bonefish or tarpon. Much of it is sight fishing: the angler moves up on the flat as soon as the rising waters allow and looks for nervous water, wakes, or other indications of fish.

Occasionally, the bass will herd anchovies and other fish into a school, then several fish will blow the water apart in an effort to get at the baitfish. If the fly caster can arrive on the scene quickly, while the big bass are still aroused, he stands a good chance of a hookup.

There is an enormous amount of infertile water on these vast flats. Therefore, if you can arrange to go with someone who knows the area and has successfully fished it, you have an advantage. Good feeding flats for stripers one year will probably be good ones the next, so patterns can be established and followed.

An airplane overhead and a striper being pulled from the water near the San Francisco airport.

Casting in open water is rarely successful, but blind casting in known hot spots is practiced among the more successful fishermen, like Dan Blanton and Lawrence Summers, who have also developed a technique for fishing the many hundreds of pilings driven into the bay bottom.

In water from four to fifteen deep, these men use shooting-taper lines. A thirty-foot head of lead-core line, or specially designed sinking shooting heads, and a thin shooting line is the standard outfit. This rig allows a long cast with heavy flies, even on windy days.

They'll locate a piling and anchor within casting distance. The best anchorage is on an up-tide side from the pilings, so you can keep the fly from sweeping into the piling, and can swim it fast or slow on the retrieve. The fly is dropped very close to the piling, allowed to sink, then retrieved in rapid two-foot pulls toward the boat. Another method is to anchor off to one side of the piling, within casting distance, and cast across-tide, letting the fly sink deep and be swept in near the piling, then retrieved away from it.

The peak fishing period for stripers in this part of California is generally agreed to be from June through November; by mid-December most of the good fishing is over. The four weeks that usually produce the most big fish are the last two weeks of August and the first two weeks of September.

Several fly patterns repeatedly take fish: the Givens Barred-N-Black, the Whistler series and Sul-Mul-Mac flies developed by Dan Blanton, the Clouser Minnow, and the Lefty's Deceiver. Most flies are weighted, so that they can be cast close to a piling in a moving tide and still get deep before they are swept into the piling. Bead chain eyes are popular on many of the West Coast patterns, but to get down deeper, some anglers use lead eyes instead. Dan Blanton claims that the bead chain eyes (and lead eyes) impart a "jigging" motion, causing the fly to rise on the strip and fall at the end of the strip retrieve.

Most flies are dressed on hooks from 2/0 through 4/0. The Mustad 34007 and Eagle Claw 318 models are standard selections, although stainless hooks in other patterns work very well.

The very best time to fish pilings is the first hour before sunrise. During this golden period just before dawn, fish will feed on any tide, but during the daylight hours, when striped bass are more reluctant to strike, a moving tidal current seems to produce better.

Neap tides, rather than spring tides, are the best tides to fish. This is especially true on the flats, for extremely low-falling water brings the flats above the surface, driving all fish from them.

Other obstructions in San Francisco Bay harbor striped bass such as duck blinds, wrecks, and rocky shorelines. Some good fishing also occurs when a local power plant outflows warm water.

A big problem when you're fishing around barnacle-covered pilings is that the sharp barnacles will slice through the line. This is often the case when a large striped bass takes the fly and gets on the other side of the piling. Keep a spare line in your box, and apply as much pressure as possible to prevent a fish from reaching the pilings once it is hooked.

Striped bass also concentrate at night in lighted areas, but remember that night fishing from bridges is forbidden by California law. Hal Jansen and the late Myron Gregory have taken many huge striped bass on a fly when fishing at night. Gregory was a real pioneer in West Coast fly fishing and had much to do with the national acceptance of the lead-core shooting taper.

A vital point to realize when fishing stripers *anywhere* is that the size of the fly is extremely important. Striped bass are among the most selective of fish when it comes to lures. *The fly caster getting refusals should alter fly size rather than pattern as a first step; often a relatively small change in length will make a great difference.*

Other areas nearby also can produce stripers. Anglers who fish the Richmond–San Rafael Bridge area feel that predawn fishing (under the lights) at the west end of the bridge is the best, and that the incoming tide seems to produce the most fish. Small bait inhabit the area, and so small flies usually take the fish best.

The Brother and Sister Islands, located in the narrows between San Francisco and San Pablo Bays, often have good striped bass fishing, particularly in the tidal rips.

The Golden Gate Bridge area is relatively unexplored by fly fishermen. The water is deep and holds swift currents, so you'll need lead heads and a big boat. This water can get nasty.

Pacific Ocean stripers range up and down the coast in the summer months. The heaviest concentration is in the area from Golden Gate to Half Moon Bay. These fish follow the schools of bait, sometimes right up into the breakers. This is tough fly fishing, since much of it is in the curling waves that break on the beach—but the fish are there.

Stripers are taken by fly casters at the mouths of several rivers in Monterey Bay, including the San Lorenzo, the Salinas, the Pajarro, and the Moss Landing Slew. At the Moss Landing Slew, a power plant sometimes sucks bait into the turbines, kills it, then spews it into the outflow, where stripers rush in to feed. It can be terrific fishing, if you time it right.

Tomales Bay, north of San Francisco, produces a lot of stripers, but they seem to be smaller on the average. Because the bay faces northwest, which is the direction of the prevailing winds, the water is often very choppy.

Coos Bay, Oregon, is about the northern limit of striped bass fishing on the West Coast. The many miles of estuaries offered by the Umpqua and Smith Rivers are perfect for stripers, although winds frequently plague fly fishermen. Blind casting the channels that drain these flats is one method of taking fish on a fly. Chumming, while generally not practiced here, could be effective.

Dick Wadsworth, a former East Coast striper nut who now fishes the Umpqua River in the Reedsport, Oregon, area, also likes the Smith River, which is nearby. Dick fished these two rivers every day in 1971 from June until August 1. "My diary tells me that I landed two fish of twenty-three and twenty-six pounds the day I arrived, and ran into fish every day thereafter," he says. "The month of June was the best month for numbers of fish. There were lots of schools of fish that averaged four pounds, and enough large fish that I was landing one to three fish a day that exceeded twenty pounds."

Dick goes on: "About the middle of June school bass become scarce, but the big ones began appearing near the surface where we could see them. These were bright, unspawned fish, fresh from the ocean. Where we were casting blind for them, we were now able to stalk individual fish. On July 9, a huge school of large fish appeared daily. They would lie off the mouth of the slough we were fishing and stay in one spot on slack high tide. These big fish would lie about three or four feet under the surface and appeared as if a cloud was casting a shadow on the water. We hooked fish from this school daily until July 30, when they all disappeared. I left for home on August 4 and my friends at Reedsport told me the big fish did not appear on the surface again until the following year . . . all fly fishing was over after July 30."

He says his favorite fly imitates the pogy, a small saltwater smelt that migrates up the river as the stripers come in to spawn. Size seems to be critical: a three-inch fly produces small fish, but a four-incher will interest the larger bass. His tie is simple and colorful: tail the same as a Mickey Finn fly, yellow then red then yellow; variegated Mylar chenille body, and a wing of white bucktail with yellow above it and a little green, topped with blue; hook size a number 3LX 3/0.

Dick feels that flies are more effective than plugs. He fishes from a twelve-foot skiff, which he admits can be dangerous, but he thinks that the silent approach to these skittish fish is a great advantage.

STRIPED BASS: EAST COAST

The East Coast fishery was in serious trouble during the 1980s, and only when the federal government stepped in and forced states to take action did it turn around. A complete moratorium was placed on fishing for stripers, both commercial and sport fishing. It is another example showing that if the environment is okay, proper controls on fish harvest can make a terrific difference. Today, striped bass range in numbers unheard of for several decades from Maine to South Carolina. But, the crisis is far from over, as I see it. The major nursery ground for striped bass is in the Chesapeake Bay. Scientists still have no firm idea as to why there are good, fair, and poor years of reproduction. Until scientists can pinpoint why, we should be careful about allowing heavy harvesting by either sport or commercial fishermen. In essence, the striped bass in the water now are our seed stock. Until we determine why stripers reproduce poorly or well, we need to conserve the seed stock. Unfortunately, commercial fishermen, through their lobbyists, have been convincing legislators and Department of Natural Resources management people to allow them liberal harvesting techniques. *Unless sport fishermen realize that they must have lobbyists who will do the same as the commercial fishermen, we stand to lose this fabulous striped bass fishery.*

The fastest-growing area of fly fishing is in saltwater. And, the greatest number of new participants to this sport are those who are fishing for striped bass along the East Coast of the United States. While there were relatively few of us who fly fished for stripers from the 1950s to the 1970s, our numbers have increased radically since the fish made its comeback. From Virginia to Maine, and especially in New England, thousands of anglers are now catching stripers on fly rods. We are catching them day and night, from the beach, the rocks, and from boats. Techniques vary for different terrains, and many improvements in tackle and flies have been achieved.

Before going into detail about how to rig for and catch striped bass, let me outline a few basic points about this fishery. Stripers are basically an inshore fish, rarely found more than a few miles away from land. They are not like tuna and other ocean roamers. Even during migrations, they tend to stay near the coastal shorelines.

The Chesapeake Bay

The Chesapeake Bay is regarded as the primary nursery ground for striped bass on the East Coast. The Hudson River and some other river systems also contribute to the stock of fish—but the Chesapeake is the main supplier of this wonderful species.

Since spawning takes place mostly in the Chesapeake Bay, the stripers that have been ranging along the coast north of Maryland (all the way to Maine) have to return to the Chesapeake. While many stripers overwinter in the Chesapeake, it is believed by many knowledgeable anglers that many of these larger bass also hold off the mouth of the Chesapeake in the

Big female stripers like this one are netted each year in the Chesapeake Bay by Department of Natural Resources biologists trying to determine why spawning success is often so poor.

Atlantic Ocean. There is some proof that a few of the stripers remain in localized northern areas throughout the year. More research is needed on this subject.

Spawning takes place in very early spring in the major river systems of this great bay. Timing is dependent upon water temperature in the spawning grounds. By late March a slow migration begins out of the Chesapeake. Stripers exit the Chesapeake Bay going south and out its mouth, or at the extreme northern end of the bay through the ship canal into Delaware Bay.

One of the triggers for the migration of striped bass is the movement of baitfish. These fish begin appearing along the coast, as far north as Maine, by early May, sometimes earlier. The general pattern is that the baitfish enter the estuaries and rivers early; by late June many of these fish have moved to the coast and even a small distance offshore. So, by mid-July you will find that many of the larger striped bass have left the rivers and the shallow bay to feed within a mile or so of the coast. However, stripers will move to the beaches and into rivers after darkness. *This means that at dusk and dawn in the summer, you often have the best opportunity to catch a big striped bass.*

Many fly fishermen tend to rush the season, and some anglers will start casting in April or earlier in hopes of catching these fish as they move northward. Rarely does any good fly fishing occur north of the Chesapeake Bay until early or mid-May. In New Jersey it's about the same. Off Long Island and even into Rhode Island and Massachusetts, an occasional striped bass is taken in late April or early May. But, the real fishing for them doesn't begin until mid- to late May, when the first schoolies of smaller fish arrive. Usually the bigger stripers are two to three weeks behind the smaller, and are the first stripers to show in northern waters. Along the shore of Long Island and farther north in early May there are often huge schools of two- to three-inch sand eels. Daytime fishing is often difficult, but at dusk and dawn, if fly fishermen use small imitations of this bait, some great catches can be had.

It is important to understand that very early in the season, the rivers and estuaries are generally more productive fishing places than along the coast. There are two reasons for this. One is that the baitfish (menhaden and alewives are two very prevalent species) seem to choke the river and estuaries very early. The second—and it's a vital point where water temperature is concerned—is that the estuaries and many shallow rivers have dark mud bottoms. This dark bottom in clear, shallow water soaks up the sun's heat. Waters in these areas can be *5 to 7 degrees higher* than in coastal areas.

The Susquehanna Flats at the head of the Chesapeake Bay are a top place to take striped bass on a fly in late May and early June. The fish are prowling these shallow flats—hungry and eager to take flies. The Clouser Minnow and Lefty's Deceiver are favorites of local anglers. I think that some of the East Coast's best striped bass fishing is in Rhode Island. In mid-May the school stripers work the Bristol Narrows, Barrington's Hundred Acre Cove, and the western shore of the mouth of the Kickamuit River.

May through September

The larger stripers usually arrive along the coast from New Jersey to Massachusetts and Connecticut in late May or early June. They tend to lie just off the coast or in deeper bays. They are attracted to drop-offs or underwater humps. As they move closer to land, they are often difficult to take on flies. The most productive fishing occurs late in the day or at dawn. These bigger fish will strike small flies. But, big baitfish imitations that are easy to cast, such as Bob Popovics's Siliclone pattern (which imitates bigger menhaden), will often produce large stripers.

This photo of Brad Burns is proof that the Kennebec River in Maine is great for early-season striper fishing. This forty-eight-inch bass was estimated at fifty pounds. Unfortunately, Brad is huge—maybe six feet, six inches and more than 250 pounds—making this fish seem smaller.

By mid-June striped bass flood into a number of rivers in Maine. The Kennebec River hosts an incredible number of fish starting in mid-June and lasting about four weeks. A boat rigged with a depth finder is a decided asset. The Kennebec is a river so deep that warships traverse it to Bath, Maine, where they are overhauled and refitted. By using a depth finder you can locate the ledges, deep drop-offs, and schools of stripers holding the area. Of course, breaking fish can also be a tip-off. The best fly lines by far for fishing this area are those that sink quickly, such as the Teeny 300 and 400 lines.

By mid-June fly fishermen can catch stripers from Virginia to Maine. Cape Cod and Martha's Vineyard become two of the great spots to fly fish through October, and even into November if the weather is kind. However, the enormous crowds make this area congested for fly fishermen.

During the summer, as indicated earlier, you can catch striped bass by seeing the fish breaking and rushing with the boat to the spot. Calm seas and bright, sunny days seem to force the stripers to move away from the shorelines. The best fishing occurs along the beaches at dawn and dusk. Stripers will take flies all night long, and in New England a great number of fly rodders fish during the summer only at night. For me, night fishing holds little charm. It is like fishing in the daytime with your eyes closed. I believe that fishing is a visual sport and I enjoy seeing everything that's going on.

In the Chesapeake Bay many of the largest fish become difficult targets

Bob Popovics with proof that night fishing for stripers pays off.

The arrow indicates a profusion of small stripers breaking on the surface of Chesapeake Bay. Drop a small streamer fly into this melee and it's like rolling a wine bottle into a jail cell.

from July through mid-September, as the larger stripers tend to hold in deeper waters off channels. Smaller fish can be found breaking throughout the summer.

But, in the Chesapeake the best fishing for larger stripers is from mid-May to late June or early July, and again from late September until late October or early November—depending on how warm the fall is. In Virginia, at the mouth of the bay, the smaller two- to ten-pound stripers can be found around the Bay Bridge Tunnel structure, along the edges of flats, and in the estuaries throughout the summer and early fall. In late October larger fish begin clustering around the rock piles of the Bay Bridge Tunnel. By early December the migrating fish have arrived and a chance to catch a trophy striped bass exists, so long as weather is fairly warm—even into early January.

A unique striped bass fishery exists in the Roanoke River in northeastern North Carolina in May of each year. It is believed that some stripers

Bill Anderson casts to one of the best striped bass fishing spots on the East Coast—the rock piles at the Chesapeake Bay Bridge Tunnel, near the mouth of this great bay.

live all year in Pamlico Sound, and that they move up the Roanoke River to spawn in late April through part of May. I have enjoyed this fishing. The river is not wide, and the fish are not huge, but it is a real pleasure to fly fish a river and hang into tough, scrappy striped bass in May. There is a ramp at Roanoke City, North Carolina, and this fishing can be enjoyed from a four-teen-foot johnboat.

In southern New England, September marks the beginning of a change in fish movements and fishing tactics. Night fishing is still productive. But, as water temperatures start to drop in mid- to late September, you begin to see a hint of migrations of ducks, shorebirds, and some stripers. Many school stripers swarm along the coast from just south of Maine all the way through New Jersey. From Massachusetts to Long Island, four- to five-inch mullets swarm in bays and along the rocky shorelines. Mullets are a favorite bait of striped bass, and large Lefty's Deceivers or other easy-to-cast streamers that represent a mullet will fool large striped bass. Mullets have a tendency to swim just below the surface, and the nervous water that they create is often a tip-off. This is a time when a popping bug can be deadly on striped bass.

October through December

October along the southern New England coast produces the best striped bass fishing with a fly rod of the entire year. Beginning sometime in July, the best action usually occurs at dusk or dawn. Maybe it's because winter is approaching, but the bass seem to feed more during the day. Perhaps they are unconsciously putting on a layer of fat for the cold months. The bass are hungry and they sometimes push the baitfish to the shorelines—

even up on the sand! Places such as Cape Cod and Martha's Vineyard can furnish dynamite fishing from the beaches. At this time of the year many juvenile baitfish are swarming and also beginning to move south. This means that in the fall there may be a number of different sizes of baitfish. While exact imitation is not necessary, better fishing can often result if you match your flies to the approximate length of the prevalent baitfish.

If October is warm and November not too cold, great fishing from the beaches can be enjoyed in southern New England as late as Thanksgiving Day. Some intrepid fly fishermen have caught stripers in early December.

Lou Tabory with a nice striper caught in the fall along the New England coast.

Along the New Jersey coast, these migrating fish begin to appear along the beaches in large numbers in early November, as they move out of New England and New York waters. If the weather doesn't turn too cold, good fishing can be enjoyed through late December.

The best fishing at the mouth of the Chesapeake Bay for trophy stripers is in December.

During the very coldest months stripers can be caught from New York to the Carolinas at spots where power plants discharge huge amounts of warm water into the estuaries. The power plants are also a draw in the summer. The huge amounts of water sucked into turbines also suck in millions of baitfish, which are chopped into bits and discharged through the outlets. This can form a gigantic chum line and fishing can be very productive.

Simon Goldseker shows off a typical Chesapeake Bay striper caught near a power plant.

SOME BASIC RULES
FOR FISHING STRIPED BASS

The following are some guidelines you can use to successfully catch striped bass anywhere I have found them. While all rules have exceptions, the following rules will prove to be true most of the time.

(1) Better fishing almost always results during tidal flow than when there is slack water. Tides carry baitfish and other morsels that stripers eat. Stripers prefer to have their food come to them. Moving tides deliver food and often concentrate it. Slack tides do just the opposite.

(2)   I believe striped bass are most sensitive to the length of the fly being offered them. If you are casting to fish and not getting hits, try to determine what size baitfish are in the area. Then, match that length with your fly. Many times varying the fly length by a few inches can make a difference.

(3)   Striped bass seem to be more sensitive to bright sunlight, especially if the water is clear, than any other species I chase with a fly rod. Stripers don't stop feeding when a low or cold weather front moves in because the front brings rain, scuddy weather, and *reduced light*. A scientist once told me that a fish that descends eighteen inches in the water has a barometric change on its body that would be about the same as going from a high to a hurricane. I think that the intensity of the light has a much greater influence on successful fishing than the barometric pressure does. Foggy, rainy, and overcast days have almost always produced more fish for me.

(4)   Points of land that protrude, as well as underwater bars that reach out from the shore, funnel bait into mini-eddies and against the shorelines. Wonderful places to drop your flies.

(5)   One of the best patterns for striped bass is a crab pattern (I prefer Del Brown's Crab Fly). Live-bait fishermen know that a crab on a hook that is free drifted is something a striper can't resist. You should carry crab patterns in floating, slow-sinking, and fast-sinking versions. It is not necessary to have large patterns. Stripers eagerly take crab patterns as small as a twenty-five-cent coin.

(6)   Underwater bars lying off beaches, where the tide flows across them, are often superior places to fish. Many can be waded. The hot spot is on the down-tide side. Water pouring across the bar forms a vertical eddy (much like a waterwheel) that traps crabs, squid, and baitfish. I have had some great success wading along a shallow bar and dropping a fly on its downside.

(7)   Many anglers don't realize that during the day striped bass will often move up into very shallow flats—less than three feet of water. They are wary and tough to stalk, but a well-cast fly can deliver some exciting fishing. This is an excellent place to cast a crab pattern.

(8)   Any rocky structure against which the current crashes is a potential hot spot for stripers. Bait is swept in with the crashing waves. But, don't just cast to the walls, study them first. The structure of how the rocks

are piled together is a tip-off. For example, if there are two huge rocks that form a wide, V-shaped opening at the top, but are joined at the base—you have a hot spot. The waves are thrown against the rocks. As the water rushes back, it flows down the V. Any bait carried with the water will be concentrated at the base of the V. Another example is a rock sitting seaward of the rocky wall, where water is trapped momentarily between it and the main structure as the water sweeps back to the sea. This spot will almost always hold bait—and a bass or two.

(9) Chartreuse is a color that stripers seem to be attracted to. Two flies I am never without when seeking stripers are the Lefty's Deceiver and the Clouser Minnow, each with a liberal amount of chartreuse in it.

(10) *The reason tide is important is that it carries the bait to the fish, or concentrates it*. Anywhere you find an eddy or a tide rip (two forces of water smashing against each other), or where the tide narrows (such as water flowing out of the mouth of a bay), you increase your chances of catching fish.

(11) Power plants can increase your chances of hooking up. They spew heated water during colder months—which many people know attracts fish. But, power plants also suck millions of baitfish into the turbines, chewing them up as they pass through the plant's system and then spewing them back into the water. Fishing such outlets is a good bet.

(12) Popping bugs are often the best flies to throw to striped bass. Because they produce a lot of noise and surface disturbance, they tend to cause fish to believe that the offering is larger than it actually is. Sometimes, when big stripers won't take your smaller underwater flies, they will strike a fast-moving popper. But, remember: on very calm days and in very shallow water, a loud popper will frequently alarm fish—so a quietly worked popper or a slider will do a better job.

(13) Fishermen new to the surf think the tidal current sweeps in from the sea directly against the shoreline, and then back out again. On most shorelines, however, the tidal flow is along the beach, not in and out. Being aware of the direction of the tidal flow helps tell you where the bait is being transported and how to retrieve your flies.

(14) Many fly fishermen tend to retrieve their flies too rapidly. There are times when a dead-drifted fly works much better. Lefty's Deceiver is

a good pattern to use. I often use a reach cast to prevent excessive drag, so that the fly drifts naturally with the current.

(15) Striped bass often hold at different heights in the water column. The fish will tend to be much deeper in the summer. To reach these fish you will need to carry floating, slow-sinking, and fast-sinking lines.

(16) Many times when a striped bass refuses one type of fly (a streamer, for example), you can switch to a popping bug, or vice versa. You can usually get the fish to take by doing the switch.

(17) Stripers holding in a large eddy are often facing in different directions, but usually the fish will face into the current. Plan your retrieve so that the fly comes to the fish as it would naturally with the current.

WHERE TO FIND STRIPERS

While stripers can be caught in many places, the two most frequently fished locales are beaches and open waters. One of the advantages of fishing a beach is that you need minimal equipment, and only a way to get to the area.

There is not enough space here to go into all the nuances of fishing beaches. But, I'll highlight what I believe are some of the most important factors in beach fishing with a fly rod.

Equipment for this is specialized and you will need it. Unless the ocean is very warm, you should have a good pair of chest-high waders and a rainsuit with a hood. That way any crashing wave can be pretty much ignored. It's always a good idea to fish a beach with a companion. This is especially true at night. Accidents can happen, and having a companion for aid is a good idea. A constant problem for the surf caster is line falling to the surf. Therefore, a stripping basket is essential.

Beaches are not generally made from smooth sand crawling up out of the sea. The average beach has depressions in it, underwater sandbars, troughs, and other features. Depressions will trap baitfish as the waves move in and out. Fish know this, so that's where you'll likely find the most stripers. It pays to learn the configuration of any beach you fish. The very best time to do this is during a spring low tide. Much of the bottom is exposed. I even recommend taking pictures of the area (with some of the shoreline included for reference when the tide is high).

The tide often flows along the beach, and many times retrieving or dead drifting the fly with the current is advised (in the same direction that baitfish would be carried along). A little chop or wave action is often better than a totally flat sea. Choppy water helps give the fly more action.

Look for baitfish—they're one of your most important keys. If you see swirls or bait leaping from the water, move quickly to the area and cast.

In New England the most productive fishing for trophy stripers is in the spring, and even better in the fall when the big fish come to the beaches to feed on bait. During much of July, August, and September, the best beach action will occur either at dusk or dawn, or during the night. Floating lines are most popular for fishing the beaches, but many anglers are now favoring intermediate or slow-sinking lines. There are some beaches with deeper water close to shore. In such places it is often best to switch from floating lines to sinking types, such as a Teeny 300 to 400 line.

If you know stripers are feeding and they are not hitting your offering, try offering a larger or smaller streamer. There are also times, especially in foaming surf, when a popping bug is the best of all flies. If a jetty juts out from the beach, or there is a river or creek that flows through the beach, you have a potentially great fishing spot. Jetties require special shoes that have rock-grabbing cleats, and a wading staff is helpful. Of all the places a shore-bound fly fisherman can get into trouble, the worst is on a jetty. Be constantly alert for crashing waves and, above all, keep an eye on the rising tide. Many anglers, busy working stripers, have found that the path they came out on is flooded, and they are stranded. *Always fish a jetty with a companion!* If a small bay or river connects to the sea through the beach, you have a great place to catch stripers. The very best time to fish such locations is when the tide is outgoing. The bait that moved up the river or into the bay will be carried back to sea on the falling tide. By fishing throughout the falling tide stage you have a great chance of scoring.

Some of the very best places to fish for stripers when you're in a boat are where waves crash against the shoreline, especially if they come out of deep water, or just off the beach where sloughs have trapped the bait and are too far out for shore-bound casters to reach. A boat lets you roam, moving quickly from one site to another, seeking breaking fish, circling birds, or any evidence of stripers.

Chumming is another deadly way to catch striped bass. Instead of chasing them, you lure them to boatside by slowly dropping ground menhaden, clams, or other baitfish overboard. I developed a fly some years ago that is deadly effective if you are using ground chum. I call it the Chum Fly

Bloody. It is often as effective as a hunk of chum meat impaled on a hook. Using a size 1, 1/0, or 2/0 hook, tie some dark brown marabou on the under-side and then on the top of the hook. When finished, the marabou should form a full skirt surrounding the hook. Don't overdress the fly; make the marabou no longer than two inches—a little shorter is often better. On some of these flies I place no weight, on others I add four to six wraps of .030 or lead wire. Sometimes I wind lead wire around the length of the hook shank. There are two keys to fishing stripers in a chum line: the fly line and the fly itself. Floating lines are virtually useless. You need either a sinking-tip or a slow-sinking line. Tie on one of the flies and *weight it to drift at the same depth as the chum being dispensed.*

Here are the three examples of the Chum Fly Bloody, so effective when using ground chum for stripers, bluefish, and a host of other species. The top fly is unweighted, the middle fly is slightly weighted, and the lower fly heavily weighted.

 ## BLUEFISH

For a number of years the bluefish furnished the best fly rodding along the mid-Atlantic and northeastern coasts of North America. There will always be bluefish, and some large ones. Scientists have told me that bluefish cycle in numbers about every forty years. The peak in numbers was reached in most areas along the mid-Atlantic and New England coasts about 1989 or 1990. Since that time we have seen a decline in the numbers, especially of the larger-sized fish. This trend will probably continue for a number of years before we again see those schools of huge, voracious bluefish slashing into the bait and our flies. Still, there will always be enough around to keep us occupied and hopeful.

Found in almost every world sea, the bluefish is a superb fly-rod quarry. One of the best things about the bluefish is that you rarely find one that isn't hungry. They can be easily chummed; they frequently chase bait to the surface; and they can be seen from a great distance breaking on the surface, with gulls and terns picking up the hapless baitfish pushed often right out of the water by the voracious blues. Casting a fly or popping bug into a school of breaking blues is akin to rolling a wine bottle into a jail cell—you're not going to get it back without an argument. There are rare times when bluefish float near the surface, and then they are very easily spooked. At such times cast from a distance with a floating line, a long leader, and smaller-than-normal flies.

Bluefish have sharp teeth, so you need heavy monofilament (60- to 100-pound) or wire leader. I favor the wire although I know that in very clear waters I will draw more strikes on monofilament shock leaders. I've lost too many bluefish of over twelve pounds to want to fish with mono again. (Smaller blues don't seem to chop through the heavy monofilament as quickly.) Number three solid wire, no longer than four inches, is advisable on big fish and usually will bring a lot of strikes. However, wire thicker than number three trolling wire often results in refusals in clear water.

I prefer to use a floating line for breaking bluefish. It allows you to get off a cast quickly, and if necessary, you can lift it from the water to throw in another direction. My second choice would be a sinking-tip. However, I would also keep a fast-sinking fly-line outfit rigged and ready. After blues stop breaking the surface, they are often twenty to thirty feet down. If the gulls haven't left the area (an indication that they expect the fish to push more bait to the top), I often just blind cast with the fast-sinking line—and it frequently pays off.

From North Carolina to Maine, bluefish move into the shallows in the spring and fall as they migrate. When the water temperatures hit the low 60s they start moving in. This can be water as shallow as three feet and the

Captain Bruce Scheible chums with ground men-haden in the Chesapeake Bay.

Three happy fly fishermen as a result of fishing in a chum line.

bluefish can top sixteen pounds! They remain (so long as there is bait) until about 71 to 72 degrees, when they depart for deeper water. The northern U.S. angler who looks for this can experience some of the best local shallow-water fly rodding of his life.

Bluefish can most easily be taken from a chumming boat, which is discussed in detail in the deepwater fishing chapter.

 **SHAD**

Winter is a long, dreary period for the angler, made livable only by reading books, tying flies in anticipation, and talking about the sport with cronies. Then, along both coasts, the first flowers of spring herald the arrival of the shad. The shad is not the biggest, toughest, or wisest fish that swims—but the shad will take a fly. If for no other reason than that it means the beginning of another fishing season, the shad is a welcome visitor to anglers on both coasts.

Shad are anadromous; they live most of their life in the sea, moving into freshwater rivers to spawn during the early spring. Their normal diet includes small baitfish, but biologists claim that during the spawning period shad do not eat. Yet, they will still take flies—perhaps they are reminded of the small baitfish they have eaten so often.

THE AMERICAN SHAD

The American shad is the larger of the two species that fly fishermen concern themselves with (a number of other kinds of shad are unimportant to the fly rodder). The average size of an American shad will run from 1½ to eight pounds; the record is over twelve pounds. On the East Coast they range from North Carolina to New England. The American shad (often called the white shad) was introduced to the West Coast by Seth Green in 1871. Fish from the Hudson River drainage were placed in the Sacramento River. Within a decade the fish had spread as far north as the Frazier River in British Columbia. On the West Coast today, the major American shad centers are the watersheds of San Francisco Bay and the San Joaquin and Sacramento Rivers. They are also abundant in the American, Russian, and Feather Rivers. A number of rivers flowing into the Gulf of Mexico hold shad, too.

American shad prefer to spawn in the larger river systems. They concentrate at the heads and tails of large pools. Sometimes they're so thick that the water seems solid with their silver bodies. Most of the time they stay close to the bottom.

THE HICKORY SHAD

The other important species of shad for fly fishermen is the hickory shad, a smaller version of the American. The hickory, called a jumping jack in the mid-Atlantic area, comes out of the water the instant a hook is impaled in its mouth. It fights well for its size and reminds many fishermen of a tiny tarpon, to which it is related. A large hickory is three pounds, and a very few reach five pounds. Hickories are caught all along the East Coast, but are less abundant than the American shad north of the Chesapeake Bay area.

Both species of shad take flies readily, and because you'll frequently fish for them in fast water (especially the American shad), you'll need flies that sink well. When fishing for hickories in smaller tributaries, where they prefer to spawn, you'll find a sinking fly less helpful.

It's important to remember that the shad has a "papery" mouth of clear, fragile tissue, so you must play it gently. Many shad have been lost because the angler "horsed" the fish along, or tried to lift it from the water by grasping the leader.

The most desirable water temperatures for shad are from 55 to 63 degrees; this is when they prefer to spawn. When temperatures rise above 66 or 67, shad will leave.

WHERE TO FIND SHAD

Because there are so many exotic and more publicized species of fish in Florida waters, few fishermen realize that there is a major shad fishery in the St. Johns River drainage. Almost any portion of the St. Johns River from Lake Monroe and Puzzle Lake south to Lake Poinsett holds shad in February and March, when the fish come up this huge river drainage to spawn. The major spawning occurs from Sanford to Lake Poinsett. The fish average two to five pounds, occasionally more. The shad like to collect in the deepwater bends on the river. Shad fishing peaks in this area in late February, but continues until late March, when the shad leave the system for the open ocean.

Standard shad flies, to be described later, are all effective. However, the St. Johns River is so large in many areas that many fly fishermen will troll with small spoons on spinning rigs to locate the shad. Once the school is discovered, the boat is anchored, and the angler uses fast-sinking fly lines to present his tiny streamers to the fish. The closer the fly is worked to the bottom—almost a universal rule for shad fly fishing—the more strikes are forthcoming.

In North Carolina the hickory shad run precedes the American shad by a week or two. The hickories begin running up the Neuse, Tar, and Cape Fear River systems in early March, followed shortly after by the large American shad. While there are many shad in these river systems, fly fishing for them has not yet caught on.

The Delaware River in Pennsylvania and New York has some excellent shad fishing, and during colonial days, the shad was a major source of food there. It was caught and eaten fresh, or sliced in half and cured in salt, which allowed the pioneers to store it indefinitely. Pollution and damming have reduced the shad fishery on the Delaware, but it's still viable for the fly rodder.

In New England about the time the lilac blooms—late May and most of June—the Connecticut River has to rank as one of the finest of all shad fishing streams. Any local fly-fishing shop can give you the latest specific information on where to fish in the area.

In California the water warms in early April and the shad swarm into the Russian, Sacramento, Klamath, American, Feather, Yuba, Trinity, and San Joaquin Rivers by the thousands. Just outside and upstream from the city limits of Sacramento, on the American River, is a fly rodders' hot spot in early and mid-June.

Oregon shad fishing is also excellent; the Coos Bay area can be great. Upriver from the public landing on the North Fork is a favorite fishing area; slack tide generally brings the first strikes. In the Roseburg area the shad will take flies from mid-May through mid-June; the Umpqua River, just below Roseburg, is especially good. The giant Columbia River, separating Washington and Oregon, probably holds more shad than any other western river. It's so big, however, that you need a local guide to help you locate the proper places to fish.

ANGLING TECHNIQUES

Shad fishing is done with the same basic techniques everywhere. In larger rivers, especially when trying for the American shad, you'll need fly patterns that are bright and flashy, sink well, and are dressed on number 4, 2, or even 1 hooks. Sometimes anglers wrap fuse wire or copper wire around the hook to make it sink quicker. Lead-core shooting heads work especially well in heavy water, although they seem to have caught on with anglers only along the West Coast.

Mylar gives off reflective flashes that help you keep track of your fly and induce the shad to strike. Fluorescent materials, both for bodies and wings, have become increasingly popular.

The migrating fish seem to follow current lines, and are frequently taken on the outsides of bends. But, once they have settled into a pool they seem to prefer its head and tail, with the lower portion the most heavily populated. A small Clouser Minnow is deadly on shad.

A dead drift with a sinking line is my favorite method of presenting the fly. Seldom does an erratic or rapid retrieve bring strikes. Adding a dropping fly often produces additional strikes, especially if you're blind fishing. Shad seem to move the most on an incoming tide, but strike more readily during slack tide periods.

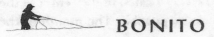

BONITO

The bonito is one of the fastest-swimming fish. There are three species: Atlantic, Pacific, and striped. The Atlantic bonito appears only along our Atlantic Coast, and the Pacific only from Baja north to British Columbia. The Atlantic bonito seems to have increased in numbers and furnishes an especially good fly-rod target in the fall, when it moves close to the beaches, feeding on small baitfish.

Bonito roam the green waters close to land but a little offshore. In Florida they are most frequently found a mile or two from the beach. They feed on small baitfish, and once you have seen a bonito splash as it feeds on the surface, you'll always be able to detect it.

On the East Coast, when you spot a school and rush to the area—much as you would for striped bass or bluefish—you cast ahead of the fish, not where they are actively feeding. Small flies, from 2½ to four inches, are best; bonito rarely take a fly larger than four inches. The best bonito fly I've tried is a 2½-inch-long Clouser Minnow on size 2 hook. I use ⅟₃₆- or ¼-ounce metallic eyes. The eye should be painted silver with a large black pupil. *This eye color is important.* Sparse, clear Ultra Hair, or better, Super Hair, is tied on, topped by ten to fifteen strands of pearl Krystal Flash and then a top wing of either pale green-blue or chartreuse.

On the West Coast bonito are fished for a little differently, although free-roaming schools near the beaches can be as successfully fished for as on the East Coast. In Monterey Bay during September, when the Japanese Current swings close to shore, a large run of bonito can be expected. Surface-feeding schools are easily seen. Bonito can be in a local area for days, and then suddenly disappear. It's usually a waste of time to blind fish for them. Surface activity is, most frequently, just after daybreak.

But the real bonito fun for West Coast fly rodders is at Redondo Beach in the vicinity of King's Harbor, in southern California. The bonito will average two to six pounds; some will top even that by a pound or two. The best fishing occurs when other fishing is nearly dead—in February—although bonito are in the harbor all winter.

The fishing is done in the harbor, which is surrounded by solid-rock jetty walls. The warm-water discharge from the electrical generating plant seems to attract the fish, but probably just as important are the anchovies constantly escaping from the live-bait receivers located in the center of the harbor. Try to cast as close to the receivers as possible. The mouth of the hot-water exit is another choice location.

ANGLING TECHNIQUES

Chumming with live anchovies is very effective, and you can rent a bait sled right in the harbor. White bucktail, polar bear, and white marabou seem to be the preferred wing materials for the flies used. Good success has been had on smaller Surf Candy flies. Mylar is recommended on any pattern you use, and the flies should not be much longer than 3½ inches; smaller is even better.

When the fish are on the surface a floating line will work. But, most of the time a sinking line, even a lead-core shooting taper, is recommended. The harbor is fifty feet deep, and fish are caught all the way to the bottom.

The proper retrieve for bonito is a matter of controversy. Many anglers feel that the fastest retrieve possible is the best; some will make a cast, position the rod and reel between their lower legs, and, bending over, retrieve as fast as possible by bringing the fly line in hand over hand. When a strike occurs they sometimes break the leader, but this method really makes a fly zip through the water. I've found that sometimes no retrieve at all, or a very slow one, is most effective. It pays to experiment on bonito.

Bonito are strong, and a run of 100 yards can be expected. Use a light drag with a reel loaded with plenty of line and you'll have a sensational time fishing these very strong, very fast fish.

LITTLE TUNNY OR FALSE ALBACORE

This fish has really become an exciting target on the Atlantic Coast, being caught in surprising numbers from New England to North Carolina. The endearing name most of us have given this fish is the "albie" or "Fat Albert." While some alba-core can be caught from the beach, the best method by far is to use a fast-moving boat. The albies push bait-fish to the surface and make miniature leaps above the water as they chase the fish. The gulls will find them before you do, so watching birds is a prime way to locate albies. After spotting them, the trick is to roar like hell in your boat to within fifty yards on the upwind side, shut down, and start casting. There are some locations where the bait concentrates during various tide phases— and so will the albacore. Tide ripping around a point forms an eddy on the down-tide side that traps bait. Some beaches will have baitfish flowing along them during a tidal phase. Anchoring up

The grin on Sarah Gardner's face tells you how much fun alba-core can be on a fly rod. Photo by Tom Earnhardt.

near the eddy or along the beach can be one of the most productive ways to fish for albacore.

These fish are built like their larger cousins, the tuna—and anything with a sickle tail means trouble when a fly caster hooks it. Albacore make high-speed runs. If the water is deep you can probably get by with 200 yards of line, but where they are taken in water less than six feet deep, you'll need a little more.

In the Martha's Vineyard area a few albacore can be taken in July and through August. In September the albacore move close to beaches all along the lower New England shores. In New Jersey it is usually October before they show up close to the beaches as they chase rainfish (bay anchovies). Albacore are the type of fish that are here today and gone this afternoon. But, when you do find them, it's some of the best saltwater fly rodding north of Florida.

The greatest albacore fishing occurs at Cape Lookout on the coast of North Carolina. Tom Earnhardt, an old fishing buddy, put me onto this. At first I thought Tom was really stretching things; then I saw the fishing. In New England and New Jersey waters, the average albacore is probably between seven and nine pounds, with a twelve-pounder a trophy. At Cape Lookout, a twelve-pounder is common and we know of fish taken of twenty-two pounds! The last trip I made there we caught several fourteen- and fifteen-pounders and one estimated to be seventeen pounds. At Cape Lookout there is a profusion of baitfish and fantastic numbers of albacore— numbering in the thousands in a relatively small area. It is not uncommon for two good fly fishermen to catch thirty albies a day!

ANGLING TECHNIQUES

The best pattern for albacore was developed by Tom Earnhardt as an offshoot of the Clouser Minnow. Using Super Hair (a second choice would be Ultra Hair), you imitate the local bay anchovies. The baitfish are about three inches long, so make the fly that length. Tie on a pair of metallic eyes (Clouser method) that are painted silver with a black pupil (the color of the eye is important). Turn the hook upside down in the vise (point up) and secure about thirty strands of clear Super Hair or Ultra Hair. Add about twenty strands of pearl Krystal Flash on top of that, then twenty to thirty strands of pale green, gray, blue, or chartreuse to complete the fly. The chartreuse pattern should be used when the water is a little dirty.

Here is Tom Earnhardt's Clouser Minnow, which is deadly on albacore and other species feeding on small baitfish.

Tuna, bonito, and albacore need to be kept in the water if possible. Never keep them out of the water—even for a few minutes. When ready to release, don't just sit them in the water. Instead, their chances are much better if they are thrown in, as demonstrated by Tom Earnhardt.

Tackle for albacore is simple. I would use at least a nine-weight; many prefer a ten-weight rod and line. While many albacore can be taken on a floating line, there are times when a sinking line will do better—so I carry both. Leaders should be about nine to ten feet in length. Since the fish have no teeth, a thin leader can be used—and should be: albies have sharp eyes. Tippet strength of ten or twelve pounds is fine.

SPOTTED SEATROUT AND WEAKFISH

The spotted seatrout, according to a state survey some years ago, is one of the most popular fish among Florida fishermen. The population has declined but the fish can be found in fair numbers on the grass flats along the East Coast from New York, all the way up to the Gulf of Mexico side of Texas, where it is one of the prime targets of fly fishermen.

Often confused with the seatrout is the weakfish, which looks somewhat like it. The largest populations of weakfish are located from North Carolina to Long Island.

The spotted seatrout, which is usually not as big as the average weakfish, lives almost entirely on grass flats of inshore waters. Here it feeds on shrimp, pinfish, small mullets, menhaden, and other little fish.

The weakfish has a more varied diet, eating almost anything small enough to ingest. Included in a long list are sand lances, crabs, mollusks, shrimp, and sea worms. Weakfish will live over almost any type of bottom, from mud flats to sandbars. They often feed as deep as eighty feet.

Both species have a delicate mouth; in fact that's how the weakfish got its name. The angler must set the hook lightly on these two species, and play the fish gently. Both species splash about on the surface but fight poorly.

Spotted trout remain in their local waters almost all year, depending upon water temperatures. Real trophy spotted seatrout are taken in the Cocoa–Cape Canaveral area of the east coast of Florida, from the Banana and Indian Rivers. In most areas four-pound spotted seatrout will draw sighs of admiration, but here it takes at least a seven-pounder to bring cameras out of the regulars' bags.

Spotted seatrout fishing is excellent in the thousands of shallow, grass-covered bays from the tip of Florida into Texas. The best technique for the fly fisherman is to use a popping cork and spinning rig with bait to locate the fish. The popping cork sits on the water; dangling several feet below it is a piece of shrimp impaled on a 1/0 hook. A yank on the rod brings a gulping sound from the suddenly immersed popper. Any trout in the area will come rushing over to see what all the racket is about and inhale the shrimp. Once the school of fish is located—and they almost always travel in schools—the fly rodder can break out his tackle and begin casting. It's a good idea to carry a plastic bottle with a cap on it, or a lobster or crab pot buoy to which are attached a long string and a weight. The largemouth bass marker buoys also work well. When you have caught several fish from a drifting boat, drop the buoy overboard, marking the whereabouts of the school. Fish near the buoy until no more strikes are forthcoming, then retrieve your buoy and continue your drift.

Weakfish are perhaps most abundant in Delaware Bay, and both species are important in the Virginia and North Carolina waters and beginning to increase in numbers north of Delaware. They are sought with the same basic fly-rod technique. Both the trout and weakfish prefer shallow bays near the coast, and rarely leave these areas unless cold weather drives them to deep water.

I have not heard of a spotted seatrout being caught on a fly at night. But, weakfish will readily strike a streamer after dark. Both species react well to ground fish chum. Anchor in an area you feel will be fruitful, and set up a chum line. Weakfish and trout are not alarmed by a boat and will come up the chum line to within a few yards of the boat.

The "papery" mouth of the trout and weakfish requires a gentle strike and fight, and the use of a landing net.

Streamer flies are the most effective for the two species. All-yellow or red-and-yellow is the universal selection of top fly rodders. All-white and red-and-white are second choices. All the flies include Mylar strips in the wing. Hook sizes range from two to 1/0.

One of my favorite methods of fishing for spotted seatrout is to locate a shallow bay with a grassy bottom and drift across it. I cast a fly dressed on a bend-back hook on a fast-sinking line, allowing the fly to bomb to the bottom. I retrieve the fly very slowly as the boat drifts. Because the fly rarely tangles, I like to crawl it right in among the grass stems. If I catch a trout I'll often anchor and cast in a circle around the boat, making sure the fly gets all the way to the bottom each time.

Bend Back flies are very effective for weakfish, too, and a Godsend in fishing over any rough bottom, where conventional hooks would constantly foul.

Spotted seatrout will readily take a popping bug—a great thrill to see—but a streamer is far more effective. That reliable Clouser Minnow is a deadly trout pattern.

CHANNEL BASS
(RED DRUM OR REDFISH)

The channel bass is one of the most popular game fish among coastal fishermen. From Texas to South Carolina, fly fishermen refer to it as a redfish. In North Carolina, small channel bass are called "puppy drum" and large ones just "red drum." All of them are channel bass. *But, for fly rodding most of us refer to it as the "redfish," especially if we are talking about channel bass of less than twenty pounds.* They're caught from New Jersey down the East Coast and around Florida, all the way up the Gulf of Mexico into Texas. In Florida and the gulf states, redfish will average from two to ten pounds, with an occasional fourteen-pounder or better caught.

But, anglers have discovered that in the spring, usually late May and early June, schools of huge channel bass work the shallows inside Oregon Inlet and the flats on either side of Davis Strait. Boats that work the shallow banks can locate schools of these husky fish in which individuals top sixty pounds. These are big fish and you need to use a very large Lefty's Deceiver–type fly, eight inches or longer and dressed on a 5/0 hook (a twelve-weight line is best to cast it), to get these monsters interested. For the northern angler who wants to catch a huge trophy channel bass, the waters inside Oregon Inlet offer a good prospect.

During the summer months and until the first hard frost in fall, smaller channel bass roam the inside or western flats in many places south of Oregon Inlet. There is terrific redfishing in the estuaries around Charleston, South Carolina. And in the lower end of Pamlico Sound, North Carolina, you can find them in water so shallow that they create a wake as they swim. Hilton Head, South Carolina, has enough of a good population of redfish on the flats to keep several top guides busy. Around Titusville there is some of the best redfishing in Florida. Poling a small boat across the flats, as they do in Texas and Florida, can produce some wonderful sight fishing.

One of the most rewarding recent events for fly fishermen has been the comeback of snook and redfish in Florida, as well as the redfish returning in great numbers to their native flats in Louisiana and Texas. This was all possible because the fishermen of that region informed their politicians that unless they created laws to control harvesting, the fish were going to be in serious trouble. As soon as better fisheries management was put into place (and the environment was in good shape), the fish came back in astonishing numbers. Redfishing in Texas, Louisiana, and Florida is better now than it has been for decades.

Florida Bay redfishing is hot from late April through October, but many redfish remain on the flats all year. They depart when a cold spell hits and the water drops into the 50s. But, they return as soon as the water warms. One of the best places to locate really big redfish in very shallow

The author with a nice redfish caught on the flats of South Carolina.

water is around Cape Canaveral. It is not uncommon to find reds here that reach more than twenty pounds.

Captain Rod Smith guided Don Leyden to this thirty-eight-pound redfish taken near Cape Canaveral. It was recognized at the time as a new world record.

Farther up the coast and along the shore of Louisiana there are many shallow oyster bars and flats that hold large numbers of channel bass. When waters are clear and the winds abate, the fly rodder can have excellent fishing. The Texas coast has miles of shallow flats, somewhat similar to those of upper Florida Bay. Redfish, along with seatrout, furnish the major flats targets for Texas fly fishermen. Here, anglers skim over the water in shallow-draft boats and fish much the same way they do in Florida. Many of the flats are grass covered, and the fish, which average a little larger than in Florida, can be seen both swimming and tailing. One good spot is the flats in the Laguna Madre area of southern Texas. The fish are there all summer, but April and May are the choice months.

Perhaps the major detriment to good redfishing in Texas is the wind. So many days are ruined by winds that can defeat a fly fisherman.

A lot of light-tackle spinning specialists in Texas have been fishing these channel bass for years. Now fly rodders are enjoying this fishing in Texas. Certainly, as word spreads, more will be seeking this husky fish with a fly rod.

Good redfishing can also be had along the coast of South Carolina, where the fish work the shallow estuaries that hold oyster bars and a lot of baitfish and shrimp. This fishery can be exciting and more anglers in the

This is a wake typical of bonefish and redfish in water less than a foot deep. Remember, the fish will be ahead of the wake, so the arrow indicates that you have to lead the fish with the cast.

region are being attracted to it.

ANGLING TECHNIQUES

Channel bass don't have the superior eyesight of permit and bonefish, and the fly rodder must cast the fly close enough for the bass to see it—but not so close that it will alarm the fish. This is best accomplished by throwing a fly six to ten feet ahead of the fish, then retrieving it so that the paths of the fly and the cruising fish will intersect.

Tailing redfish can be cast to the same way as bonefish. Drop the fly in front of the fish, eighteen inches or closer. As the fish tips back to a normal swimming position, move the fly slowly in front of it. Redfish will take almost any color fly, but combinations of chartreuse and white, orange and red, olive and brown, olive and yellow, and red and white have all been productive. These patterns are also easy for the angler to see, so he can easily keep track of the fly's course as it approaches the fish. The Clouser Minnow has become the most popular of all patterns for redfish. Since reds are often found on grass-choked flats, a weed guard is often put on the fly.

Flip and Diane Pallot prove that a canoe can get you into water so shallow that other boats can't get those redfish feeding in the grass.

In Florida Bay you can see channel bass swimming right in the grass. At low tide they will often be swimming in just six inches of water. Conventional flies, however, work poorly, because they are constantly entangled in the grassy bottom. Two underwater patterns have been developed that work exceptionally well. The Bend Back is one. The wing is made from a large amount of bucktail or fluffy marabou in the colors mentioned earlier. An ample supply of strips of Flashabou or Krystal Flash aids the redfish in locating the fly. It's a simple fly, but you can drag it through the grass with only a rare hang-up or two. Most people who fish Bend Back flies tie body material on the hook shank. But, I have determined that Bend Back flies that carry a bare shank and only a wing are more weed-free. Make a comparison. Tie two identical Bend Back flies, then fish them in grass-filled or other waters that would tend to grab them. You'll be surprised how many fewer times the bare-shanked Bend Back gets snagged.

The other fly pattern, the Seaducer, is a hackle streamer. This fly is tied on a conventional hook, usually 3XL in length. Six to eight saddle hackles are attached to the tail, then the full length of the hook shank is wound with as many saddle hackles as can be tied on it. The whole thing resembles a multilegged caterpillar with a supple saddle hackle tail.

It works something like a dry fly in that the palmer-wound hackles along the hook shank support the fly so well that it simply does not sink far below the surface. In fact, if several false casts are made, the angler frequently has to jerk the fly to get it to drop below the surface. Once under water, the fly sits almost suspended, with the hackles on the shank flexing back and forth and the saddle feathers at the rear working in a manner that excites any channel bass that sees it. The fly, because of its buoyancy, can be manipulated along in inches of water, and the palmer-wound hackles usually brush the fly away from most grass, making it relatively weedproof. In dense grass a weed guard is often used on the fly.

A popping bug or Dahlberg Diver works wonders at times, and scares the hell out of the redfish on other occasions. It should be tested each day to see what the fish's reaction will be. Channel bass on the flats will pounce on a popper most of the time; color seems unimportant. The trick is to cast four to six feet away from the fish then make soft popping sounds, instead of loud splashing ones, to attract the fish. The problem with poppers and Dahlberg Diver–type patterns, however, is that missed strikes occur frequently. The mouth of a redfish is located low on its head—so it can

A Dahlberg Diver fly fooled this nice redfish.

Redfish often carry one or many small, dark spots like these.

feed well on the bottom—and it often has difficulty grabbing a popper or Dahlberg Diver.

The redfish is not known for its fighting ability. The fish will make short, determined runs, then stand on its head and try to rub the fly out against the bottom. Shock leaders of fifteen- to thirty-pound test are frequently used because of this grubbing trick, but most of the time the channel bass can be taken on a straight leader tippet.

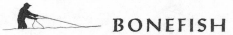 ## BONEFISH

Most bonefish must die from ulcers. They feed and swim in a constant state of alarm. Bonefish do *not* have lockjaw, super-sensitive noses, or any sort of radar that can pick up an enemy angler from half a mile away, although all of these possibilities may seem reasonable to a bonefisherman at some point during his career.

Bonefish are scattered throughout much of the world. Fly fishermen have pursued them in Central America, the Caribbean, Christmas Island,

and the Florida Keys. Each year more places to catch bonefish are being discovered in the South Pacific. *Christmas Island has to be the best place I know of to learn how to catch bonefish.* You'll cast to more bones in a day there than you will in most other areas in a week. You learn by your mistakes and your successes. The fish are usually in schools, but also frequently in singles or pairs—and there are incredible numbers of them. It will be a long time before these bones become overfished. I'm sure there are bonefish in many other areas of the Pacific, as well; some of the flats simply remain to be explored. I have fished just about anywhere anyone can for bonefish—which are by far my favorite fish to catch on a fly. If I had to choose the place where I feel the best-quality bonefishing exists, I would suggest Andros Island in the Bahamas. By quality bonefishing, I mean that there are a lot of fish and you'll have a very good chance to catch large ones, too. There are certainly many other fine places to seek bonefish: the rest of the Bahamas, Los Roques, parts of the Yucatán Peninsula, and Belize, to name a few.

The Bahamas represents some of the finest bonefishing in the world—and it's close to the United States.

Unfortunately, bonefish have been drastically depleted in areas where they were once so numerous as to stagger the angler's imagination. Natives spread Clorox in the water, which chases the spooky fish off the flats and into their waiting nets. The Clorox also kills much of the life on the flats—leaving it a virtual desert for a long time to come. Other areas allow netting of bonefish—or, where it is illegal, the authorities turn their heads. The fish are then sold in local markets for very little. Local governments have been extremely short sighted. Not only do they deplete a natural resource, but they also lose the revenue generated by camps catering to tourists from across the world, which bring more money in a week or two than is generated by all the sales of the netted bonefish. Perhaps some of these countries will make an effort to protect the bonefish, and it will surge back.

In the Florida Keys, perhaps the best bonefishing occurs in Biscayne Bay. However, there are big bonefish from Key Largo all the way down to Key West. It's peculiar that the flats in the Key West area, which would appear to be excellent bonefish territory, have very few bones, but teem with the wily permit.

Three locations in the world consistently produce the largest fly-caught bonefish. In late January, huge bonefish, full of milt and roe, move onto the flats on the east side of Bimini in the Bahamas. These fish will remain there until sometime in late March or early April. The southern end of Biscayne Bay still holds some of the biggest bonefish you're likely to encounter as a fly fisherman. Shell Key, on the Florida Bay side of Islamorada, is another hot spot for trophy bonefish. But, these are some of the toughest to catch anywhere. A fourth area where I have seen and caught huge bonefish is on the west side of Andros Island.

In April and May giant spawning bonefish invade the flats of Biscayne Bay. Captain Bill Curtis, who has perhaps the most productive record of all the bonefish guides who take fly rodders, works the flats of Biscayne Bay, within sight of the skyscrapers of downtown Miami. It's not unusual for one of his clients to catch six or more bonefish with a fly in a single day, and they consistently catch bonefish of from eight to twelve pounds.

Fish caught in Biscayne Bay will range in weight from five to nine pounds. This is trophy size in many other areas. If I couldn't get to Bimini, and I was interested in catching a world record—or at least a trophy—on a fly, I'd probably fish in the southern end of Biscayne Bay. It may have produced more record and outsized fish than any other body of water in the

The bonefish—the author's favorite fly-rod quarry.

world. No one seems sure why this is so. The fish have had to accommodate water-skiers, fast-traveling pleasure boats, and other invaders, but they have adjusted admirably well.

As with other kinds of angling, knowing the strong and weak points of the bonefish and using this knowledge to advantage is the road to success. The bonefish is a tough quarry; it's hard to deceive, and gives a good account of itself once it is hooked.

When learning how to bonefish, there's no substitute for spending time with a guide or angler experienced at the art. Watch him, listen to everything he says, question him constantly about his techniques, and learn all you can about the habits of the bonefish. Just one day with a guide or good bonefisherman is worth a year of study on your own.

Bonefish are very sensitive to water temperatures; you'll see almost none on a flat if waters are cooler than 68 degrees. At 70 degrees a few fish will be around, but they'll be reluctant to strike, even at a tasty shrimp. Once the temperature rises above 73, however, the fish become very active. After the temperature gets above 80, some bones will desert the flats. I have experienced good bonefishing in water temperatures as high as the upper 80s.

In Florida and the Bahamas during July, August, and September, bonefish feed best at dawn for an hour or two, and then very late in the evening. *In the heat of summer, or in the winter, the best flats are those that are close to deep water. Deeper water is not heated by the sun or chilled by winter as much as the flats' water.* Each tide sweeps cooler water from the depths into the

Women especially enjoy bonefishing. The tackle is light and the fishing is exciting. They usually do very well at it. This is a ten-pounder that Lynn Fuller landed at Andros, in the Bahamas.

flats in the summer, and warmer water in the winter. Flats located far from deep water tend to be hotter in summer and cooler in winter than those close to deep water. This is something to consider when going on vacation to a distant place, or even when fishing local waters during these times of the year.

Bonefish travel in schools, in singles, and often in groups of two or three fish; the extra-large fish are almost always loners. Even if there are several on a flat, they seem to prefer being alone. Single bonefish are much more difficult to approach and less likely to strike a fly. School fish are apparently more competitive in their feeding habits and accept a fly more readily.

Many people have caught bonefish on bare, white sand, but in these cases the fish are usually crossing the sandy area either to get to a food source or to return to their sanctuary in deeper waters. When over light sand, the fish are almost always more easily frightened, so the fly must be cast much farther ahead than normal.

Bonefish are bottom feeders; their mouth is located on the lower portion of the head so they can easily suck up food. One scientist wrote a description of a bonefish that, while accurate, was certainly unflattering: "The bonefish has an elongated, torpedo-shaped body with a slender head and a small inferior mouth." Bonefish feed on crabs, shrimp, many types of worms, small minnows found on the flats, and almost anything else they can swallow. Many good bonefish flats hold turtle grass. This plant resembles lawn grass, except that the stems are about three-eighths of an inch wide and from a foot to eighteen inches long, and dark green. Turtle grass is a breeding ground for small sea life, vital in the food chain.

Some flats are *hard*, that is, firm enough to wade; others have a mushy bottom. Bonefish feed on both types, but if you prefer to wade it's a good idea to select a hard flat.

FINDING BONEFISH

It's easier to spot a bonefish on flats that are light in color. Some of the best bonefish flats, however, are completely carpeted in turtle grass, and the dark bottom makes it very difficult for all but the most expert to see the fish. Bonefish apparently can adjust their coloration somewhat to suit the bottom they feed upon. Bones that feed regularly over dark turtle grass will have a back that is dark in color; those that live over light sand or a bright bottom have few pronounced vertical markings and are almost pure silver in color.

Wading for bonefish is one of the special joys of fly fishing.

Bonefish are often hard to see—it takes practice. The arrow indicates a ten-pounder cruising in front of the angler.

Polarized glasses are a must when looking for bonefish. The tint preferred by Florida Keys guides and anglers is yellow-brown, which offers a functional compromise good on both bright and dark days. Bright yellow glasses are wonderful on dark days, for they build contrast and so actually appear to brighten the scene. However, these same glasses can cause headaches for some people on a sunny day. Smoke-colored glasses work well on hazy days. The inexpensive polarized glasses found on most drugstore counters will work for a limited amount of time, but the soft lenses scratch easily and you must take extreme care to keep them in good condition. Most old-timers have purchased glasses that have a polarized section sandwiched between two pieces of hard-to-scratch optical glass, and such glasses, with a little care, will last for years. I have one pair that has gone through two pairs of frames and is still usable.

If the angler is being poled across the flats, the boatman should be careful about placing the foot of the pole on the bottom. Many bonefish have flushed when a boatman "clanked" the pole against the hard coral. Even the type of clothing you wear when bonefishing is important. Dark clothing forms a dark silhouette against the sky, making it easy for the bonefish to notice an angler standing in the bow. White, pale blue, yellow, and green are cool to wear and don't contrast as much against the sky. If the bonefish follows the fly toward the boat you should crouch low, to avoid casting a high silhouette that will warn the fish. Should bonefish suddenly appear close to the boat, without detecting you, make all your casting motions at a slow pace. A quick drop to the deck or a fast rod movement will surely flush the fish.

The water depth determines a great deal about how you should look for a fish. If the water is very shallow (less than a foot deep) look at the *surface*, not at the bottom. In such shallow water the bonefish's progress can be detected by the dorsal or tailfin above the surface, or by the distinct wake it makes as it moves across the flat. Bonefish will often stand on their heads and rub their noses in the bottom or blast a jet stream of water at the bottom to dislodge a crab or other morsel. The whole tail will protrude above the surface, one of the most exciting sights in light-tackle fishing. If you miss the tail exposed above the surface, you may see a telltale puff of mud made by the bonefish's water jet.

If the water on the flat is more than a foot deep you should be looking at the *bottom*, not at the surface. Under water, bonefish resemble a light gray shadow. Their course is never steady; they'll move a few yards in one direction, then suddenly dart off to the side. One of the greatest problems in presenting a fly to a bonefish is that often, about the time you have decided where the fish is going and made a cast, the fish will bolt off in another direction, and a hasty backcast and another shot must be made.

A school of bonefish traveling in a foot or more of water will cause ripples (called nervous water) that are at variance with the surrounding surface. This condition is difficult to describe, but once you have seen it you'll recognize it in the future. Bonefish moving in a school also produce distinct wakes, even in water three feet deep. Look for ripples moving *against* the wind and wave pattern, a sure tip-off that fish are below.

Watch for stingrays working on the flats. Often permit and bonefish will track alongside a slower-moving ray, which is scouring the bottom, flushing food in its path. If a crab or shrimp darts away from the ray, the swifter bonefish simply slips in and grabs it before the ray has a chance.

In the 1960s Joe Brooks taught me another trick in looking for bonefish. We were fishing with Captain Jack Brothers near Key Largo. Jack cut the motor well away from the flat and poled us up in the clear, shallow

The arrow points to a ray that is "muddling" on the flats. Many fish hover over these rays and can be easily caught on flies.

water. Joe offered me the casting platform, but I refused and insisted that he take the first try at a fish. Joe stepped up, stripped line, made a false cast, and stripped the line back onto the deck. He held the fly in his left hand and looked over the flat. Nothing was said for perhaps ten minutes; only the war dripping from Jack's pole interrupted the silence. Joe suddenly turned and smiled at us. "We should see some fish here," he said. "There are lots of sharks around. I've noticed that when sharks are missing from a flat, or no stingrays are working, few bonefish are around." Since that day, I have verified his observation many times. In fact, if I begin poling a flat and it is devoid of fish life, I give it five minutes to produce; if nothing happens, I move on.

There is no single best tide for bonefishing, despite the many articles maintaining that bonefish are best taken on a rising tide. It really has to do with the terrain. Usually flats located directly against deep water are most productive when the tide begins to rise and fish in the deepwater sanctuaries come out to feed. Portions of the same flats located several hundred yards from the deep water may not be productive until the tide has risen almost to its peak, simply because the fish cannot swim that area on lower stages of the tide. Flats on the far side of deeper water are often best late in the tide. In many areas bonefish will feed on one flat as the tide rises, move to another flat during high tide, then cross over that flat and move to a third on the falling tide. Bones frequently will feed only on a certain portion of some flats, always ignoring the other parts of them. Why this happens is not really understood. But, it clearly illustrates that you need the services of a guide or a skilled bonefisherman if you are new to a specific bonefishing area.

In bonefish waters around the Bahamas, Cuba, and portions of Central America, you'll find huge muds. (I've never seen big muds on the Pacific.) They are usually depressions in the flat that hold some water at low tides, maybe a blind channel, a pothole, or a similar feature. Bonefish that have been feeding on the flats collect in these holes as the tide lowers, and continue to feed. Their thrashing about creates a thick yellowish mud. The angler who sneaks up on such a mud—often several hundred yards in size—and casts his fly around its edges can frequently catch a number of bone-fish.

Bonefish seem to be in a constant state of alert, ready to flee at the slightest alarm. They're always moving. Should you see a greenish fish resembling a bonefish in color, but lying perfectly motionless on the flats, it will almost surely be a barracuda. If a cuda starts tracking your fly, slow it down or stop the retrieve. Let the fish look at it and it will move away. Speed up the retrieve, however, and the cuda will move in, make one snap of its jaws, and collect your fly. In the South Pacific, milkfish are often confused with bone-fish. Milkfish look almost exactly like bonefish—particularly in the water. Only after observing both for some time will you be able to tell the difference.

A crab fly is a great pattern for bonefish. This is a Del Brown Crab Fly, also called the Merkin—the author's favorite. The author ties this in several color combinations.

On any flat bonefish seem to prefer swimming *against* the tide or the wind—whichever is stronger. Frequently you can follow the path of a bonefish by the silvery showers of minnows that flush in front of it. Many flats have little runs or depressions in them, maybe just a few inches deeper than the rest of the water. Bonefish prefer to swim in these places. Some areas of the world, such as Belize or Christmas Island, have a reputation for growing only small bonefish—and the majority may indeed be small. But, by wading or poling the channel edges of a flat, you will frequently find that much larger bones will come up from the depths, feed on the channel edges, and then drop back to safety.

Think of bonefish as you would a bird dog. The setter or pointer begins downwind and moves into it, picking up the bird's scent wafted to it on the breeze. Most of the time, flats fish—and especially bonefish—will feed *into* the tide if they can, locating crabs, shrimp, and other food as the current brings their scents to the fish.

ANGLING TECHNIQUES AND TACKLE

The type of tackle for bonefish varies slightly with conditions. You should have a reel that holds a minimum of 150 yards of backing. The backing can be twenty-pound-test Dacron or Micron. If you're fishing on calm, wind-free days, you may want to use a rod that carries a weight-forward 5 through 7 line. Since very small flies are used, this tackle is adequate when there is little breeze. But, on windy days a line as heavy as a weight-forward 9 may be called for—to buck the wind. If you have to choose only one bonefish rod, I'd recommend an 8-weight.

For bonefish the reel should not be a slip-clutch type—*instead it should be a direct-drive.* You never need more than a pound of drag to restrain a bonefish. On a long run there may be as much as 125 yards of line stretched across the flats. A slip-clutch reel originally set at one pound will not exert enough pressure to retrieve the line. Rods for bonefish range from 8½ to nine feet. My favorite is a 9-foot Sage 8-weight rod that comes in four pieces. It is a delight to travel with and to cast. Bonefish rarely swim more than a few yards in any one direction. Many times a cast is made and the fish turns. This calls for an immediate pickup and a recast in front of the fish. You will often need a 9-foot rod with some reserve power to make a quick pickup, change direction, and cast quickly. If the bonefish runs through line-cutting coral, a 9-foot rod helps hold line aloft to, hopefully, prevent a cutoff.

The angler can locate a fish more quickly if the guide has him point to the fish. The guide can say, "Move more left—more—stop." The angler can look down the rod and locate the fish much faster.

On calm days a rod of about nine feet that throws a 6 or 7 line is a good choice. But on a windy days a nine-footer that will throw an 8 or 9 line is ideal. There is no one rod that's perfect for bonefish; you should match the rod/line combination to the existing fishing conditions and your own skills.

Leaders can be simplified. Many people connect the butt section of the leader to the fly line with a nail knot—and that's okay. However, I make a whipped loop in the fly line and then use a surgeon's loop in the butt section. I find it the most practical method and have never had a problem with it. Nail knots, epoxy splices, or needle knots all work—you have to decide what suits you. The reason I prefer the loops is flexibility. On calm days, over tailing fish, I have effectively used leaders as long as sixteen feet to keep noisy line impact on the surface away from the fish. But, on a windy day I may unloop the long leader and replace it quickly with one eight or nine feet in length. Some anglers like to build a portion of the middle section of fluorescent yellow monofilament to give a better idea where the fly is— others feel this spooks fish. I've tried it, and the bright yellow mono does- n't seem to bother the bonefish. One important factor about leaders is often missed. A big bonefish fly may be a 1/0, though most anglers prefer size 2 or 4. Attaching a small fly to a fifteen- or twenty-pound tippet destroys the natural action of the fly. If a tippet of twelve pounds or heavier is used, I suggest using the nonslip loop (see pages 54–55). This knot, when tied correctly, delivers full line strength, and the loop, even with a heavy tippet, allows the fly to move about freely. For most bonefish an eight- or ten-pound leader is best. Because of the coral, sea fans, and other sharp objects on the bottom, using a leader tippet of even six pounds is touchy, and while many bonefish have been taken on 4-pound test, if that taut fragile strand touches anything sharp—the game will be lost. The most popular tippet size for bonefish is a ten- or twelve-pound test. The flats at Christmas Island are as white as snow. The native guides there, who know little about monofilament, have determined that darker-colored leader tippets deter strikes. I suggest using clear or a pale-tinted leader when fishing over a light-colored bottom.

While all shades of colors exist for bonefish lines, almost all the top bonefishermen I know prefer a brightly colored line. I favor chartreuse, since it can easily be seen on overcast days. While you may not think it, you are monitoring your cast as it unrolls toward the target. A dull-colored line is difficult to see, and accuracy suffers. If you don't think having a visual picture of the line unrolling is important for accuracy, try this trick. Make several casts where you can easily see the line in flight to the target. Then make several casts where, halfway through the forward cast, you close your eyes. You will be amazed at how inaccurate the last few attempts are. Don't worry about the bonefish seeing the line. If you cast properly and have at least a ten-foot leader, the fish shouldn't see the line. On calm, bright days I never use the overhead cast if I can make a side cast. This keeps the line, leader, and fly low to the water. It accomplishes two things: it diminishes the chance of the fish seeing anything, and the low cast lets the line, leader, and fly fall quieter.

Shooting heads or shooting-taper lines are not recommended for bonefishing. Since most fish will be caught within sixty feet of the boat, distance is not a problem. But, more important, you lose the ability to correct a bad presentation quickly. With a conventional bonefish taper or saltwater taper, if the fish makes a change in direction after the cast has been delivered, a good fly caster can pick up most of the line, make a hasty recast, and get in another presentation. Shooting tapers require that the running line be retrieved all the way back to the head before a cast can be made, and this almost always eliminates the chances for a second cast.

Bonefish Flies

The diet of a bonefish is varied—it will eat about anything it can swallow. This includes crabs, shrimp, minnows, and many types of worms that inhabit the flats. Stomach analyses have revealed that bonefish frequently eat long, skinny worms. But, their mouths are small, and they usually won't ingest a six-inch plug or huge fly. Flies no longer than three inches are probably the best choice. Bonefish feed mostly on the bottom, but they will take food throughout the water column. While working as the manager of the Met Tournament in Florida (during the 1970s, this tournament was responsible for much of the advancement of light-tackle fishing in salt water), I looked through old photos and saw several of bonefish that had been caught on the Ballerina fishing plug—on the surface. Bonefish are opportunists, and it is possible to catch them on occasion in very shallow water with bushy dry flies. However, I hasten to add that for each one that takes a dry fly, perhaps a hundred will accept one under water. Ask any experienced bonefisherman where he manipulates his fly, and almost to a man he'll say on the bottom. Perhaps the single most important criterion for bonefish flies is that they sink quickly. The most effective spinning jig ever used in the Florida Keys for bonefish was a Hampson, a one-quarter-ounce, lead-head jig with a 2½-inch tail. So, very tiny flies aren't necessary. While they allow a softer impact on the surface, they have a disadvantage: hooks of size 6 and smaller often grab very little of the fish's flesh. On a long run, these small hooks often pull free. For most bonefishing situations, I prefer hooks no smaller than size 4. Fly patterns designed with the hook riding up—so it can be crawled along the bottom—are especially effective. There is a basic rule you can go by for an initial fly selection on a bonefish flat. If the flats are bright colored (such as marl or sand), then use a bright-colored fly. If the flats are covered in olive green turtle grass, a dark fly will almost always produce better than a bright one. Think about it. Any creature that has lived there, if its coloration contrasted with the bottom, would probably have been eaten eons ago. Match the color of the fly to the color of the flat you're fishing and you probably won't go wrong. The only exceptions to this are bonefish flies that carry chartreuse on the wing. Don't ask me why—but they certainly are effective.

Many variations of the epoxy fly became all the rage a few years ago. It does have some fine characteristics. Today, however, few bonefish flies are made almost entirely of epoxy, although some popular patterns do incorporate it. Flies made almost entirely of epoxy have an objectionable impact when they hit the surface, and on the retrieve they have little lifelike action. Most experienced bonefishermen prefer flies made with more flexible and lifelike materials.

Perhaps the most popular fly used by bonefishermen all over the world is the Crazy Charley. Back in the 1980s Bob Nauheim, a California fly fisherman with vast experience in salt water, developed this fly. He was fishing with his guide, Charley Smith, at Charley's Haven on Andros Island in the Bahamas. The fly was so deadly that the guide kept saying, "Dat's sure a nasty fly," so Bob named it the Nasty Charley in honor of the lodge owner. Later, a large commercial fly-fishing company renamed it the Crazy Charley and the name stuck.

This fly is tied with bead chain eyes, but it is important to secure the eyes on the *under*side of the hook, so that the point rides upright. This fly casts like a dream and dives instantly, and bonefish eat it. The protruding bead chain eyes, however, limit where it can be fished. Over white sand or clean, bare flats it's a dynamite fly, but where there's debris or turtle grass, the bead chain eyes often foul in the grass. The original fly was tied with a half- to three-quarter-inch tail of six to ten strands of pearl Flashabou and a body of silver Mylar, over which was wrapped clear, fifteen- to twenty-pound monofilament. A pair of bead chain eyes is secured at the front, and then four white saddle hackles (or white calf tail) are used to build a wing slightly longer than the hook. The fly can be tied in many color variations. One of the best is a gold Flashabou tail, a gold body overwrapped with clear monofilament, and a tail of dark brown calf tail. A variation of the Charley is the Gotcha, which is basically a white Crazy Charley with about one-quarter of the hook length behind the eye built up with bright pink thread. *I would rate this one of the 4 or 5 all-time great bonefish flies and I am never without it on the flats.*

I now tie all my Crazy Charley– and Clouser Minnow–type bonefish flies *with no body, just a bare hook shank.* I find that the fly has a quieter impact on the water. It is much easier and quicker to tie. Best of all, it seems to be just as effective with a bare shank and a wing as it does with the fancy body, which often takes longer to tie than any other part of the fly.

I also prefer lead eyes to bead chain eyes. Because the lead eyes are much smaller, they make less noise when they hit the surface. They also sink the fly faster.

Snapping shrimp live on many bonefish flats by the millions and are a major food source for the fish. The Snapping Shrimp fly is available anywhere bonefish flies are sold and is another must-have pattern, especially if you fish where there is turtle grass. This pattern is so well publicized and is sold by so many fly-fishing outlets that I won't go into much detail here. Almost always it is weighted, and usually size 4 is preferred.

Another fly should be mentioned. Back in the 1960s Pete Perinchief, a superb Bermuda light-tackle angler, began the technique that is today applied to tying almost all bonefish patterns: a reverse wing. The fly will ride upside down, with the point up, reducing the chance of snagging the bottom. *His series of Horror flies (he told me he named them after his daughter) are still among the most effective bonefish flies ever used.*

There are occasions when bonefish are in very shallow water that is as flat as a mirror. This often occurs early and late in the day when the tide is starting to rise, or near the end of its fall. The fish, often with their dorsal fins protruding above the surface, are working the shallows. In such a situation a normal bonefish fly often hits the surface with too much noise. I developed a pattern I call the Tailing Bonefish Fly. This is tied with either no body or a thin one. The key to this fly is the wing. I use twice as many materials as you would normally put in a bonefish fly. I favor bucktail for a wing material, simply because it is buoyant. When cast, the wing dries and the fly comes to the water as if it is a parachute. Using a fourteen- to sixteen-foot leader, I have dropped this within a foot of a bonefish swimming in inches of water without frightening it. Many times you have to retrieve a bit of line before it dives below the surface. I carry it in two colors: one with an all-white wing and one with a brown wing, usually with a yellow-dyed grizzly saddle hackle on each side. I would never be without this pattern; it has served me so well on thin-water flats. Incidentally, I developed the fly on a standard hook, but I now tie this on a bend-back-style hook. This makes it difficult to snag on the coral even in inches of water.

But, if I were forced to fish with only two bonefish flies the rest of my life, the choice would be easy. I would select the Clouser Minnow with a white-and-chartreuse wing and the Clouser Minnow with a white-and-light-tan wing. I remember sending some of these to Flip Pallot, of *Walker's Cay Chronicles* TV fame. He carried them around for months unused. One day, when the bonefish refused all his offerings, he reluctantly placed one of the

Clousers on his leader. The results were so astounding that Flip's fly box is now filled with these two patterns—and only a few other bonefish patterns.

This Clouser Minnow is a bit longer than most bonefish flies, ranging from two to 2¾ inches in length. It is an extremely simple fly to tie. Place a size 2 hook in the vise (for bones smaller than three pounds I use a size 4 hook) and attach lead or metallic eyes one-quarter inch behind the head. Turn the hook over in the vise and secure about twenty to thirty strands of white bucktail. On top of that add ten to twelve strands of pearl Krystal Flash the same length as the wing. Add the same amount of bucktail in either chartreuse or light tan and you have the finished fly.

Another fly pattern that for some time I tended to ignore, to my regret now, is a good imitation of a crab. While many crab patterns work, I have had such luck with the Del Brown Crab Fly that now I use it exclusively. Bonefish feed extensively on crabs, so it follows that this pattern works well. If you fish it where there is a grass-covered bottom, or where the bottom is studded with coral, a weed guard is recommended. On many white flats there lives a ghost crab that is a creamy white. Bahamian guides have told me that bonefish desire this white crab above all other foods. A cream-colored Del Brown Crab Fly the size of a penny can sometimes be deadly when bonefishing on light-colored flats.

Everyone who bonefishes eventually determines that he has solved the mystery of what bonefish eat. Some anglers will carry many bonefish patterns. The truth is that if you present and retrieve a fly properly, most of the time bonefish will accept your offering. After many years of pursuing bonefish all over the globe, I am convinced that the following few patterns are all you really need to successfully fish for bonefish almost anywhere in the world. I long ago discarded the boxes with huge numbers of flies and now only carry these patterns. If the fish are small, I dress the patterns on 6 or 4 hooks. If the fish weigh more than four pounds I tend to dress them on a 4, or, even better, a size 2 hook.

Here is my suggested list of the *only* bonefish flies you will need: Clouser Minnow (both in white and tan and white and chartreuse), Gotcha, The Horror, a Bend Back, Tailing Bonefish Fly (a white-wing and brown-wing pattern), Crazy Charley White, Crazy Charley Tan, Snapping Shrimp, and Del Brown Crab Fly.

Bonefish have a soft, leathery-tough mouth. This means that your hook should be sharp. Many experienced bonefishermen don't like to use a triangular or diamond-shaped point, fearing it will cut through on a long fight. (I have never had this happen.) Many prefer to sharpen the point slightly. Another method is to stroke the file only on one side of the point, as though you were making the first stage of a triangulated point. This results in removing metal from only one side of the point. It works very well not only for bonefish, but for many other species as well. Some of the finest guides in Florida use this single-side sharpening method. I think most hooks need some sharpening, and certainly, during fishing, hooks will dull and need attending to. *The most important factor, I believe, when sharpening any hook, is to sharpen only the first one-eighth inch of the point.* Sharpening more than that can leave a cutting edge, and it may also weaken the point, so that it tends to curl if it hits a rocky bottom, or if it strikes bone on contact with the fish.

Presentation, Reeling in, and Releasing

Most bonefishermen work their fly too violently. They retrieve in six-inch to two-foot darting strips, which usually frighten most bonefish. The most successful technique for me has been to cast six to eight feet in front of the bonefish. The fly can be dropped a little closer if the water is choppy, or a little farther away if the surface is calm. Let the fly fall toward the bottom. If you sense that the bonefish hasn't seen it, make two long, quick strips, which will almost always alert the fish. Then drop it close to the bottom and make a series of short strips on the line. Don't make a series of long strips—this almost always frightens the bonefish. Once the bonefish has seen the fly and begins tracking it, I have learned to use a retrieve that has doubled my number of hookups. When you know that the fish is very close to the fly (this is often indicated by the fish tipping its nose downward), you want to begin a *slow* retrieve.

To digress for a moment: many times when bonefishermen are stripping line they feel a few little pecks on the line, as if the fish is trying to get it. What I think happens is that as you finish one strip on the line, and then drop the line to reach forward to grab it again, the bonefish grabs the fly! As you recover the line you feel those quick little pecks, and assume the fish didn't get a grip on the fly. Actually, what you felt was the fish dropping the fly that it had grasped while your hand was off the line.

To double your hookups on bonefish, try this. Cast the fly well in front of the bonefish. Make the two quick strips and allow the fly to fall near the bottom. Then, begin your retrieve. As the fish moves in very close to the fly, grasp the line and slowly—very slowly—start drawing backward on the line. *What you want to do is keep the line and leader taut and very slowly drag the fly along the bottom.* Keep drawing on the line until your hand is as far back as you can go. If the fish still hasn't taken the fly, quickly drop the line, come forward, recover the line, and repeat the slow draw. If the fish hasn't taken by then (and that is unlikely), make two quick long strips, and again begin the slow draw. By slowly drawing on the line you have kept everything tight, and if you do it correctly the fly will ooze along the bottom at a very slow pace, even stirring up little puffs of sand or mud, as if it's trying to hide. You do have to be aware of the boat's movement. If the tide is sweeping the fly toward you, or the boat is closing on the fish, you will have to draw on the line faster. What you are trying to do is keep the line and leader tight. When the fish strikes, all you need do is give a firm, short pull back with the line.

During any retrieve it is necessary to keep the rod tip pointed at the fly. Never manipulate the fly with the rod tip; this creates slack that will cause missed strikes as the rod is dipped back to the first position. Don't hold your rod high above the water and retrieve. Even though your line hand gives but a twitch, the slack hanging down from the rod to the water will sag and cause the fly to swim when you wanted it to stop. For bonefish, keep the tip nearly in the water—or even in the water. This results in better fly manipulation and more effective striking.

If the fish is tailing, the fly should be presented within a foot of it, and may have to be dragged right under its nose before the fish will see it. When a bonefish is swimming along in a foot of clear calm water, though, the cast should be at least eight feet in front of it. But, be ready—if the fish changes direction, as it is likely to do, you must quickly pick up the line from the water and make another cast. The fly should be directed at least a foot or two above the surface of the target area; driving the fly into the water will create too much disturbance. It pays to be *down-sun* from the fish when you cast, to prevent throwing a line shadow over the fish. Should the fish swim into or under the leader or line, stop retrieving. If the fish strikes a moving leader or line, you've had it! Once it has passed under the line, you can gently pick it up and make another presentation.

One of the major reasons fly fishermen fail to catch the bonefish they are casting to is that they make an improper second backcast after they have presented the fly. Here's what happens: the cast and retrieve are made and the fish refuses the fly. Another cast is made in front of the fish and the fish flees. What happened is that when the fly was lifted from the water, the backcast was made while some (even a foot) of fly line was still on the surface. Surface tension grips any fly line. If you make a backcast with any line left on the water, you rip the line free from that surface tension. This causes an alarm sound that spooks fish. *Never make a backcast when the fly line is near a fish if any of the line is still on the water.* Make sure you have raised the rod far enough that only the leader is in the water. During false casting many fish are spooked because the fly hits the surface during the backcast. This will almost certainly frighten the bonefish.

My favorite of all bonefish casts reduces fish spooking to a minimum, although you take a chance that the fish may change direction and you may have to recast. When a hungry barracuda has been prowling nearby, or sharks are aggressively working the flats, or there are very calm conditions, bonefish can be exceptionally spooky. Even a cast softly dropped fifteen feet in front of one may cause it to flee in panic. Under such conditions here is the cast that works best. Anticipate the direction the bonefish is swimming. Try to throw *thirty or forty feet* in front of the fish, where the impact of line and fly will not startle it. What helps is to drop the fly near some sort of reference point. This can be a piece of coral, a little tuft of aquatic grass, or any object you can easily see. Watch the bonefish, and when it gets within about six feet of the fly, gently twitch the fly (remember these fish are extra-spooky) so that it moves a few inches. This is the safest way to avoid spooking the bonefish.

After you spot a cruising bonefish you frequently have a maximum of about ten seconds—often less—to make a cast. Remember that you are standing in the boat, holding the fly and leader, with much of the fly line lying on the deck at your feet. The procedure for making a quick cast is outlined in chapter 8; study it well. Before you make your first trip tarpon, bonefish, or permit (all three are flats dwellers), you should practice at home until you can make that delivery in ten seconds or less. And don't forget that casting speed is not all; you must get the line into the air, all the while calculating the speed and direction of the bonefish. Then make the presentation of the fly at the right spot, at the correct moment. Regardless of what the guide or companion is shouting to you, *take your time*. The difference between you rushing a ruined cast and making the cast at your best top speed may be only two seconds.

When you think that the fish has taken the fly in shallow water, *never strike up with the rod*. If you miss the fish, the fly leaps from the water. Instead, either strip strike or move the rod to the side. If the fish misses the fly, it simply darts a few feet along the bottom and drops back in front of the fish—encouraging another strike.

When you set the hook there will be yards of line on the deck, which will soon disappear through the guides. Once the fish has been hooked, your immediate concern is to clear that line—which will be *smoking* through the guides in an instant. Hold the rod high, then form an O ring around the line with the first finger and thumb of your other hand. As the running line begins tearing up off the deck, keep your eye on it (disregard, for a moment, the escaping fish), and with your fingers in the shape of an O ring, feed the line from under your feet, off the gear on the deck, and allow it to flow smoothly through the guides. Remember to keep the rod hand higher than the hand feeding the line. If the rod is lower, the line can tangle around the reel or the rod butt.

Once the fish has pulled all loose line from the deck, fight it from the reel. The drag pressure should be set at no more than a pound. My favorite way to set a bonefish drag is with my lips. *Make sure that your lips are dry.* Grip the fly line between your clenched lips just in front of the reel. By holding the line as tightly as possible in your lips, adjust the reel drag until you reach the point where you just can't cause the drag to slip. This isn't much drag, but it's all you need for bonefishing. *It's vital that you do nothing*

Drags should be set lightly for bonefish. Susan Schultz demonstrates the author's favorite way to set the drag for bones. Clench the line as firmly as possible with dry lips. When you can no longer pull the line off, you're done.

to restrain a bonefish during its first long run—which will be from fifty to more than 100 yards. As soon as the fish has ended its run, immediately begin to pump the rod and recover line. Generally the fish will fight sluggishly back to the boat. But, when it sees you it will make a second run, which is almost never quite so long or fast as the first. The fish may repeat this several times before it tires.

Bonefish fight until they are totally exhausted, so you must revive the fish when you release it. If you simply unhook it and drop it back, it will usually sink to the bottom and die. To revive it, grasp the fish around the lip firmly. Gently rock the fish back and forth. This method holds the mouth open and, on each backward rocking motion, opens the gill covers wide, allowing life-giving oxygenated water to flow across the gills. It's the fastest way I know to revive a bonefish. Don't worry about how to tell when the fish has recovered; when a bonefish is ready to leave, you'll know.

Getting to the Fish

The most popular kind of bonefishing is done from a boat poled across the flats. A guide moves the boat with a long pole, to which a shoe of some sort is attached to prevent the pole from sticking in the bottom. The angler stands on the front casting platform, line carefully coiled in readiness on the deck, holding the fly in his hand. When a fish is sighted, the guide manipulates the boat so that the angler gets a clear shot at the bonefish. Use of a boat allows the angler to cover the most amount of water and to view the flats from a high angle—a definite advantage. The disadvantages are that fish can feel the boat as it moves through the water, and they can see the elevated angler.

Wading is the second important method. Here, a boat is often used to get to the flats, and then the boat is generally moved until fish are actually sighted. Then the angler steps out and carefully wades to within casting distance. Wading is for some a pleasant preference; at other times it's a necessity, because the boat cannot approach the bonefish if the water is too shallow. Wading lowers the angler's profile and allows the fly fisherman to get very close to the fish. I have been able to catch bonefish by kneeling with only two or three feet of fly line outside the rod tip. Wading has the disadvantage, however, of restricting the amount of area you can cover. By being so low to the water your vision is restricted as well, but fish will approach closer than they would to someone in a boat.

A third method of taking bonefish is by staking out, or anchoring in, a choice spot that bonefish frequent. You can stand alert and wait for expectant bonefish to arrive, or you can chum them into your area. Some guides position the boat by sticking the pole into the bottom and tying a short rope to it. If your guide does this, make sure he has inserted the pole into the flat at a very low angle. If he hasn't, the fly line will surely catch on the pole on your backcast.

Chumming is an effective method of bringing bonefish to the boat, but it does require some knowledge of the area. You can't chum bonefish if there are none around. Once you've determined that a flat is a good spot for chumming on a particular tidal phase, cut up half a dozen live shrimp and throw them into the area you want the bonefish to come to. Shrimp have gotten pretty expensive, so many anglers and guides use a foot-long piece of 1¼-inch plastic pipe with caps and many half-inch holes drilled into it. A long cord is attached to one of the caps. The pipe is filled with cut pieces of shrimp and the ends sealed with the caps. The pipe, attached to a cord, is thrown where you want to fish. The holes permit the juices to flow to the sensitive noses of bonefish, which are attracted to the pipe. If no fish come, you can retrieve the pipe, drop it in a bucket, and go to another location without using up all your expensive shrimp. It's a good idea to chum a bright spot, so that you can see the fish more easily when they arrive.

Be sure to anchor the boat on the upwind side of the area chummed, and, if possible, on the up-tide side, too. Captain Bill Curtis has raised this chumming technique to a high art form in Biscayne Bay. He instructs each angler to cast to the feeding bonefish, place his rod tip under water, and then strip the fly in, only an inch or two at a time.

I have read articles that claim catching a bonefish is a snap. The writers obviously hadn't done much bonefishing with a fly rod. Joe Brooks rightly called the fish "the gray ghost of the flats." Bonefishing with a fly rod is one of the most intricate challenges in the sport of angling. It can also be one of the most satisfying. I was once asked to write a magazine article about what I would fish for if I had only one more day to fish. "Think about it a few days and call me," the editor said. I answered, "I don't have to think about it. I'd go for bonefish at the Andros Island Bonefish Club. Bonefishing is my favorite form of fishing with a fly."

PERMIT

The permit is perhaps the supreme challenge to fly fishermen in shallow water. This fish is warier than a bonefish and nearly as fast, swims even more erratically, is infinitely stronger, grows bigger, and has incredible eyesight. For years we simply didn't know how to catch permit. I remember the first one I caught back in the late 1960s. It weighed less than five pounds. After I had cast to hundreds, that one finally took my fly along the north side of the Marquesas Islands, west of Key West. I was so delighted that I kissed the fish before I released it.

PERMIT FLIES

Fortunately, fly fishermen have now developed solid techniques for taking permit in the shallows with specially designed flies. The first glimmer of a breakthrough came when Captain Nat Ragland, of Marathon in the Florida Keys, developed a fly called Puff The Magic Dragon, whose name was soon shortened by most anglers to just the Puff. While this fly did catch some permit, it still wasn't the answer.

Permit seem to prefer crabs to any other type of bait. Flies imitating crabs have been around for years, but none really seemed to produce. Finally, tiers began to create some that did a good job. The first pattern that really took a lot of permit and gained popular

As far as the author knows, Joe Brooks caught the first permit on the fly. This one was taken in the mid-1960s by Joe. Don McCarthy, the Bahamas public relations officer, was with him.

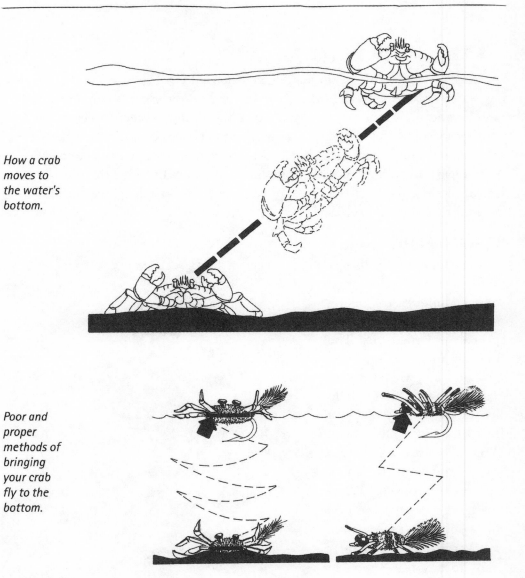

How a crab moves to the water's bottom.

Poor and proper methods of bringing your crab fly to the bottom.

acceptance was the McCrab. While this was an effective pattern, it had some liabilities. The heavy, hard coating on the base of the fly made it difficult to cast and it landed on the surface with a very audible splash.

A good permit fly should have several characteristics. It should be relatively easy to cast; if you can't cast it well, your chances are reduced. Second, it should land on the surface with a minimum of disturbance. Third, it should resemble a crab. And fourth, it should sink properly.

When a permit approaches a crab, the crab understands that unless it hides quickly, it's probably going to be eaten. So what the crab does is tilt to one side and head for the bottom in a steep, diving decline. For this reason the best crab imitations are weighted only on one side. As soon as they contact the water and slack is given in the leader, they tilt to one side and sink quickly, just as a natural crab does. This is an important point!

Crab flies that have a hard base material spread across the bottom are not only difficult to cast, but hit the water with a resounding splash. They also tend to sink like a saucer that is placed in a dishpan full of water: in a wobbling, back-and-forth motion. This lengthens the time it takes for the fly to get to the bottom, and is an unnatural swimming motion for a real crab. Well-designed crab flies have a soft material on the bottom and are weighted only on one edge.

There are two fly patterns that fit this bill perfectly, and fortunately, both are easy to tie. They are the Jan Isley Wool Crab and the Del Brown Crab Fly, often called a Merkin. Isley's fly is made mainly from wool, with lead or metallic eyes on one end and a few rubber bands to represent legs. It is a terrific fly and, by selecting different colors of wool, you can match it to the color of the crabs in the area you fish. Many light-colored flats have the aforementioned ghost crab in abundance. The Del Brown Crab Fly tied with cream-colored yarn is a good imitation of this crab.

The Del Brown Crab Fly (which is a tremendously successfully pattern on a host of fish) is my personal favorite. This fly is made from rug yarn. It is easy to tie, and by using different colors of rug yarn, you can vary the color of the fly. Some anglers feel that head cement, glue, epoxy, or even hot glue gives off an odor that causes permit to ignore the fly, but I don't subscribe to this belief.

Del Brown has caught more than 350 permit on this pattern. See page 76 for more information on this fly.

TACKLE

Tackle for permit fishing is pretty simple. Most anglers prefer a weight-forward floating line, although a few will use a slow-sinking or intermediate line. The Bonefish Taper and Saltwater Taper seem to be the best line designs. The most popular line size is either a 9 or a 10. Some people prefer an eleven, and a few will opt for an eight line. However, a big permit might be too much for a size 8 rod. A nine-foot rod that matches the line you use is a good idea. Leaders should be between nine and eleven feet long.

The team of Captain Steve Huff and Del Brown has probably caught more permit than anyone else.

The butt section should be at least forty- or even fifty-pound test, since you are often forced to cast at short distances with a heavy fly. The heavier, stiffer butt section tends not to collapse under this situation. Most anglers use about a fifteen-pound-test tippet. I have not found permit to be especially leader-shy. The reel should contain a minimum of 150 yards of backing plus fly line. Few permit make seriously long runs. They tend to bolt away and then circle, often expending their energy within fifty yards of the boat. However, they are powerful fish and must be played with some finesse.

FINDING PERMIT

Many fly fishermen (including myself) regard fishing over wrecks as not having the same attraction, nor requiring the same skills, as catching permit in the shallows. Therefore, I will not touch upon the subject of wreck fishing for permit.

Permit are not as sensitive to chilling waters as bonefish. It depends upon the guide that you talk to, but some of the ones I respect so much agree that permit are best seen on the flats when water temperatures are somewhere between 72 and a little more than 80 degrees. Since flats often heat up in the summer, the best fishing is usually during spring tide weeks. That is when the most tidal flow occurs during the month, more water is pulled from the flats on the falling tide, and more water is brought in from deeper areas on the incoming tides. In the Keys, March may be the month with the best water temperatures, if you can get a break with the wind. Permit like enough water to swim well in. This means a depth of about eigh-

Chuck Walton was one of the pioneers who first began to successfully catch permit in the early 1970s.

teen inches to several feet. I have seen permit lie on their sides like a flounder and swim in the shallows, but I don't think they like it.

If you were to have the best of all conditions for permit fishing you would want these: water two to four feet deep, fairly bright sun (for good visibility), a little breeze to put a slight chop on the surface, and a water temperature of between 72 and 80 degrees. Calm water and clear skies are tough times to fish permit. They seem to be able to see you faster, and dropping a crab pattern on a flat calm surface often spooks permit.

Almost all of a permit's body is silver in color. This acts like a mirror and reflects back to the viewer the type of bottom the fish is swimming over. Thus, on a dark green flat the fish appears dark green, and on a light flat it appears light colored. Along the back and tail, however, there is an almost black coloring. This is what most people see when they locate swimming permit. It resembles a thin, dark Y.

Most permit on a flat will be traveling in the same general direction. If the first few you see are traveling diagonally to the south on a flat, chances are most others will, too. Permit tend to travel in small troughs or ditches on the flats, or along a ridge, where crabs and other prey can be trapped. On a flat where the tide enters or falls through an opening, the permit will often cruise back and forth on the down-tide side of that opening, intercepting bait as it is funneled through. On the later stages of tide, permit will frequently prowl the edges of channels, taking crabs and other food that is swept from the flat to deeper water. Permit often seem to enjoy moving up on a flat early in the morning when there is an incoming spring tide. Perhaps they didn't eat well the day before and they need a quick breakfast.

Deeper holes or pockets well up on a flat will often hold a school of what are called "floaters," permit that seem almost suspended or moving slowly around in this deep hole. Permit, and especially larger ones, are often found well off the keys and shoreline on flats sometimes a mile or more out in the main bays. These fish will cruise the edges of flats, and when water is deep enough, ride right up on them.

One of the most frequent ways permit are located is through nervous water, or ripples or wakes moving across a flat. If you see low-flying birds, such as cormorants or pelicans, when fishing a flat, keep an eye on them. If they pass over a permit, it will almost always show itself by flushing away

Del Brown with one of his world-record permit, taken on his crab pattern. Photo courtesy of Marshall Cutchin

from the bird. It will usually run a short distance, slow down, and begin feeding again. This gives you an opportunity. I have often been fooled by a lone permit swimming along near the surface. You see that back-and-forth wobbling motion so similar to a swimming shark that you think it is one.

For some unexplainable reason permit seem to disappear from the flats in Florida and parts of the Bahamas in late spring (usually in May). Many fishermen think that they may be moving offshore to spawn. There can also be a brief time in October when the same thing occurs.

Permit can be found from Florida all through the Caribbean. There is even a Pacific version of the permit, but not much is known about it by fly fishermen. The Yucatán Peninsula area probably holds as many permit as anywhere (Ascención Bay and Es Spirito Santo Bays are two great spots), and you often see schools of them there. Most of the time the permit are small, as little as half a pound and not many of more than twelve pounds. However, a few very large permit can be found there. If you are seeking a trophy permit on a fly, then the Florida Keys flats from Marathon to west of Key West may be the best in the world.

PRESENTATION

Presentation of the fly is an important part of hooking up with a permit. When it comes to catching permit on a fly, there is no greater angler-guide combination than Del Brown and Captain Steve Huff. Steve is generally regarded as the finest guide in the Florida Keys. Del and I have fished in several parts of the world and I can attest that he is a great angler. Pair these two and you have a deadly combination. Del fishes with other guides, of course. But, most of his days on the flats seeking permit are with Steve on the poling platform. The number of permit Del has caught constantly increases—at last count it was well past 300 on a fly! No other angler comes close to this accomplishment.

I have fished with several top-drawer guides who have successfully gotten their clients permit. Most agree on the basic techniques of enticing a permit into striking your fly. All agree that permit are less spooky in deeper water. Permit do sometimes "lay up," that is, just float or suspend in the water. But, most of the time they are traveling in a zigzag swimming motion, and often moving very fast. To take advantage of every opportunity, the angler must stand on the bow, ready to make a cast immediately. Del Brown has a neat trick. He makes a long black mark at fifty feet on his fly line with a permanent marking pen. Stepping up on the casting platform, he strips out line until he reaches his mark. Rarely do you need to cast farther than that, and if there is extra line on the deck it can cause all sorts of problems. Most anglers and guides think that your chances are better if you encounter from one to four permit. If a school appears and one fish is frightened by the fly's movement, it will flee, taking the rest of the permit with it. A point made by several permit guides is worth noting. Crab flies, even the Isley and Brown patterns, are a bit hard to cast, and those with epoxy and other hard materials are even more difficult to throw. Since you will be required to cast quickly and with little line, you need to practice your accuracy before going fishing. Accurate casting is a vital part of successful permit fishing, and it pays to practice casting crab flies when you are not fishing.

To catch a permit on a fly, you need to imitate the natural motions of the crab, one of its favorite foods. There is some disagreement here, but Steve and Del have caught so many permit that I believe their method is the best to follow. When a permit is seen, they believe you should drop the crab fly as close as possible in front of the permit. This means that, if you can, you should drop the fly within one to four feet of the permit's head. "One of two things will happen if you do this," explained Steve. "The fish will either grab the fly or run away."

Del explained, "I try to drop the fly right on the fish's nose, and as soon as the fly hits the surface I lower the rod to let the crab sink toward the bottom. It's important to keep the line under control as the fly sinks, so you feel the fish pick up the fly in case it is grabbed on the fall. If the fly is inadvertently cast behind the fish, I let it swim far enough away that I can pick up the fly and make another cast. Sometimes, when a permit is going away from you, by dropping a fly three to five feet behind the fish it hears the splash and turns and takes."

Both Steve and Del feel that manipulating the fly once it is close to the fish is a mistake. The secret, they think, is to cast close to the fish and then let the crab sink—with no manipulation by the angler. *Stripping the fly usually frightens the fish and both men feel that any stripping motion, even when necessary to get the fish to see it, is chancy.*

Del Brown carries his Crab Fly pattern in several weights, including an unweighted version. I have learned to follow his advice and it pays off. Most of the time he casts his pattern with a pair of 1/24-ounce lead eyes. But, when he is fishing shallower water, he will tie on a fly with 1/36-ounce eyes. There are times in all permit areas when a tremendous hatch of crabs will be seen.

Almost all permit are released, as their numbers are not large.

The best fishing for them seems to be in channels on a rising or falling tide, where they are being carried along in a sort of conduit. The crabs will be riding near the surface. This is the time to use an unweighted crab; I even coat the fly with a paste fly flotant. A reach cast helps make the fly drift naturally, which, again, is what you want.

When the fish takes the fly, almost all the good permit fishermen I know use the strip strike. The hand holding the line is firmly gripped, and a slow drawing back with the hand is used to set the hook into the fish.

A few successful guides ascribe to the above—but, when they see a cruising permit, they prefer to throw the fly well in front of the fish and then let the fish come to the fly.

 ## TARPON

I was a striped bass addict for most of my early fly-fishing life. Then I caught a tarpon. I have boated nearly every species that will accept a fly.

While I prefer to fish for bonefish most of all, nothing offers more fishing excitement than a big tarpon I have just put a hook into.

Tarpon come in many sizes. You can fish a canal ditch with a 4-weight fly rod and line for tarpon as small as freshwater trout. Or, you can stake out on a tarpon flat in the lower Keys in the spring and toss a streamer to a 150-pound giant. There are few fishing experiences that compare with standing on the casting platform of a skiff, armed with only a fly rod, and seeing a log of a tarpon coasting across the flats. The big ones, more than 100 pounds, make you feel inept and foolish as you stand there, poised with a three-inch streamer fly in your hand, wondering how in the hell you are going to win over these six feet of scale-encased muscle—so big that you can describe the fish by its *width!*

Costa Rica offers a brand of tarpon fishing that is unlike many other places. Here, in murky waters, giant tarpon are caught in good numbers by fly rodders.

Legs become rubber, arms inoperable; your eyes misjudge. If the fish actually takes the fly, you'll probably strike too hard. The tarpon catapults from the water like a giant jack-in-the-box, sometimes throwing water all over you.

FINDING TARPON

Tarpon are found along the southern coast of the United States and all through the Tropics, on the Atlantic side. But it is from lower Florida through Mexico and the Central American countries that tarpon are considered the king of fish for fly fishermen.

Tarpon are sensitive to cold, and in the winter only a few fish will be found in the shallows, even in the Florida Keys. As waters warm in late February or early March, the giant tarpon, on their annual migration, move up onto flats. There is probably noplace in the world where such large fish can be so easily fished for with a fly as the Florida Keys. By late April, the Florida Bay side of the Keys teems with schools of giant tarpon, many in excess of 140 pounds. By June many of the fish have moved to the Atlantic side of the Keys and may remain there well into July before disappearing.

During the summer months tarpon in the five- to forty-pound class frequent many of the shallow basins, channels, and pockets among the Florida Keys. Throughout the year you can find some tarpon in the lower portion of Florida, especially along the coastal area of Florida Bay that touches the Everglades and Charlotte Harbor on the west coast of Florida.

During late May a migration of large tarpon appears off the lower southwest coast of Florida, beginning in the sloughs and estuaries around

Lefty Kreh holds up a tarpon caught by Harold LeMaster. Hal and several other Clearwater anglers fished the Homosassa area of the west coast of Florida for years before it was discovered by the Florida Keys guides.

the Shark River (in Everglades National Park), where fly rodders can take them by blind fishing with a sinking fly line and a bright-hued streamer fly. The fish move on up the coast off Punta Gorda in June, then swim on to Grand Isle, Louisiana, in mid-July. A few weeks later they arrive off Port Aransas, Texas. But, north of the Shark River in Florida's Everglades the tarpon are usually in deep water, where dead baitfish, crabs, and mullets are the best bait. Then, the silver king shows up along the coast of the Yucatán Peninsula in the fall, and by winter is working its way through the waters of Belize, Panama, and Colombia. While this is not certain, it is suspected that the tarpon at that point cut across the Gulf of Mexico to start the cycle all over again in the lower Florida Keys.

The largest tarpon that can be taken in shallow water are found offshore from the Crystal River, in the Homosassa Bay area. I was lucky enough to fish this several years with Hal LeMaster, Kurt Smith, and Dr. Dee Mitchell, men who fished here for years without anyone knowing about it. Then the Florida Keys guides found out, and now the spot is a crowded annual pilgrimage for some of the top fly rodders in the world.

The peak months for a fly rodder seeking a real trophy tarpon in the Florida Keys are May and June, although fish in good numbers are in most of the Keys by March and linger through July. The most popular locations are the Islamorada area, near Marathon, and down in the Key West waters. Excellent skiff guides, who thoroughly understand the fly fisherman's problems, are available. The boats are tailored for fly fishing, with large open casting platforms and no line-entangling gadgets aboard.

Some large and small tarpon remain around the Florida Keys and other fishing hangouts through the Tropics throughout the year.

Soon after I first moved to Florida, I told Vic Dunaway, who was then outdoors editor of the *Miami Herald*, that I had finally figured out a bunch of tarpon I had been fishing for several weeks. He smiled, and with a condescending air said, "Lefty, about the only thing you can be sure of about a tarpon is that it is a tarpon." The next week I again fished the tarpon I had "figured out," and never got a strike. I have often thought about Vic's remark. No fish is more unpredictable.

TACKLE

The outfit for big tarpon is a specialty tool. The single most important piece of equipment is a stout reel with a superb drag. The drag must be whisper smooth, for it is not uncommon for a big tarpon to run 200 yards at full bore. Any lurch in the drag could mean a broken leader.

The reel should carry a minimum of 250 yards of Dacron or Micron backing. Most anglers prefer thirty-pound test. To obtain a little more room for backing, many anglers will cut ten to fifteen feet of running line from the rear portion of the fly line. The new braided polyethylene lines, such as Spectra or Spider Wire, work well as backing lines if they are used in the correct manner. These lines are not monofilament nylon or Dacron, but a different breed of line. They are super-thin for their line strength. You can put 50 percent more of this backing line on a reel than you could with Dacron. The most important factor is that you must install this Spectra-type line very firmly on the reel spool. If you don't, the line will dig into the bedding when you're fighting a fish, and you'll break either the leader or the line when the fish takes off on a long run. I recommend using no less than fifty-pound in these new lines as backing. Lighter lines are so thin as to cause problems. Many fishermen put Dacron or Micron on first, the remainder of the spool with the poly line, and then attach the fly line.

The leader should be at least six feet long. Most of us now use the quick-change leader. This is a three- to four-foot section of thirty- to fifty-pound butt leader that has a loop in the forward end. The class tippet usually has a twelve-, sixteen-, or twenty-pound tippet section looped to it, which is attached to a twelve-inch section of eighty- or 100-pound monofilament—the shock or bite leader that connects to the fly. Some experienced captains feel that it's beneficial to use a fluorocarbon leader as the shock or bite leader for big tarpon. Fluorocarbon leaders are supposed to be more difficult to see, and using this material in the eighty- to 100-pound size may draw more strikes.

The rod has to be stout. When that fish is lying five or six feet below the boat, exhausted, the only way you can claim your trophy is to lift it, and this takes a rod with enormous power. While fish of more than 150 pounds require a 12-weight rod, a modern graphite rod in size 10 or 11 will catch almost any giant tarpon you'll ever hook. And, they are lighter and easier to cast. An angler who has never fished for giant tarpon may pick up a rod designed for a 12-weight line, heft it, and shake his head in disbelief. He'll think that no one could ever cast such a rod all day long. He's right. But, no one does. You cast to a giant tarpon only after you have seen the fish; on a good day of fishing these giants, you may have made only two dozen casts.

The rod is primarily a fighting tool, and as long as it can deliver the fly to the fish, that's all that's required. Good tarpon fly rods have large snake guides—bigger than anything used in freshwater fishing. Two reasons: the fish exerts tremendous pressure on the guides as it fights and is lifted from the water, so the guides have to be large and held securely on the rod; and, an escaping tarpon will frequently bolt away after the strike, causing the line coming off the deck to go through the guides in a knot or clump. If the guides are tiny, the line catches and the fish breaks off.

The reel seat on a tarpon rod should be stout, either chrome on brass, high-grade anodized aluminum, or tough plastic. It should carry double-locking rings to ensure that the reel doesn't fall off in the middle of the fight. Another trick is to run a little tape over the reel-locking rings to make doubly sure that the seat will not loosen.

Most fly fishermen now use one of the commercial Tarpon Taper lines. These have a short heavy section up front that permits the angler to get the fly quickly to a tarpon at short range. Others use a saltwater taper, which closely resembles the Tarpon Taper. Three types of line are used for tarpon fishing. The floating line is perhaps used most. Since most giant tarpon are caught in five to ten feet of water, the angler can usually cast his fly far enough ahead of the fish to make a good presentation. However, when floating grass clutters the surface, floating lines funnel the vegetation right to the hook on a retrieve.

The intermediate (slow-sinking) line sinks very slowly, unless dressed with a flotant. This line gets the fly down quicker to tarpon in deeper water, and it tends to settle through floating grass. There is one disadvantage to using an intermediate line, however. If you make a cast and the tarpon suddenly veers off course, you must get the fly back quickly and make another presentation. The intermediate line has often sunk so deep that a hasty backcast is impossible. Another intermediate line that some anglers and guides prefer is the clear monofilament line, which is fished much like an intermediate and seems less likely to spook tarpon swimming near it.

The third line, used rarely on the flats but often in deep water, is the extra-fast-sinking. This line will bomb a fly to the bottom of a hole or channel and crawl the lure before the tarpon. It must, however, be brought back close to the boat, and a roll cast must be made to lift the fly from the water before another presentation.

TARPON FLIES

No fish takes a fly better than a tarpon. It still amazes most of us that a giant tarpon will move ten feet out of its way to suck in a three-inch streamer fly. Along the west coast of Florida the fish seem to go for a relatively large fly, perhaps six or seven inches long. But, in most places I have fished in Florida and the Tropics, the big fish in clear water will take a streamer from 2½ to 3 inches in length.

I've come to the conclusion that there is no one best tarpon fly—at times they seem to go for a myriad of patterns. Clear-water tarpon flies are all tied using the Keys Tarpon Style, which means placing a few feathers at the rear and a short palmered collar in front. The palmered hackle is generally laid back toward the wing. This makes a fly that simply doesn't tangle. In clear water most experienced anglers prefer to fish flies that are bright in color. In darker waters, those slightly cloudy, or those over dark turtle grass, many anglers prefer using a slightly darker fly pattern.

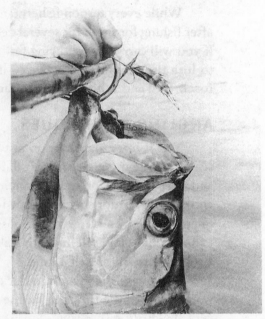

It surprises many fly rodders when they see how small a fly a giant tarpon will strike.

There are a few generalizations about flies that hold true most of the time. Black flies, or those black with a tinge of orange or yellow, can often be deadly. Grizzly feathers dyed in a host of colors and combined with other feathers are always worth throwing at tarpon. Strips of rabbit fur undulate like a wild thing when tied to a properly manipulated fly. For years all flash material was eliminated from tarpon flies. Now, many guides put several strands of Flashabou or Krystal Flash in the wing, believing that it makes tarpon strike quicker.

I suppose if I had to be limited to a single pattern, it would be the Cockroach, which is a Keys-style tie with grizzly wings of six to eight saddle or neck hackles at the back, and then a collar made from brown bucktail. It was developed by that great angler Captain John Emery. The fly is actually a variation of the Lefty's Deceiver, and it is a great pattern on many fish other than tarpon.

For giant tarpon, hooks from 2/0 to 5/0 are used, with the 3/0 the most popular size. Since these hooks are difficult to set into the concretelike mouth of a tarpon, the points must be well sharpened. The triangulation method of sharpening the hook, which makes three supporting cutting edges, is preferred by many. I like to sharpen the hook on the outside bend into a V shape.

While every tarpon fisherman has his favorite patterns, I'm convinced after fishing for them for several decades that you need only a few patterns. If you will carry the following few patterns, you will almost always be able to lure the tarpon into striking—if you make a good presentation: Cockroach, Red and White, Stu Apte Tarpon Fly, Blue Death, and Chinese Claw.

ANGLING TECHNIQUES

You fish for giant tarpon in two ways in the Keys—or anywhere you search for them on clear-water flats. A guide can pole you along the banks and over the flats, or you can anchor or stake out the boat at points along an underwater uprising and wait for the fish to come to you. Tarpon frequently breathe air from the atmosphere, as we do. They rise to the surface, exhale, inhale, and roll under. In calm waters, an experienced angler can see a rolling tarpon for half a mile.

Fish moving along just under the surface will create a wake or nervous water. Most of the time the fish lie rather motionless in the water, or move very slowly, in either singles, pairs, or large schools. If you see a school of moving fish you should cast in front of all of them; that way, if you get a refusal from the leading fish, the remainder of the school will still have a chance to examine the fly. Also, casting *into* a school of fish can alarm them. A fly line, delicate as it is, dropping over a tarpon will usually cause it to panic. If the fish is alone, the fly should be cast far enough ahead to allow it to sink to a depth that will enable it to meet the fish on a collision course.

There is another very different area where giant tarpon have been caught by the hundreds. This is along the northeast coast of Costa Rica. Casa Mar is a superbly run tarpon camp located on a lagoon near the mouth of the Rio Colorado. The river here pours its silt load into the ocean, and it's been estimated that more than 45,000 tarpon live either just outside the river mouth—or in the river. Perhaps nowhere on earth can an angler catch more tarpon in a day than at Casa Mar and nearby fishing camps. While it is certainly a rare occurrence, there has been a report of two anglers in a week battling more than 100 tarpon, and these fish averaged sixty to ninety pounds. But, this is an entirely different kind of tarpon fishing, and requires different techniques and flies. Unless it's calm and you can get out on the ocean, the fishing is in the main river, which usually runs from cloudy to muddy. Since the fish live and feed here all the time, they will take flies. But, the methods used on the clear-water flats of Florida don't work well here.

It took anglers from California to develop the techniques that are now standard for catching fish in such waters. They found that the tarpon lie on or near the bottom of these swift, dirty rivers, and that blind fishing a lot of water was required to find them. Sleek flies didn't do the job. Instead, you should use the Whistler series designed by Dan Blanton, as well as other dark flies that "push" water, giving off vibrations that the tarpon can locate. These flies are usually heavily weighted with both number

Fishing a Tarpon Daisy Chain
In the spring tarpon will often form a daisy chain—one fish following another, head to tail, in a tight circle. Never attack these fish with your flies. If tarpon are circling, as shown in the drawing and you throw your fly to the right side of the circle, the fly will be coming at (or attacking) the tarpon. If you throw the fly to the left side, however, as the fish approached the fly it would appear to be trying to escape, and it is more likely that the fish will take it. If you use a long leader you can throw the fly into the middle of the daisy chain—but, this cast must be gentle, so that the impact of the fly line doesn't frighten the tarpon.

two or three lead-fuse wire and heavy bead chain eyes—and they do the job. These same flies work very well in the deep harbors and channels of the Keys and Central America. Most beginners work the fly too fast. The tarpon likes a fly that swims along, undulating slowly up and down.

How should you strike a tarpon? The fish will either approach the fly from the side, rolling away as it strikes, or come from directly behind and

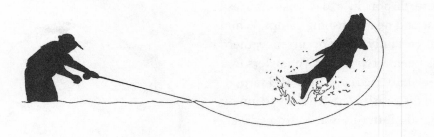

Dipping the Rod

When a fish is under water it is somewhat like a man in a swimming pool. The hooked fish has to push against the water as it fights you. This reduces its violence against the purchase of the hook in its mouth. But, when that fish leaps into the air, it can exert all its thrashing weight against the hook and your leader.

To reduce the chances of losing a jumping fish, some people bow to the fish to create slack while the fish is in the air. But, sometimes some bowing will create enough slack for the leader or line to wrap around the fish. Many years ago, the fly fisherman who had caught more tarpon than any other, Harry Kime, developed the dipping technique, which I feel is superior to bowing. When the fish jumps, simply point the rod at the fish and dip the rod tip under water. This forms controlled slack that will not tangle on the fish.

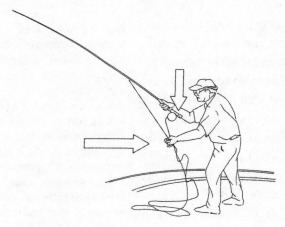

Clearing Loose Line

When a fish strikes, there is often loose line on the deck, which will surely tangle if not attended to. As soon as you sink the hook into the fish, close your thumb and first finger around the flowing line to form a large circle. Then, forget the fish—it's been hooked. Look at the fly line on the deck and begin clearing it so it will run smoothly through the guides.

This same finger method is used when casting for accuracy or sight fishing, such as when bonefishing or fishing for tarpon or permit. Many people simply cast, let go of the running line, and, after the fly strikes the water, look down to locate the running line. After they locate the line they look up—and often can't find the fish. Instead, make the cast to the fish, and let the running line pay out through the finger ring. As soon as the fly touches down, keep looking at the fish, and you will be ready to start your retrieve.

inhale it. If the fish comes from the side, you're lucky. As it moves away it will drag the hook against its mouth. But, if the fish is stalking the fly you must follow a definite pattern. The fly is moving at a certain speed, which the tarpon has already determined; as it moves in, it expects the fly to continue at that speed, so it times its strike accordingly. Watch the tarpon; as it moves in to swallow the fly, cease stripping. If you do this the fly will go deeper into the tarpon's mouth and guarantee you a better hookup.

There is a myth that says you should wait until a tarpon turns after taking the fly before striking. But, many tarpon coming from directly behind the fly grab it and continue straight ahead. *When the tarpon closes its mouth, strike.* Don't pull back in a long sweeping arc with the rod, however. The tarpon may decide to go in the opposite direction at the same moment and a broken leader will be the result.

It is at this point that the knots you tied get their test; only the best of knots will pass. If you plan to fish for bigger tarpon, then you should master the knots. Guides spend as much time and care building their leaders and knots as they do on anything else. It pays to keep a number of extra leaders made up, ready for use. Should you break a fish off, it will take only moments to re-rig.

You can determine a tarpon's swimming direction when it's rolling. The arrow indicates the direction this tarpon is moving.

Flip Pallot prepares to release a baby tarpon caught on a freshwater trout outfit.

If you fish from an anchored boat rather than one that is poled across the flats, you should have a release anchor attached to the anchor line. This is simply a quick-release snap tied to the anchor line. To the snap is attached a buoy of some type. If the tarpon is hooked and begins tearing away, your companion can unsnap the anchor line and begin chasing. Later, he can return to the buoy, retrieve the anchor, and reposition the boat.

The cast to a tarpon, bonefish, permit, or any other fish moving on the flat must be very accurate—and it must be made immediately.

There are, of course, other kinds of tarpon fishing than fishing for the giants. One of the most interesting is night fishing for tarpon, especially in the Florida Keys. All during the warmer months of late spring, summer, and early fall, tarpon roll and feed under most of the bridges in the middle Keys. Usually a silent two-minute wait will tell you if tarpon are around. In the

For a few minutes, this baby tarpon in Mexico gave Jennifer Carley all the action she could handle.

quiet darkness you can hear them rolling and crashing on bait. It's best to fish when the high slack tide begins to move from the gulf toward the Atlantic; you can catch fish throughout the fall of water. This is not to say, however, that you can't hook fish on an incoming tide as well.

Blind casting, since there are often large numbers of the fish, is fruitful. Be sure to fish the up-tide side of the bridge. Most of us prefer a moonlit night.

In the Gulf of Mexico along the Yucatán Peninsula coast the flats hold thousands of smaller tarpon, in the ten- to forty-pound class. The fish can easily be seen swimming in four feet of water, and they take flies well. An 8 or 9 rod is preferable. It's possible in some of these areas to hook and jump forty or more tarpon a day.

In the Turneffe Islands off Belize, large schools of tarpon live in channels from February until May. They feed in the deeper channels that cut through the island, and fast-sinking lines do the best work. There are some clear-water basins that produce the same kind of fishing you can find in the Florida Keys.

One of my favorite methods of catching small tarpon is with a medium freshwater trout outfit, throwing a number 7 or 8 line. Using scaled-down tarpon flies about two inches long, I like to pole on high spring tides around the little mangrove islands of the Florida Keys and other tropical areas, looking for the five- to thirty-pounders that lie back under the mangrove roots. It's tricky fly casting—and the best of sport when one of these twenty-pounders hits that fragile rod. Many of them make several jumps through the bushes and are gone. Enough leap toward open water to encourage you to try again.

 ## SNOOK

The snook has made such an astounding comeback in Florida, due to new regulations managing the species, that it is now one of the most popular of all fly-rod fish in that area. There are several reasons why fly fishermen hold the snook in such high regard. The most important is that it acts so much like largemouth and smallmouth bass. Northern anglers visiting Florida (and the thousands of fly fishermen who have migrated from the North to the state) instinctively know how to fish for them.

Snook, like freshwater bass, hold in, or under, cover and then blast out to grab their prey. They will hide along undercut banks, back in a myriad of mangrove roots, close to bridge pilings, around channel markers and buoys,

The snook—one of the most highly prized of all shallow saltwater species.

White holes like these on the flats will often hold snook, as well as barracudas and large seatrout.

or wherever they can remain unseen by their prey. On the flats snook often suspend in what fishermen call "white holes." These are depressions in a flat, free of grass and light in color. Snook frequently suspend in such a hole, ambushing bait. Cast a fly across the white hole and retrieve it, and you stand a good chance of hooking up. Redfish will also frequent such white holes, though not so much as snook and seatrout. Like freshwater bass, snook feed a lot at night.

Snook are very sensitive to drops in temperature. I remember back in the mid-1960s when the air temperature dropped to 29 degrees! It was during a spring tide week and the flats at Flamingo in Florida Bay were exposed during the night. As the tide rose, it began to flow across these flats that had stood in the freezing air. The resulting water temperature, drastically chilled, killed many species. To my surprise the fish to die were sharks and jack crevalles, which I would have guessed to be among the least affected. The other species that died by the hundreds was the snook. And, just as surprising were the numbers of huge snook (more than twenty pounds) that had been living and prospering in the Flamingo marina area, where hun-

Canoes are one of the best ways to penetrate the mangrove backcountry where many snook live.

dreds of boats traversed weekly. If there is a temperature drop, the snook will generally leave the shallows and head for deep water in creeks, channels, or bays. Most snook habitat has a dark bottom. As soon as the air temperature warms and the sun comes out, the water on these flats rises quickly and the fish, now hungry, will move back fast. This is a great opportunity for fishermen to reap a bonanza.

The best snook fishing in this country is in Florida. And in Florida, the best snook fishing is probably along the lower west coast and in the Ten Thousand Islands area that borders on Florida Bay, and almost all of it lies within the vast Everglades National Park. This is ideal habitat for snook. There are thousands of islands, channels, oyster bars, rivers, flats, and bays. These furnish mullets, crabs, shrimp, and a host of other foods that snook can eat. The standard fly-fishing method is from a boat poled along the shoreline. The flies are cast in among the mangrove roots. On a falling tide the snook will wait at the openings of small ditches to grab bait being carried to the main watershed. These will eagerly take your flies. Many snook are caught when sight fishing—perhaps the most thrilling way to catch them.

ANGLING TECHNIQUES

Because snook are found so often near hook-snagging cover, a weed guard is recommended. A fly that has become very popular with many guides is the Glades Deceiver. This is a variation of the Lefty's Deceiver. It's about three inches long with a wire weed guard and a wing made from calf tail. Most of the time you can cast it in among the tangled brush and mangrove roots; the wire weed guard allows you to drag it through this dangerous territory. Another fly that results in great success is a Clouser Minnow of about three inches with a wire weed guard. When you want to fish slowly where the waters are very shallow and weed-free, use the Seaducer.

Snook will take a host of flies and each angler develops his own selections. But, if you carry the following flies in several sizes, you'll be well armed for most places you fish snook: Glades Deceiver, Seaducer, Bend Backs in several colors, Clouser Minnows in several color combinations, Lefty's Deceivers in several color combinations, popping bugs, and a few Dahlberg Divers.

Favorite tackle for most snook fishing is a weight-forward floating line in size 8 or 9, matched to a 9-foot rod. When snook are found around bridge pilings or deep in channels, a Teeny 300 or 400 line is often most effective.

Another very different kind of snook fishing is after dark. Many bridges in the lower half of Florida have lights that fall on the water. Bridges tend to constrict the flow of water from one large body or bay to another. This concentrates bait as it flows with the tide. Snook will hold on the uptide side (the side that the tide is

Ted Juracsik caught this huge forty-two-inch snook in the Ten Thousand Islands on a Clouser Minnow.

coming from) and grab shrimp and other bait being swept to them. Where the snook hold is important to the fly fisherman. Lights on the bridge create a shadow line at the places where the bridge shields the light from falling on the water. *You want to fish the area just inside the shadow line on the up-tide side.* These fish can be seen, once you get the hang of it. Get on the bridge and look down. Study the darkened shadow area closely. You will see the snook almost as a gray shadow. Once they're located, you can fish for them. The best method is to use a boat and anchor and hold up-tide of the bridge. Locate the fish, cast a Seaducer or Lefty's Deceiver a few feet above them, and try to let it drift back naturally with the tide. Once hooked, a snook will try to get to the bridge pilings and cut you off. Be prepared as soon as you set the hook to try to lead the fish away from the obstructions.

A favorite method for catching snook, which I enjoy greatly, is fishing lighted boat docks at night. Cruise the waterways and locate a lighted boat dock that has minnows and sometimes breaking fish under the lights. Cast small streamer flies armed with weed guards right under the dock. This can reward you with ladyfish, jack crevalles, and some dandy snook!

 ## BARRACUDAS

These are among the most exciting fish you can encounter on the flats—and you can meet them big! Barracudas inhabit all the tropical seas, in both the Atlantic and Pacific. For years we really didn't have much luck catching them. We failed more often than we succeeded when trying to entice them to strike a fly.

Before explaining how I think you should fish for cudas, let me state a few fact about this grand fish. You can never retrieve fast enough to fool a cuda. Their speed is incredible. I have watched a cuda as I presented a fly. I saw the cuda before it struck and as it hit the fly, but the interval between was so fast that I never saw that fish in the act of striking. So, you can forget trying to make high-speed retrieves to deceive a barracuda.

ANGLING TECHNIQUES

Cudas are predators, but other and larger fish feed on them, too, so they can easily be spooked. Throwing a fly right in front of them and beginning a retrieve is almost always fatal. Even worse is to drop a fly line—or leader—over a fish. Skinny flies made of strands of synthetic materials to resemble needlefish are inferior flies for standard cuda. They will catch fish,

Irv Swope with a nice cuda that took a fly in the Bahamas.

but there is another pattern that I believe is much superior, for several reasons.

The best barracuda fly I have ever used comes in two color combinations and is easy to tie. It never fouls the wing in flight. That's something you can't say of almost any other barracuda fly! Here are the two patterns, both tied with the same method. Place the hook (1/0 to 3/0, depending upon the size of the cudas) in a vise upside down (point up). Then, tie on a wing of the longest orange bucktail you can find, so that it circles halfway around the shank. Turn the fly over in the vise and add in twenty to twenty-five strands of gold Flashabou. Make sure that the Flashabou is at least half an inch longer than the bucktail wing. Complete the fly by putting enough of the same orange or red bucktail (same length) on top to form a full skirt around the hook. I usually add epoxy to the head for durability. The second color combination is tied the same way. The lower half of the fly is made from white bucktail and the upper half from chartreuse bucktail, with the same Flashabou in the middle.

Here is the method I now use to fish these cuda flies; it works more than half the time, which is the best percentage I've been able to get to date on barracudas. You need a floating line, preferably a weight-forward type.

After you locate the cuda, make a cast so that the fly lands about five or six feet in front of and just beyond the cuda. As soon as the fly contacts the water, make a long, slow pickup and a backcast. What you have done is dropped the fly in front of the cuda, then caused it to streak rapidly past the barracuda's face and disappear. This usually excites the fish. Repeat the operation one or two times, so as to really aggravate the cuda. Then, drop the fly in the same spot—only this time, just begin an erratic but not-too-fast retrieve. More than half the time the cuda will hit the fly almost immediately—the rest of the time it flees in panic.

Another fly that has worked well for me on cudas—though not nearly as well as the just-mentioned pattern—is a popping bug. With this fly, *the cast is made ten to fifteen feet in front of and beyond the cuda.* Begin the retrieve as soon as the fly strikes the water, and keep it moving. It doesn't have to be retrieved too fast—just make sure the bug is never still.

 ## SHARKS

One of the most difficult fish to catch on a flat with a fly rod is a large shark. Not because of its power and ferocity—it's more complicated than that. In very deep water sharks can be taken by chumming them to the boat. This certainly is exciting, but I think that catching big sharks on the flats is infinitely more exhilarating.

Throughout the Tropics and extreme southern Florida, sharks get up on the flats and cruise, seeking food. Occasionally, they swim in water so shallow that their huge dorsal fins stick above the surface, reminding me of black sailboats cruising the flats. They may not seem to be moving fast, but you'll soon find that it is very difficult to keep up with them when you're poling a boat. To make things tougher, they rarely swim a predictable course.

Sharks have poor eyesight, and this really causes problems for the fly fisherman. The angler must cast the fly so it lands near the eye and alongside the head, *not* in front of the fish. Then, during the retrieve the fly must be kept there as long as possible, to give the shark ample time to see it. *If the fly is positioned in front of the shark, it will never know it's there.*

Since the amount of time the fly remains near the shark's eye is crucial, the boat's and the angler's positions prior to the cast are important. If you cast to a shark that is going away from you, the fly, no matter how well placed, will zip by so quickly that the shark will either not see it or miss it on the strike. You need to approach the shark at such an angle that it swims toward you. Then you can make your cast and maintain the fly near its eye. As the shark moves close to the boat you should kneel, for, although its vision is poor, the shark *can* see a silhouette. And, in stalking a big shark silence is vital.

Flashabou or Krystal Flash built into the fly helps the shark locate it. Since it is also necessary for the angler to know the location of the fly, so he can keep it near the shark's eye, a fly with a dash of bright orange or red is helpful, too. I like the same fly patterns that I use for barracudas. Sharks take such a fly well, and you can see it easily, as well. Sharks have powerful jaws and can crush a small hook easily. For sharks of more than forty pounds, hooks in the 3/0 to 5/0 size are recommended. Popping bugs will certainly draw strikes, but because the shark's mouth is located so far back on its underside, it has difficulty grabbing the bug. Too often the front of the fish's head just pushes the popper away.

Sometimes, when stalking a shark you'll find that it is moving away at such a speed that you'll lose your chance for a cast. Stick the first two feet of the fly-rod tip under the water and swish it rapidly back and forth. The vibrations may attract the shark, and it will often turn and approach the boat.

Another good trick is to catch a small fish of several pounds, tie it to a twenty-foot length of heavy line, and allow the dead fish to drag along the

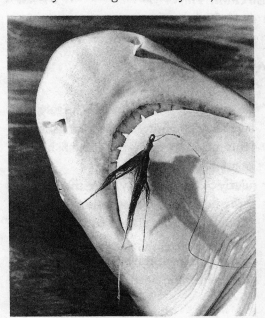

bottom behind your boat as you move across the flat. Keep an eye on the bait, for sharks will frequently show up and try to seize it. Naturally, you should then retrieve the bait and cast immediately to the aroused shark.

If you live in an area where the waters are slightly murky, or the water is deep enough that the sharks cannot be clearly seen, you can still

Note how far back the mouth is located on a shark. That's why it's important to retrieve the fly near the eye instead of in front of the fish.

Sharks are among the finest flats trophies a fly fisherman can catch.

take them on a fly. Establish your boat along a sod bank or other points sharks frequent. Set up a chum line of blood (hatcheries and slaughterhouses can supply it) or ground fish chum. The sharks will often be attracted enough to come within a few yards of the boat.

Once hooked, sharks can provide terrific excitement on a fly rod.

 ## KING SALMON

I have never fished for king salmon in salt water, but Bob Edgely, Dan Blanton, and Lawrence Summers have sent me photos of giant kings, as well as a great deal of information about this magnificent fly-rod game fish. What follows is distilled from my correspondence with them.

Most of those who fly fish regularly for king salmon agree that the best time to fish the Pacific Northwest is the first week in November. This offers the best chance at a really big fish, though there are always fish in the rivers by the end of October.

Two very popular rivers to fly fish for king salmon in the Pacific Northwest are the Smith River in northern California, near the Oregon border, and the Chetco, also located near the Oregon-California border.

The Chetco River is a short coastal stream that has a good run of kings. The fishing starts a little earlier than on the Smith River. You can figure on taking fish from around the beginning of the second week of October up through November. The fish run a little smaller but there seem to be more of them, maybe because of the salmon hatchery on the Chetco. Since the hatchery was built, the run on this river has increased greatly.

The average salmon in the Chetco will range from eighteen to twenty-five pounds, with a few fish running larger. A sixty-five-pound fish was taken in 1971 on hardware, but it was an exception rather than the rule. Fishing with flies takes place from the mouth of the river to a point about five miles upstream. Most of the best fishing occurs within a mile of the river's mouth. You fish from a small, eight-foot pram, casting your flies toward the shoreline from a point a short distance offshore. The flies drift with the tidal currents, and most strikes occur during the drift, rather than on the retrieve. The area between Highway I and the entrance to the harbor is a very good one. Cast your flies toward the harbor jetty wall.

There are a few holes upstream from the Highway 1 bridge. One is the Morrison Hole—large salmon hold well in this one.

The Smith is a beautiful river. The heavy annual rainfall is about 100 inches; the rains begin sometime in November. The stream has not been ruined by clear-cut logging or damming. One inch of rainfall in late October and November in a twenty-four-hour period will fill the river with king salmon. Give it maybe twenty-four more hours to clear and the river will be perfect for fly fishing.

King salmon usually enter the Smith during the bottom of the outgoing tide, when the current is at its strongest. The strong current helps the fish find their way over the bar and into the river's mouth—but, the kings won't come into the river if the surf is extremely rough. Once the fish are in the tidal lagoon area of the river they will mill around until the tide starts in, and then move upriver with the rising water. The river area that is called the tidewater extends from the mouth to Woodruff's Hole—this is the water influenced by the tides.

The average size of Smith River king salmon is between twenty-five and thirty-five pounds, with plenty of fish in the twenty-five to forty-five-pound class. There are some fifty-pounders, too, but they're hard to nail.

The best holes to fish on the upper Smith River vary from year to year, but the most consistent ones are the Cable Hole, the Society Hole, and the Buck Early Hole.

ANGLING TECHNIQUES

The fly gear used for king salmon is the same as that used for West Coast steelhead, or in some cases a little heavier. The rods must be able to handle a number 10 or 11 line and twenty-six to thirty feet of twenty-pound-test lead-core line that has been made into a shooting head. These are big, strong fish, and it takes a good strong rod to tire them. Reels should be large, with ample line capacity, and a good drag, too. Tippets are generally ten-, twelve-, or fifteen-pound test, and leaders run about nine feet.

A boat of some kind is needed for just about all the fly fishing, with the exception of two holes. A moderate-sized powerboat will work, but a one-man boat is the only practical choice to use upriver. The boat should be stable enough for a man to stand up in; keep in mind that there are rapids to shoot and that currents can be strong.

Fly lines used in the tidewater are Hi-Density and fast-sinking shooting heads. The upriver fishing requires the use of a lead-core shooting head; the holes are deep and swift, and the lead is needed to get the fly down to the fish. Leaders can be shorter for upriver use, too. On the Chetco a lead-core shooting head is mandatory.

When fishing in tidewater you locate the fish holding in certain depressions or holes. You can often locate the salmon as they roll on the surface. Anchor your boat a long cast away from the fish. Never cross over a school with the boat or you'll scatter them. Cast your fly across the fish and let it sink close to the bottom; counting as the line sinks helps you find the level where the fish are holding. Retrieve the fly at various speeds until you find one that the fish seem to prefer.

The strikes of king salmon are not spectacular; they just stop the fly. Salmon that are hooked fairly well rarely jump, but will take off on several long runs and fight deep. If a salmon jumps several times right after hookup, or if it porpoises, it will, without a doubt, be foul hooked and should be broken off. It's not legal to land a snagged fish. You can't help snagging an occasional fish if you are working a large school of kings, and breaking off the fly doesn't seem to bother them a bit.

Salmon prefer to hold in deep slow pools and backwater eddies, rather than in the fast tail slicks that steelheads prefer. They will mill around in the deep hole, sometimes thirty to forty feet deep, waiting for the river to rise so they can continue upstream. The perfect situation is when enough rain has occurred to get the fish up to the pools and then the river drops some, isolating them in their respective holes. The best way to fish these river pools is to fish your fly "down the shoot"; a shoot is a slot in which the fish are holding. You anchor above and cast a lead-core shooting taper almost straight downstream, then retrieve the fly straight up-current. Be sure the fly is near the bottom.

The two holes that you can fish by wading are the Cable Hole and the Water Gauge Riffle, but you must fish a lead-core shooting taper there. You can fish the Society Hole by standing on the rocks—which get crowded.

Two basic types of flies produce well for king salmon. Various shrimp patterns, tied on 3X-strong hooks, number 2 in size, are effective. The shrimp are generally tied using brown bucktail as the tail and carrying this over the back to the head, with a body of silver Mylar. The head is brown tying thread, alone or with a tuft of bucktail.

A Comet-series fly is also extremely effective. Bright colors are used, usually fluorescent. The tail is bright orange or sometimes black, either bucktail or calf tail. The body is Mylar, either silver or gold. A collar 1½ inches in diameter of yellow, yellow and red, or red is tied in palmer-style right in front of the Mylar body. As on most West Coast flies, a bead chain pair of eyes adorns the front of the pattern.

All king salmon flies are weighted to make them sink faster.

 ## CALIFORNIA SURF FISHING

California coastal fly rodding can be exciting and is available to almost everyone. A meager amount of equipment is needed to fish in the surf, although Pacific surf is on the average much heavier than Atlantic, and this calls for some specialized gear. Floating fly lines are a poor choice in most surf conditions. They tend to get swirled in many directions by the turbulent waves, which spoils the retrieve and the pickup for another backcast. Instead, either a lead-core or at least a fast-sinking line (shooting tapers or heads are best—the monofilament shooting line has little drag in the surf) is called for when the surf is crashing. There is almost always a breeze, and lead-core lines penetrate the breeze much better. Some lead-core lines carry a plastic coating, but too often the line gets rolled in the sand, scouring the plastic from it.

Nick Curcione is California's acknowledged expert at surf fishing with a fly rod. Nick uses a shooting basket made from a plastic waste can. The box should be large enough to easily drop the line inside, but not so big that you have difficulty carrying it. It's attached to your side with a belt that runs through a few slots made at the top of the container. The shooting basket is a must, for you have to keep your line out of the suds or it will be rolled into useless tangles. For more on stripping baskets, see page 154.

It pays to study the beach area you plan to fish at low tide. Knowing where to find sloughs or depressions close to shore that will be covered at high tide means you will know the location of fish, for they seek out these places. Usually the last ninety minutes of incoming tide is the prime period—that's when fish are closest to the angler and in a feeding mood.

There can be some exciting moments on lower tides. As the water clears, corbina cruise the shallows looking for sand crabs. But, these fish can be as spooky as any bonefish, so this is a place where a floating line, a long leader, and a delicate cast are called for.

Two major surf species exist along southern California's beaches. From late fall until early or midspring barred perch roam the suds and can be taken with small flies. From late spring until fall, corbina feed well in the surf. Farther south on both sides of the Baja Peninsula there is a large variety of rockfish, groupers, and other species that can be taken casting either from the shore or from a boat worked tight to the shoreline.

Small flies in sizes 1, 2, and 4 are generally used for barred perch and corbina; in Baja a slightly larger fly will take bigger fish. A small white Lefty's Deceiver is a proven killer, but simple streamers with short wings, often red and yellow, are good patterns, too.

In central and northern California the surf holds fifty-two species of rockfish—most of these will take a fly. It helps to have a small boat to fish around the kelp beds or the rocky points, but some casting can be managed from the shore. Rockfish are generally found in schools, and they prefer open water or areas around kelp beds. Sometimes they can be taken on popping bugs, but small flies that imitate baitfish work well. A Bend Back–style fly, or another with a monofilament weed guard, often helps because of the kelp.

The rockfishing slows in the summer months but comes right back after that. These fish are greedy and will hit a large variety of patterns, which should be from four to six inches long. The main problem is locating the rockfish and getting your fly to them. Lead-core lines are used frequently when the fish are deep, but on occasion a floating or intermediate line will do.

A NEW WORLD OF SALTWATER FLY FISHING

There is a vast and unexplored world out there that is starting to get the attention of fly fishermen. These are the inshore waters of the South Pacific and Indian Ocean, and the waters off Africa. Some of us have fished these lightly. I have fished the exciting waters off northern Australia and New Guinea, and have talked to others who have fished many of the small islands that dot the South Pacific. I have friends in Africa who are enjoying fishing for many species we are unfamiliar with in the United States. I have friends in South Africa who are having great success with a number of species. Some of these are known to Americans. Would you believe there are ladyfish on the African coast that top fifteen pounds? A big one in Florida or the Caribbean is a four-pounder! There are tarpon larger than 200 pounds roaming here, and some heavier than that have been caught on regulation tackle.

BARRAMUNDI

In the South Pacific there are a number of fish that offer great potential for fly fishing. One of the most sought after by local anglers, and sure to become a coveted trophy for many fly fishermen from other parts of the world, is the barramundi. I am no scientist, so I can't say for sure that it is a first cousin to the snook. But, it has the same sloping head and sharp-edged cutting plate on its gill flap. It has the same basic overall shape, too, and a strong lateral line. And, its flesh tastes like snook. More similarities exist. It seeks the same cover as snook, hiding under fallen trees, old stumps, and similar structure. It can be found at the mouths of estuaries or miles upriver.

There are places in New Guinea, and other areas of the South Pacific, where no one has ever thrown a fly to these fish—and they can reach more than fifty pounds! I was with Ed Givens, the great saltwater fly fisherman from California, when he boated a thirty-pound barramundi on the Bensbach River in New Guinea. What a fish!

Ed Givens strains to lift a huge barramundi caught in New Guinea. This fish is very similar to the snook in Florida.

Some of the most exciting action I have had with barramundi has been on rivers where I knew that few if any fly fishermen had ever cast to them. There is a certain thrill to such fishing.

THREADFIN SALMON

In the same waters roam two other fish. One is the threadfin salmon. This is a fish shaped much like a bonefish, with a powerful tail and silvery in color. Few fish you'll catch on a fly could be confused with it: it has six long barbels dangling from its lower jaw, much like those of our catfish. Threadfins can top forty pounds and inhabit inshore tropical waters of northern Australia. They fight like hell and can be taken by sight fishing, just as you would bonefish. They also hang around drainage areas on a falling

This is a threadfin salmon, a wonderful flats fish found in Australian waters.

tide and you can blind fish for them at such times. They will eagerly strike Lefty's Deceivers, Clouser Minnows, and Whistler patterns. They are a great flats or shallow-water fly-rod target.

TREVALLY

The jack crevalle is revered as a tough opponent. A big jack would be one of twenty pounds; a monster would be forty pounds. But, in the South Pacific there roams a fish that looks exactly like a jack crevalle called a trevally. There are about three dozen different kinds of trevally, but the one that can reach more than 150 pounds is the giant trevally. I saw two of these fish caught on fly rods at Christmas Island by Randi Swisher and Cary Marcus that were around the seventy-pound mark. Once, when I was offshore of Christmas Island, at the mouth of Cook Island, there were huge groundswells—maybe thirty feet high. As one swell approached a giant trevally ran across in front of us on its forward side. As that fish moved across the wall of water, it was like looking in a store window. I gasped and asked

Rod Harrison is releasing one of the toughest fighters in saltwater shallows—a giant trevally.

the boat captain how big he thought that trevally was. He looked and said, "I'd swear that fish approaches 200 pounds."

Trevally will attack flies, especially popping bugs. It can sometimes be difficult to get them to strike. One method that has worked well for me is to make a cast with a popping bug and begin a fast retrieve. If the fish refuses to take it, I backcast quickly and start another retrieve. As the fish approaches I lower the rod at the fish and, holding the line, sweep the rod so that the bug streaks through the water. This almost always draws a strike!

NIUGINI BLACK BASS

Some years ago I made a trip to New Guinea to be in a film that involved outdoors writers Rod Harrison and Dean Butler, and cinema photographer John Henke—all Australians—each with a great sense of humor. Rod and Dean began extolling the terrible ferocity of a fish they called the black bass or Niugini black bass. (*Niugini* is the way the people in Papua New Guinea spell *New Guinea*.) They told me I would need fifty-pound-test leaders, and that the fish's tooth-filled mouth would destroy my flies. I could write an entire chapter on this great fish. *All I will say is that it is the*

Sam Talarico with a big Niugini black bass. Only a handful of fly fishermen have ever caught this fish or its cousin, the spot-tailed bass. This is perhaps the strongest fish that swims. It lives near river mouths that enter New Guinea seas. The Australians have a perfect name for it. They call it River Rambo.

strongest fish for its size of anything I have ever hooked—and that includes yellowfin tuna. If you seek this fish, which lives in the brackish river mouths of New Guinea, go prepared! Use a forty-pound-test leader straight off the fly line. Have extra-stout hooks and get a *very* good grip on the line when you set the hook. Up the same rivers is a cousin of the Niugini black bass called the spot-tailed bass. It is nearly as strong. At this writing I believe that less than a dozen of us have caught both of these species, and perhaps less than three dozen anglers have caught the Niugini bass on a fly rod. So, the opportunity is there!

MILKFISH

The final inshore South Pacific fish I would like to address is the milkfish. It can be found through much of the Pacific, in places such as New

Rod Harrison holds up a milkfish, often confused with a bonefish. This South Pacific species is much stronger (and grows much larger) than a bonefish, and eventually we will figure out ways to take this vegetarian on fly rods.

Guinea, northern Australia, the Philippines, and southeast Asia. This fish looks so much like a bonefish that few people can tell the difference. Years ago the International Game Fish Association recognized a world-record bonefish that was later determined to be a milkfish. But, there are several differences between a bonefish and a milkfish. A monster bonefish would be one that topped eighteen pounds. A very large milkfish would be close to forty pounds! I have only hooked three, but others who have caught them agree with me that milkfish, pound for pound, are much stronger than bonefish. The major difference between bonefish and milkfish is their feeding habits. The milkfish is a vegetarian; I have watched it apparently eat algae.

Just as we faced a challenge when trying to discover how to effectively fish for permit, we face the same type of problem with milkfish. On my last trip to Christmas Island (where there are many milkfish), I tried a fly I had tied in an attempt to imitate the algae they feed on. To tie it, I made a loosely spun body of Antron, then palmer-hackled the entire fly. Hackle was trimmed from the top and bottom; I teased the Antron so it projected outward from the hook shank. It was then dressed with dry-fly oil, so it would float in the surface film. It worked fairly well (I hooked three fish, which all ran away and cut me off on sharp corral), but there is much experimenting to be done. Someone in the future will work out a formula for catching milkfish. When he does, we will be able to fish for one of the greatest inshore trophies in all of salt water.

OTHER SPECIES

Both the inshore and near offshore waters of the South Pacific are filled with a huge number of species that most fly rodders have never heard of. There are narrow-barred mackerels, which can weigh more than 100 pounds and leap twenty-five feet through the air. These fish can be caught both close to land and well offshore. Dogtooth tuna prowl in big schools, as well as the biggest cobia I've ever seen. There is a great species called the queenfish that roam in packs as the bluefish do on the northeastern coast of the United States. I never met one that wasn't hungry, and, when hooked, I've had them actually jump in the boat with me.

I have been lucky enough to catch most of the fish people would like to catch on the fly rod. The only fish I have not yet taken is the dorado (the

The narrow-backed mackerel, often called the Spaniard in the South Pacific, is similar to the king mackerel and abounds in these waters.

natives call it the "golden fish") of the freshwater rivers of Peru. I have tried, but jungle rains roiled the rivers while I was there.

If you are looking for new frontiers, the South Pacific, the Indian Ocean, the waters off Africa, and a host of other locations are yet to be really tested by fly fishermen. Be one of the first!

SUMMARY OF SOME TIPS FOR FISHING THE FLATS

(1) **Lines should be cleaned before entering the boat.**

Dirty lines will often drastically reduce casting distance and can mean lost opportunities. Many new fly lines have a thin outer coating that won't take the abuse that older lines did—such as being scrubbed with Bon Ami or other abrasive soaps. *Modern fly lines can be cleaned by washing with warm water and a gentle liquid detergent.* Just make sure you rinse them well enough to rid them of all the soap.

(2) **Your footwear should not have big shoestrings. Moccasins are the worst line grabbers of all.**

I can't tell you how many times I have seen a cast foul in midflight because the shooting line tangled in a shoestring. I tie a square knot in the strings on my sneakers. I clip off the ends and place a drop of cyano-acrylate glue on the knot. Then I just slip my foot in the shoe, as I would into a slipper.

(3) **Always wear a hat with a dark underbrim.**

Many fly fishermen stand on the bow of a flats boat wearing no hat. The glare from the sun will reduce how well you can see. A hat is certainly an aid. But, if it has a pale underbrim, then light bouncing off the water, up and under the brim, and then into your eyes will also impede you from seeing well. A cap with a dark underbrim is a real plus for seeing.

(4) **Clean your shoe soles before entering a boat.**

This will not only endear you to the guide, but also help your own angling: dirt carried on board tends to stick to a wet fly line. This will greatly reduce casting distance as well as causing wear to the rod guide and fly line. You want the deck to be super-clean at all times.

(5) **Pull off only the line you will need to cast to a fish.**

Too many anglers step up on the casting platform and then pull off seventy to eighty feet of fly line. Never pull off more line than you will need for your next cast. Any extra line lying on the deck is a potential trouble source. Del Brown, master permit fisherman, came up with a great idea. He figured that fifty feet of line, and a ten-foot leader, was all he'd need for most situations. So, he made a foot-long mark at fifty feet on the fly line. When he steps up to the casting platform, he simply strips off line until he reaches that mark.

(6) **Stretch all coils from the line before making the first cast.**

Fly lines stored on the reel will usually come off it in tight coils, and this can cause tangles on the cast. One of the quickest ways to rid the line of coils is to hold about eight feet of it in your hands so that it hangs down to the deck. Place your foot on the bottom of the loop and give a firm upward pull with both hands.

(7) **When standing in a flats boat, make a cast with all the line you have stripped from the reel and then retrieve it.**

When you first strip line from the reel, the forward end of the line is on the bottom, and as you continue to drop line from the reel it ends up on the top of the pile of line. If a cast is now made, the forward end of the line on the bottom usually tangles. By making a long cast and then retrieving the line, the back of the line is on the bottom of the pile.

(8) **Whenever possible, do not drop the retrieved line on the deck where you are standing.**

Any flats fisherman can tell you of scores of times that his cast was made, only to be ruined because the line was underfoot. The perfect casting platform on a flats boat (in my opinion) is one where there is a relatively small, two- or three-inch elevated platform for the caster to stand on. Behind that is a lower platform where the line is placed. I recommend that when you are on the average flats-type boat, stand a little back from the bow and drop the shooting line in the well or on the main deck below the casting platform.

(9) **Clear the deck where you will drop fly line.**

Protruding fly-rod handles, spinning-reel handles, and other items in the boat should always be placed so that fly line won't grab them on the shoot.

(10) **Constantly check the line around your feet for tangles.**

No matter how carefully you have placed the line on the deck, it somehow always moves around. Keep checking to make sure it's not underfoot or trapped on something in the boat.

(11) **On windy days, use a stripping basket.**

It is unfortunate that only in the northeastern United States do fishermen use stripping baskets in boats. Anyone who has fished on windy days on tropical flats knows how often the wind blows the shooting line around and ruins the cast. Try a shooting basket and you may be pleased.

(12) **Flats fishing requires a speedy cast that is accurate.**

When you're flats fishing, you're sight fishing, and most of the time you must make your cast soon after locating the fish. The time to practice speedy casting is at home—even on a lawn. Far too many northern fly fishermen don't practice, so they fail when the opportunities arise.

(13) **Don't stare at one spot when you are searching for fish.**

Constantly shift your eyes when you search the shallows for fish. By staring at one place you fail to see tiny wakes, moving fish, skipping minnows, tailing fish, and so on.

(14) **A great tip-off for locating fish is to watch low-flying birds.**

Gulls, cormorants, and other birds either see fish moving around and go there, or they spook the fish by flying close overhead. Usually, a spooked fish will only swim a short distance and settle down. On some flats where there are lots of shrimp, you will see gulls inches above the surface. These gulls are grabbing shrimp that have been pushed up by redfish, snook, and other species.

(15) **Use your rod to locate a fish the guide is trying to show you.**

When the guide says the fish is at ten o'clock, point the rod in that direction. The guide can then tell you to move left or right. This is the fastest way for you to locate a fish the guide is trying to show you. See pages 92–93 for more information on this fish-location method.

(16) **Don't cast until you see the fish.**

Unless the guide insists that you cast, never throw your fly where you only *think* the fish is. This almost always results in a bad cast.

(17) **If a fish is straight ahead of the boat (at the twelve o'clock position) don't cast until the guide has moved the rear of the boat to one side.**

If you cast straight ahead, you will almost always hook the guide—not a good idea! Give him a chance to move the boat off to the side before you cast.

(18) **Don't cast too soon or wait too long.**

Making a cast too soon means you will probably have to frantically retrieve line and recast. If you wait too long, however, the fish is frequently too close and will see the boat. Cast when the guide tells you to.

(19) **When you do cast, if the fish obviously doesn't see the fly, cast again.**

Most of the fish we seek on flats with a fly are sight feeders. If you make a cast behind a fish or too far to one side—or for any other reason the fish is not likely to see it—don't continue to retrieve. Instead, quietly pick up and cast again.

(20) **If the fly hits the boat pole, motor, or any other hard object during your cast, check the fly.**

Make sure that the point hasn't been dulled. It's also a vital rule that if you strike two fish and don't get a hookup, you should check the hook point.

(21) **Never make a backcast if there is *any* line on the water.**

Surface tension grips your fly line in contact with the water. When making a backcast in the shallows, you should always make sure first that all line is off the surface. Even if only a foot of line is on the water when you make the backcast, the line, ripping loose from the surface tension, makes a noise that will frighten many fish. This is one of the major reasons why many people fail to catch fish in the shallows.

(22) **When false casting, never let the fly hit the surface.**

This happens often when bonefishing, where lead or bead chain eyes make flies a little difficult to cast. After you pick up and false cast, you make another backcast and the fly strikes the water between you and the fish. This ruins many opportunities.

(23) **Retrieve the fly with the rod pointed at the fish.**

Don't hold the rod tip well above the water. The sag in the line will create too much slack on a strike and can spoil the retrieve. Never use the rod tip to manipulate the fly. This also increases the chances of having too much slack when the fish strikes. Keep the rod pointed at the fish and manipulate the fly by stripping in the line.

(24) **Never strike upward on a fish in shallow water.**

When a fish accepts the fly in shallow water, the tendency is to flip upward with the rod tip. If the fish misses the fly and you flip up, you have missed the strike, and you have also removed the fly from the water. Another cast may spook the fish if it is close by. To properly strike, move the rod sideways or use a strip strike. A strip strike is done simply by grasping the line during the retrieve and pulling back a few inches to set the hook. If the fish is missed on a side or strip strike, the fly is still in the area near the fish.

Being aware of these things will increase your chances for success when fishing the flats.

A PROBLEM MOST FLATS FISHERMEN FACE AT SOME TIME

If you have fished the flats very often it's highly plausible that you and your partner have become very frustrated at times. Usually, when fishing from a flats boat, one person stands at the bow and is ready to cast. The other person either poles the boat or sits and watches while the guide poles. Either way, one person is fishing and one is watching.

What often happens is that one angler is more skilled or experienced than the other. So, he generously offers the lesser-skilled friend the first opportunity to catch a fish. Many times the unskilled person is really charged up about catching a fish. Because of his lack of skills he ruins a number of opportunities, while his friend sits.

Before long both people become frustrated. The unskilled angler knows he is blowing everything, but he's so anxious to catch a fish that he's reluctant to step down. The generous friend doesn't want to insult his partner, so he keeps his mouth shut, but he becomes more frustrated with every spoiled presentation. I have been in the position a number of times where I sat for most of the day while my companion blew one chance after another. He got all the good fishing. I got a brief shot at the platform. Both of us were unhappy at the day's end.

What can you do to eliminate this situation? I have a solution that now works well for me. The tides are changing constantly. This can affect how the fish act or react. The time allotted on the front deck should be about half an hour. The first individual is allowed on the platform for half an hour, or until he hooks a fish. *Once he hooks a fish, or lands one, he steps down— regardless of whether the half hour is up. Every half hour you change positions if nothing has been hooked. The key is hooked, not cast to!* If you allow each person more than half an hour on the platform, the good tide (when fish are really moving) may be gone.

Try this and I think you'll find both companions are happier at the day's end.

CHAPTER 10

Deepwater Fishing

The excitement and mystery of deepwater fishing make it a superb challenge to the saltwater fly fisherman rugged enough to lock his knees under the gunwale and versatile enough to present a fly to a host of species not considered fly-rod fare. It is a true frontier, and there is more opportunity for the thinking fisherman to develop new techniques than in any other area of fresh- or saltwater fly fishing.

The sudden appearance of the huge body and dorsal fin of a fast-swimming sailfish a few feet behind the boat, ready to take on that long streamer fly, will make an angler's knees quiver and his heart beat at double speed. So will the location of a prowling school of savage bluefish—jumbos tearing a frightened pod of baitfish to shreds. You know that the instant the fly hits the water, you're going to have a fish on, and you can bet you won't have an easy time landing it. And when a companion has teased a heavy-shouldered amberjack or husky cobia to boatside with a live bait and you're ready to drop a silver-dollar-sized popping bug to that wildly excited fish, the singular thrill is one that has to be lived to be completely understood.

Deepwater fishing should be defined as fly-rod fishing in water depths exceeding twelve feet. Much of this type of fly fishing is actually running the boat in search of fish or fighting dusty weather to come home. But when it's right, no other angling compares to it.

Unlike shallow-water fishing, where a silent approach is generally mandatory, and casting must be done with care, the emphasis in deepwater fishing is on locating the fish and then getting something in front of them that they will strike. Your lure can be a fly or popper dressed on any size hook—from a tiny number 4 to a huge 7/0. The length of the fly can range from a mere two inches to eight or nine, or even longer if you can cast it.

Deepwater fish sought by fly fishermen can be divided roughly into two categories. The first are roamers; these fish, mostly pelagic, move great distances in a short time, working over bait today in one area, moving twenty or fifty miles away by the next day. This type of fish may be offshore in abundance for a few hours, a day, a week, even a month, and then suddenly disappear. They are constantly on the move, searching for the right water temperatures and enough baitfish to feed upon. Temperature and availability of bait determine when these fish will move into your area, and when they will leave.

The second category includes the fish that remain in a specific area for long periods of time. Such fish can often be located easily, and a scheme devised for duping them into taking a fly.

The roamers would be represented by such fish as albacore, bluefish, oceanic and Atlantic bonito, cobia, dolphins, the jacks (crevalle, barjack, and

On calmer seas you can often see billfish basking on the surface.

horse-eye), mackerels (cero, Spanish, Atlantic, Pacific, and king), marlin (blue, black, striped, and white), salmon, wahoo, sailfish (Atlantic and Pacific), yellowtails, false albacore or little tuna, and other tuna (blackfin, bluefin, Allison, Atlantic, and Pacific bigeye). These are only some of the major species available to fly fishermen who work deep water. Some roosterfish and striped bass are in this category.

The second group are homebodies. They sometimes appear in schools, but may also be solitary denizens, or accompanied by only a few companions. Among this notable group of fish are African pompano, barracudas (Pacific and great), rockfish, groupers, amberjacks, and snappers. This list does not seem nearly as long and impressive as the one for roamers—but remember that fifty-two species of rockfish occur in California waters, and that groupers and snappers are divided into several dozen subspecies. Not all rockfish are in water regarded as deep, but for practical purposes, the methods used to catch deepwater species will in most cases succeed for nearly all rockfish situations.

 ## FLY RODS

Two basic fly rods will form the nucleus of the offshore angler's tackle requirements. A rod that handles a weight-forward number 9 and 10 line is ideal for your light stick. This rod is great for salmon trolling on the West Coast and for casting to bonito, many jacks, mackerels (except king mackerels), yellowtails, false albacore, and many other smaller open-water species. These fish are fast, capable of a 100- to 200-yard run, but do not dive deep and exert the tremendous strain on tackle that fish like amberjacks, billfish, and larger tuna do.

The second rod is a fish-fighting tool, and it's described in another chapter on tackle. The original fish-fighting rods were great at beating a fish, but terrible casting tools. Modern rod designers have given us sticks in graphite and boron that not only cast well, but are every bit as good at fighting fish. One of the greatest advancements in fly-fishing tackle has occurred with these fish-fighting fly rods.

If you have used rods no heavier than a 9 or 10, you may want to at first reject a rod that is designed to cast a size 12 to 15 fly line. But, when you tangle with a sailfish, amberjack, roosterfish, or some other hard-pulling deepwater species, you'll appreciate the fish-lifting power of these big sticks.

There have been occasions when I hooked a very large fish on too small a fly rod and found that had I fought the fish in a normal manner the rod would probably have broken. In such situations I put my forearm and hand under the blank behind the stripping guide to provide extra support for the flexing rod. You will also find that some of the fish-fighting rods in size 12 or larger have a foregrip for this purpose. Some anglers swear that it hurts the rod's action and that it's just not needed. Manufacturers have been able to make rods in which the action is not affected. Frankly, if you fight a fish for more than an hour, the foregrip can be quite a help in relieving angler fatigue—the choice is really up to you.

 ## FLY LINES

Lines for offshore range from size 9 through 15, with the weight-forward 12 probably the most popular. There are occasions, such as in offshore chum lines, where I've found that even a rod as light as a 6 is dandy for small bonito and other little species.

Since many times the fish are found at or lured to the surface, floating lines have their place. But in deep water, quick-sinking lines generally have greater application. The fast-sinking weight-forwards are very useful. Especially useful when you want to plumb the depths with your fly is either a lead-core shooting head or one of the commercial heads weighing from 400 to more than 600 grains that sink almost as fast. When fishing offshore with these heads, don't use monofilament for a running line, use the new, strong, shooting line sold by several line manufacturers. The thinner mono will cut your hands during the fight.

 ## REELS

Fly reels have been well covered in the chapter on tackle. Those with at least 250 yards of thirty-pound Dacron backing are recommended, and some of the models that carry as much as 500 yards of backing are appreciated on long runs. When retrieving a great deal of line the large-diameter reels are very helpful.

The angler who runs to the blue water and knows nothing about fishing it will wonder how anyone can find fish in such vastness. Everything

Frigate birds are good indicators of larger fish cruising near the surface on open seas.

looks the same. Yet to the knowledgeable angler there are exact places to go, and definite procedures for finding these hot spots.

Birds can be a quick tip-off. Gulls, terns, and other waterbirds are—as described earlier—indicators of feeding fish; the man-o'-war or frigate bird is especially important when you're after larger fish.

Many species of fish will feed briefly at the surface, often for just a few minutes, then disappear, popping up somewhere else a few minutes later.

It pays to get to a feeding school of fish as quickly as possible, before the fish sound or the baitfish scatter. If you arrive late and see no fish activity, make several casts anyway. Often a few predators are still around.

Remember to approach a school from the upwind side, so you can throw your fly downwind. And *never* run the boat through a school of breaking fish.

Remember also that one of the greatest tricks the fly fisherman can learn about casting to breaking fish after a fast boat approach is how to hold and release his line. The fly rodder, if he casts with his right hand, should stand at the right rear quarter of the boat. The forward taper or belly section of the line, plus the leader and fly, is streamed out behind him in the boat's wake. When the boat reaches the fish and the motor is chopped, the fly rodder can make a quick forward cast.

If the boat is large, with spreading outriggers, the fly rodder should request that they be folded out of the way before the action begins. If that's not possible, a side cast can be made. But, the angler should always remember those 'riggers and anything else that might be in the way.

When no birds are about, the surface of the ocean can often reveal your quarry. Schools of fish swimming just below the surface will often show color. Many skippers can tell the species of fish by the peculiar coloration of the water. Multicolored dolphins and rainbow runners are often a stirring sight as they swim in the clear waters of the sea.

Schools of baitfish are often revealed by the shimmering light reflected from their sides. Another tip-off is flying fish soaring quickly out of the water. When baitfish are under attack, the school will shower into the air, creating a stirring sight and sound. Sudden boiling of the water at the surface may indicate that a large fish just turned there. And nervous water may mean large fish swimming below.

Sails, marlin, and sharks often bask on the surface. Resting, maybe even sleeping, these big fish lie motionless so that their tail- and back fins protrude above the water. In the Sea of Cortez and along the Pacific Coast, there are numerous occasions when scores of striped marlin and sailfish can be seen basking on the surface. A very silent approach is necessary, for such fish are easily alarmed.

Floating weeds harbor myriads of tropical fish one to five inches in length. Baby amberjacks, little bonito, and thousands of other tropical fish rest and live in these floating weeds. Because of wind and current action, the weeds often form lines miles long. Weed lines are formed mostly during calm periods, since wave action tends to break them apart. In the Atlantic, the Gulf Stream's current forms the weeds in dense lines, especially when there is an easterly wind that gently blows them sideways to the current.

The first weed line encountered offshore is rarely the most productive. Unless you see visible fish action at the first line of weeds, it's a good idea to head farther offshore, looking for the next weed line.

Another method of locating offshore fish is to look for floating debris—logs, sticks, boards, anything that offers shade. The Central and South American rivers spew millions of tree branches and whole trees down from the jungle forest to the sea. These provide a haven for dolphins and offer some of the finest dolphin fishing in the world. Wahoo frequently lie under such debris. I heard of one party that took seven wahoo and nineteen dolphins from under one huge tree using spinning tackle.

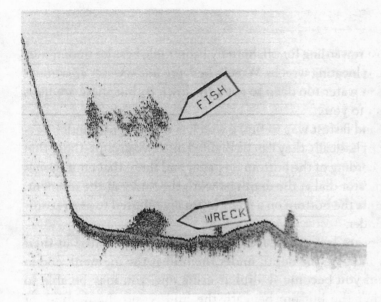

Modern depth finders can locate wrecks and tell you exactly where the fish that hover nearby are. With Loran C or GPS (Global Positioning System), once a wreck is located it can be marked and you can return anytime you wish.

When feeding under the surface, many fish create a slick of the chopped bodies of the oily baitfish they are consuming. An oily slick on the water should definitely be investigated.

Saltwater fishermen should either know the bottom characteristics intimately or carry charts. Charts reveal the sudden drop-offs, ledges, bumps in the bottom, wrecks, and other fish-producing areas. Fish do not usually live on a plain bottom. They will generally be found where an upcropping of rocks occurs, or a shelf drops off to form a hiding place for the food that they prey upon. Studying a chart will reveal such places.

Many years ago, one angler used to fish out of Ocean City, Maryland, and return later in the day with a spectacular catch of white marlin. No one could figure out how he did it. After following him one day they discovered his secret. About twenty-five miles offshore, this man had located an underwater plateau that rose from the ocean depths. The smaller fish the whites fed on lived along this uprising, drawing the marlin during the summer season to this particular area, now called the Jack Spot. Ocean City has now become the "White Marlin Capital of the World," and is vitally interested in pursuing a program of catch-and-release of these great billfish.

Well-marked charts will reveal many such uprisings, as well as drop-offs, where the bottom descends rapidly, forming vertical walls that accommodate the crabs and other crustracea, small fish, and other foods that predatory fish feed upon. Vertical drop-offs are always prime fishing possibilities.

Perhaps most rewarding for offshore fly fishermen, besides finding sur-face-feeding fish, is locating wrecks. Wrecks become underwater apartment houses. Many lie in water too deep to get a fly down to, but there are ways to bring these fish to you.

The easiest and fastest way to find a wreck is with a depth finder. Several types exist, but basically they can be divided into two groups: those that print an actual recording of the bottom on paper and those that emit flashes of light on an indicator dial at the depth beneath the finder at the moment. The type that paints the bottom on a chart is usually referred to as a record-ing-type depth finder.

Flasher types are less expensive. However, they are limited in their usefulness. They indicate the depth under the hull at the moment, and in some situations, if you become skillful at using one, you may be able to determine whether the bottom beneath the hull is soft, hard, mud, or rock. The better ones will indicate any fish beneath the boat with weaker flashes, but the operator usually needs some skill and practice before he is aware of the fish sightings. And if he isn't watching the machine at the instant the flashes occur, he has no way of knowing that he has passed over fish.

The recorder types are far superior. The recorder actually paints the bottom on a moving chart, so you can see the profile of a ship's hull on the bottom, or rock piles and other bottom configurations. But the recorder does more. It clearly paints on the chart the exact depth and size of the school of fish, and will even indicate a single large fish between the recorder and the bottom.

Some recorders offer a liquid crystal display, where no paper chart is required—but the paper does give you a permanent record you can refer to. Obviously, the liquid crystal display eliminates the cost of paper—you have to make your own choice as to which you want.

If you drift or cruise slowly over a potential wreck site, a flasher type will indicate how deep the bottom is beneath the hull. But recorder mod-els will furnish the exact and continuous outline of the bottom with all fish schools between you and the bottom, so that after you have made a pass across a wreck you can stop to examine the chart and see a photographic record of what is down there.

The compass and the depth finder are serious tools for the offshore fly fisherman.

The depth finder has the advantage of allowing you to return home in dense fog or low-visibility weather with comparative safety. Your charts tell you the water depths. As you return, the recorder can monitor the bottom, indicating where you are and preventing you from running aground. Many anglers, when moving slowly in deep water, run their recorders, hoping to pick up uncharted hot spots. Depth finders are useful in reading the bottom when you are approaching known good areas, too. If you are aware that a certain good drop-off occurs at forty-eight feet, with the recorder you can tell when this depth is reached.

Depth finders are now being rigged on many boats in the sixteen- to twenty-four-foot class. On these small boats they should be firmly installed to reduce vibrations, and an adequate cover should be maintained to keep salt spray from the sensitive working parts.

Loran C units have been developed that are small and inexpensive enough to be used on smaller boats. Many offshore boats and skiffs that can afford to go offshore in fair weather carry Loran. Once a wreck is located Loran allows you to come back *exactly* to the spot—even in total darkness.

Once you have located fish you must either cast far enough to get a fly to them, or bring them to you. Naturally, when fish are crashing bait on the surface, the only problem is getting there while the action is still going on and tossing a fly into the feeding mass—a simple problem to solve.

Real problems occur when you know fish are deep down, and you can't reach them. The lead-core line offers one solution. Make the longest possible cast and allow the super-fast-sinking line to bomb right to the bottom. Count as the line sinks; note how long it takes the line on the first cast to get to the bottom. Lead-core lines can be fished well to a depth of fifty feet if there's no strong current. Once you are aware of the time span—let's say it took a count of twenty-two—then make each succeeding cast at that count or just short of it if you want to work on or close to the bottom.

Myron Gregory, the late West Coast saltwater fly-rod pioneer, was the foremost advocate of the lead-core line technique. He began fishing with it in the 1950s, and it has become a standard procedure on the West Coast.

It's almost impossible to lift a lead core from the water with a normal pickup. Use instead the water haul. Strip in most of the head, raise the rod until most of the line is out of the water, then roll it out straight on the surface. When the fly contacts the water, begin a slow draw rearward with the rod, and when the fly begins moving make a strong backcast—the water

You can tease fish up from underwater wrecks by suspending a large and frisky fish on a pole (as shown). The dark spots are cobia and amberjacks that have been lured to the surface. The angler is throwing a large white popping bug to the fish, which are in a frenzy.

helps load the rod. You can shoot line on that final backcast, and then go to well over 100 feet with the cast.

Fishing submerged wrecks is a totally different kind of deepwater fly fishing. Wrecks are always excellent places to fish. But if you find one in eighty to 100 feet of water, how can you bring these fish within reach of the fly? Perhaps one of the simplest methods of attracting snappers, cobia, and big amberjacks in tropical waters is to light several firecrackers and throw them overboard. The concussion never harms the fish, but the loud noise will often draw to the surface fish that will not respond to other techniques.

The most exciting method of luring fish topside from a wreck is with a teaser. Florida anglers have developed this technique in recent years to a high art. Al Pflueger Jr. was one of the pioneers. You obtain a number of baitfish before going to the wreck; blue runners are preferable since they're so lively and tough, but any fish of from six to sixteen inches will suffice. Tie a short length—maybe four feet—of fifty- to sixty-pound-test monofilament to a gaff handle, heavy-duty rod, or pole, and attach a 4/0 to 6/0 hook to the other end of the line. Hook the baitfish in the center of the back, taking care not to strike its backbone and kill it.

Lower the teaser over the side and allow it to splash on the surface. If no larger fish appears within a few minutes, another angler can take a rod and violently swish it back and forth in the water. Apparently the vibrations set up by the rod and the swimming fish bring out the killer instinct in many fishes. Cobia, amberjacks, dolphins, barracudas, big snappers, and other wreck dwellers are drawn by such tactics. I have never met anyone who has tried this trick on roosterfish, but I'll bet it would work for them, too. Of course, sharks move in also.

Once the fish arrive on the scene you follow a prescribed routine. Swish the teaser back and forth right in front of the hungry fish. Sometimes the game fish become frantic and move so close to the boat that they charge, miss the bait, and actually run into the side of the boat. It's advisable when catching your bait to get an ample supply. When a dozen or more amberjacks and cobia are milling around the bait, you're going to lose baitfish. What usually occurs is that, while you're busy teasing the fish and keeping the bait away from several of them, a larger and wiser fish will sneak under the boat and ambush the teaser before you get a chance to yank it away.

Observe several rules for this type of fishing: a stout fly rod is mandatory; the lure that has performed consistently best in this situation is a huge 1¼-inch across-the-face popping bug made of Styrofoam, with a well-sharpened 7/0 hook. Put just the leader and a few feet of fly line—rarely more than seven or eight feet—outside the rod tip.

I remember one day when my son, Larry, Jim Lopez—a great saltwater fly rodder—and I stopped alongside a black Key West harbor buoy to get blue runners for bait. We had thirty-one of them in the live well when Jim got the idea to go to a little-known wreck that lay more than twenty miles out in the Gulf of Mexico. He fired the engines and headed northwest. I complained that we should take time to get more bait; Jim felt we had more than enough. We found the wreck with no trouble. The gulf was as flat and green as a pool table. Jim rigged five feet of sixty-pound-test mono to a gaff handle and tied a 5/0 hook to the other end of the line. Larry rigged a stout fly rod with a number twelve line and a Styrofoam popping bug with a face the size of a half dollar.

I climbed to the bridge and took a light reading for my cameras, then nodded to Jim that I was ready. He dropped the teaser bait overboard and it began to struggle and fight. Within two minutes I began to see dark shapes emerging from the depths below. Up came more than a dozen big amberjacks and seven large cobia; all the cobia were more than forty pounds. Within minutes Jim had lost four of the baits to the savage fish. Larry, casting like a madman as the fish swirled alongside the boat, hooked two in the next twenty minutes. Both fish wiped him out in the wreck more than sixty feet below. Both weighed well over seventy pounds, and despite the twelve-pound-test tippet and heavy rod, Larry simply couldn't keep them out of the wreck. He handed the rod to Jim and began to tease the jacks and cobia.

Having done this many times before, Jim waited until the fish were about as excited as they were going to get, then dropped the line in and made several loud water-gulping whooshes with the bug. A good amberjack grabbed the bug and streaked into the wreck below. A large cobia repeated the trick a few minutes later. Jim managed to get a bug in front of the smallest amberjack in the pack. After a stirring battle I gaffed the fish for Jim. It weighed forty-eight pounds. Then I realized that we were out of baitfish. Those thirty-one blue runners had disappeared in less than an hour.

Offshore towers, like those on the Gulf Coast and those offshore from the Carolinas, harbor big cudas and cobia, which can be lured with a teaser bait. Some of the fish that live around these towers become extremely smart and are difficult to fool with a fly. Norman Duncan has developed a technique for taking cudas after they have been excited by a teaser bait. Barracudas are incredibly swift and have keen eyesight. They quickly realize that a fly is just that—an artificial bait.

Norman teases the cuda until it takes a bite from the bait. He allows the bait to lie motionless in the water, then throws his fly right beside the mutilated bait. You must let the current sweep your fly without any manipulation by you—*the fly must float dead in the water.* Apparently the cuda thinks the fly is another hunk of the baitfish that is being swept away.

If you have no bait aboard, and you are over a wreck or near an obstruction that might harbor large fish, you can often tease them into striking a fly with the use of a "chugger" plug. This is a lure with a face that is deeply scooped to pick up "gallons" of water on a jerky retrieve by the angler. The lure carries no hooks. The chugger is cast out and brought back in swift jerks of the rod, causing the lure to make great gulping sounds, which attract many kinds of fish.

As the chugger is worked rapidly through the water the fly rodder watches the lure intently. If any fish appear near the plug a cast is made so the fly falls near it—and it is almost always eagerly accepted by the stalking fish.

Sometimes the chugger is very effective around buoys and markers, as well as wrecks and towers. I remember fishing one day with my son, Larry. Returning from a good day offshore, we passed through the Key West harbor, and I mentioned that we should check some of the buoys for cobia. Larry didn't really think it would be worthwhile, but reluctantly agreed to try—just to please me. It was sundown and we had only a few minutes to try. I stood on the casting deck of the eighteen-foot boat while Larry began to cast the chugger around the buoy. Suddenly, an amber shape arose and began to follow the plug. Larry jerked the plug away as it neared the boat and I asked him if he wanted to cast to the fish. He leaped to the platform and grabbed the rod. The cobia had dropped back into the channel depths but I was sure I could bring it back again. I cast and began to work the plug noisily. Larry saw the fish first. It was only twenty-five feet away, but Larry, a fine caster, was so excited that he had to make three casts before the fly plopped right in front of the fish. The fly was a seven-inch Lefty's Deceiver, which I have had great luck with when fishing cobia. The white hackles and Mylar inched along in front of the fish, which slowly moved up and inhaled the fly. Larry struck hard, and fifteen minutes later I gaffed a 37½-pound cobia for him.

Kites provide a new and novel method of teasing fish into position where the fly rodder can make a cast. Though kites have been used in the South Pacific since before the time of Christ, Harlan Major is usually credited with establishing kite fishing in this country back in the 1930s. It died out as a fishing technique shortly after that, but in the past few years it has been revived and now promises to become more popular than ever.

The kite is flown from the boat by a special reel; the separate line allows the angler to put aloft a square kite that remains in a steady position. Dangling from the line near the kite is a clamp similar to a clothespin. Another reel is held by a companion, and from it the line runs up through the clamp and down to the surface beneath the kite. At the surface a live bait is dangled so it can splash and remain in one position on the water; naturally, this attracts any predator fish that is nearby.

In regular kite fishing when the predator grabs the baitfish it pulls the line from the clamp, and the fisherman winds in the slack, strikes, and fights the fish. Fly fishermen employ the kite in a slightly different manner. The line holding the bait can be drawn through the clamp without falling from it—allowing the angler to adjust his bait to move it up or down in the air. Should a fish accidentally grab the bait, the line is secured to the clamp so the fish cannot pull the line free; when a fish is merely attracted to the bait, you can elevate the teaser quickly under the kite. The now-frantic fish will often accept a fly cast to the area where the baitfish disappeared.

One of the truly pioneer fly-fishing experiments is the successful procedure for taking sailfish and marlin on a fly developed by Dr. Webster Robinson with his wife, Helen, and Captain Louis Schmidt, of Panama. Once these fish were considered beyond the realm of the fly fisherman.

Doc Robinson's efforts to take blacks finally resulted in the plan to boat billfish on a fly. Fishing in Panama for black marlin, Doc became frustrated by the scores of sailfish that were attacking his baits and destroying them. In desperation he fashioned a wooden plug without

The two men who pioneered the teasing techniques for luring billfish to the fly: Dr. Web Robinson (left) and Captain Lefty Reagan with a nice striped marlin they landed in the Sea of Cortez.

hooks, which was trolled behind the boat near the larger marlin baits. It was hoped that the sailfish would attack the smaller lure, and they did. In fact, the sails were so aggressive that when the hookless wooden lure was reeled in, the fish would often continue to attack the lure. Sometimes they'd flee when they saw the stern of the boat, but often they were so intent upon killing and eating the wooden lure that they remained within a few feet of the transom.

Why not try for sails with a fly? Doc was not the kind to just fling a fly at a billfish. Instead, he went home to Key West, Florida, and devised a strategy.

Since he belonged to the famed Rod and Reel Club of Miami Beach, Doc determined to fish according to club regulations, which meant a leader with a breaking strength of twelve pounds, and a shock leader attached to the fly that did not exceed a foot in length. Knowing full well that sailfish often plunge to the depths then streak toward the sky in a leaping jump, Doc was aware of the terrific strain that would be placed against the leader as the fly line was dragged through the water. So he adopted a very old tactic, used by salmon and bass fishermen for many years, of cutting thirty feet of fly line from the back portion. This helped reduce the strain on the leader from line drag as the sailfish made its plunges.

He also studied the inside of the sailfish's mouth and found that it and other billfish had a softer area in the upper jaw than they did in the lower. This meant he'd have a better chance of a hookup if the hook point rode up.

On January 18, 1962, Doc stood on the deck of the *Caiman*, while his wife, Helen, held a trolling rod. Skipping in the wake behind the boat was a strip of bonito belly that had been cut and then sewn into a shape resembling a fish. The bait carried no hooks.

"Watch it!" screamed Captain Schmidt, as a sailfish rose behind the skipping lure and began to track the bait. Mrs. Robinson had already seen the fish; she was ready. The fish moved forward, then lunged and slapped at the bait with its bill. Mrs. Robinson fed a little line back and the sail got a good taste of the bait. Suddenly, she jerked the bait from the sail's mouth and reeled it closer to the boat. Enraged, the angry sail moved forward and again inhaled the bait. The whole act was repeated several times, until finally the fish was within casting range. Doc called out for Captain Schmidt to stop the boat dead (so that he could make a legal cast) and for Mrs. Robinson to remove the teaser bait. She snatched the bonito belly out of the water and Doc swept the six-ounce rod forward with a muscular snap. The white popping bug fell ten feet to one side of the sail. The big popper swirled in the water; Doc popped the bug and the sail moved toward the fly. No one on the boat was breathing as Doc gave the bug another gurgling pop. The fish hesitated, but its large dorsal fin was aglow with color. Doc raised the 9-foot rod a little, and the fly skittered on the surface. That was too much! The fish leaped forward and came hissing down through the air, the fly disappearing under that thrusting beak.

Robinson struck, and the sail, less than forty feet from the boat, skyrocketed out of the cobalt blue Pacific with a giant leap, then began greyhounding in and out of the water as it tore line from Doc's reel.

Screaming at Captain Schmidt to get the boat around and chase the sail, Doc watched his line almost disappear from the spool before the *Caiman* finally came around and began to pursue the fish. Finally the fish stopped running, changed tactics, and began circling the boat, leaping frequently. Rhythmically Doc pumped and wound, pumped and wound. After forty minutes of the most brutal fly-rod punishment Doc had ever applied to a fish, the sail was ready to be boated.

Boating the sail was a problem that Doc had fretted about long before the trip. He realized that conventional boating would be out. Normally, the long leaders can be grasped by the mate and the fish controlled to some extent. With a little more than twelve inches of twelve-pound-test leader, and a ten-inch wire shock leader, Doc knew that no one should grab the fly leader while boating a billfish. The fish was gaffed and heaved aboard.

The fish weighed 74½ pounds—not a big Pacific sailfish by Panama standards, but truly a prize. Doc had taken a billfish on a fly. He went on to capture fourteen other Pacific sailfish during the next three years; his largest was 107½ pounds.

One factor in Doc's success was that he used bonito belly, rather than a wooden plug. After the sail had tasted the fresh belly bait (minus hooks, of course) it wanted more. Natural bait is far superior to an artificial teaser. Some modern anglers have forgotten Doc's basic lesson and are using artificial lures, which are probably not nearly as effective.

Successful with Pacific sailfish, Doc decided to try a bigger billfish. Blue and black marlin were certainly too large for any fly rod, and white marlin were not as big as the fish he had already caught. He finally decided upon striped marlin. They were bigger than sails, yet small enough to offer at least a fighting chance on fly gear. His tackle would be the same—twelve-pound-test tippet at least a foot long, no more than twelve inches of shock leader, and a six-ounce fly rod.

He decided to test his ideas at Baja California, where he knew that great concentrations of striped marlin could be found. He took along his own captain from Key West, Lefty Reagan, one of the most experienced light-tackle skippers in the world.

They got a surprise on the first fish, and soon learned that marlin are considerably harder to excite with a teaser than sailfish. Once they're excited, it is difficult to get them to sustain their eagerness to get that teaser, even if they have tasted it. Once the marlin decided it liked the taste, however, it was an easy task to draw the fish to the boat.

"The first time I hooked a marlin," Doc said, "I remember telling myself I would be damn lucky if I managed to salvage any part of my equipment from the fly right down to the butt cap."

He fought the first marlin for two hours and lost it when the leader finally parted from fatigue. He then hooked four more. He worked one within gaffing range of the boat, only to lose it in the rough seas. Finally, one bright midday he boated the first marlin ever taken on a fly rod, and rewrote the saltwater fly-fishing books. The giant billfish weighed 145 pounds.

During the next two weeks he fought many striped marlin on a fly. He lost count of the strikes he missed and the fish that threw hooks, but he knew that he lost nineteen of those white popping bugs to striped marlin. He ran completely out of twelve-pound-test leader material and used the next lightest material he had, twenty-pound-test. With this leader, which is slightly higher than the weight acceptable for world records, Doc boated a 178-pound striped marlin.

Lee Cuddy, a close friend of the Robinsons, and one of the real pioneers in fly fishing, boated the first Atlantic sail ever taken on fly gear. Lee was fishing with Captain Bucky Stark out of Islamorada. He fought the fish in a terrible squall that saw one engine go out and everyone on board get drenched. His sail weighed forty-eight pounds.

Doc Robinson used a popping bug and hookless bait for a teaser. Since that time there have been tremendous improvements in both tackle and technique used for teasing and catching billfish.

Perhaps the first major breakthrough or advancement after Doc's original work was devised by Captain Jim Paddock and mate Rick Defoe. Working on the boat *Stormy* in the rich sailfish waters off the west coast of Costa Rica, these two innovative anglers devised what is now considered the basic tackle for billfish.

One of the major problems with catching a billfish on a fly rod is that after the strike they run so fast that the drag against the line breaks the leader—that's why Doc shortened his fly lines. Another serious problem is that when a fish leaps the angler should try to throw slack—but a billfish may be way out there and leaping away from the boat. The leap is completed before the angler realizes he should have bowed. Jim and Rick solved this problem very neatly, and it can be used anywhere in salt water where huge fish are lunging against the leader and you need a safety shock absorber.

Here is the way they rigged the fly line for billfish. No more than fifty feet of Scientific Anglers Hi-D (fast sinking) was used as the shooting head. This was usually an 11- or 12-weight line. It has a thinner diameter than a floating line, reducing drag. To this was added approximately thirty feet of level floating line with a strength test more than that of the leader. Both Cortland and Scientific Anglers now make a shooting line for heads that test at least thirty pounds.

One of the key elements in their method was the built-in shock absorber they developed. Behind the shooting line they attached 100 feet of twenty-five-pound-test monofilament. Under a stout pull this will stretch yards before it comes tight—just what was needed to absorb the shock of a big fish leaping away from the angler. Behind the 100 feet of twenty-five-pound mono is standard thirty-pound Dacron or Micron backing. It was soon determined that the *color* of the shock-absorbing monofilament used was vital. Fluorescent or high-visibility monofilament was needed to prevent the captain from running over the line when chasing a fish. Conventional mono was simply too difficult to see.

The original popping bug devised by Web Robinson often turned upside down, was hard to cast, and frequently missed fish on the strike. Here again, major improvements have been made. It was discovered after trial and error by a lot of anglers that streamers worked well—but if you could make a little noise with them, the billfish found them quicker. Anglers began using Ethafoam (made by the Dow Chemical Company) or upholstery foam, cutting a cylinder-shaped piece about three-quarters inch thick and about one inch long. A hole was seared with a hot wire in the center of the foam. This was inserted onto the shock leader and pushed down to the hook eye. What resulted was a streamer with a popper head. I lost a sailfish because the popper head slipped up on the leader during the battle and a toothy critter struck, cutting the leader, so I now secure the popper with a bit of Dacron.

This lure works wonders. It can be thrown at the fish and popped, yet it swims like a baitfish. If you want to remove the popper after a refusal, simply rip it off and recast the streamer.

A number of streamer flies work very well. Large Lefty's Deceivers are still probably the most preferred. One way to make a huge Deceiver (eight to twelve inches) is to tie on some FisHair to form the long wing, then add the longest saddle hackles you can find to build up each side of the FisHair. Chico Fernandez ties a baitfish imitation from all Fishair that has taken a number of sailfish. Winston Moore (the king of the billfish fly rodders, who has caught more than 100) often used an orange bulky streamer of FisHair of approximately eight inches. Some people incorporate a stinger hook turned upright and hidden in the rear of the wing—claiming that it helps connect better on the strike.

Winston Moore knows more than anyone in the world about catching sailfish. Some of his advice is worth heeding. I think one of the most important things he ever told me was how he sometimes is able to increase the number of strikes he gets when the action is slow. Incidentally, his method works well for trolling for many kinds of offshore game fish too.

"The one thing that raises more sailfish than anything I know," Winston explained to me, "is that I finally learned that many of the billfish were coming up from deep water and I had already passed by them with the teaser before they got to the surface. I now have my captain never travel for more than five minutes without making several very tight turns and figure eights. It's been interesting to me how often this works for me when others in the same area are not getting fish into the baits or teaser."

Winston also feels that most anglers troll their teasers too fast. He explains, "In a twenty-five-foot Mako with a single diesel engine we troll at about 700 RPMs. When a fish is raised, we slow to about 400 to 500 RPMs. I think the main reason is that when we slow down we create less white water, which lets us see the fish better."

There are many occasions when you are either cruising looking for fish, or have seen them and must run quickly to the spot. You lose too much time if you wait until you arrive on the scene before peeling off line for a cast. To keep line stored under control, pull off as much line as you can and still cast comfortably. Just before reaching the school of fish, pick up the rod and get ready. Earl Leitess is casting here. The line in the bucket flows smoothly out.

Another bit of advice that is well to heed is that he takes his time teasing the billfish. "I think that a fish teased too quickly to the boat will not take the fly. I am never in a hurry to make the cast: allow the fish to worry with the bait and pull it from its mouth a number of times before the cast is made."

Many of the most successful billfishermen believe that plastic lures work fine as teasers. Some do add a piece of meat inside the teaser. Others feel that real meat works better and when you can get a bonito or dolphin belly, it's probably best.

Harry Kime, who also is skilled at catching billfish, feels that matching the teaser bait to the fly is important. If a certain teaser is used, he feels more strikes result if the fly matches it in color and size. Harry has one trick that I am certain aids the angler when manipulating the bait or lure. Rather than use the standard short boat rods, Harry employs a ten- to twelve-foot surf stick and a large-capacity spinning reel that allows him quick recovery of the line. With this rig he has greater maneuverability of the teaser bait, can retrieve line faster when he wants to, and, most important, with the long rod he can whip the lure away from the fish just before the cast is made. The long rod and high-speed reel allow him also to get the lure back to the fish quickly—if it's called for.

One other trick helps, and it's a good one to use anytime you need to be ready for a cast while a boat is under way. Throw the fly as far as you feel you will need. Then strip the line back in, dropping it in a five-gallon bucket. This prevents the line from being blown all over the deck, and the line will usually come out of the bucket tangle-free. Add one more idea too. Since the flies thrown offshore are often large and resist sinking until thoroughly wet, have a smaller pail sitting beside the five-gallon bucket. In it, place about an inch of water and drop the fly inside. This keeps the fly presoaked and it will slip beneath the surface quickly.

Teasing billfish to the transom and getting a good shot at one with a fly is a cooperative effort. The captain must know where to troll and how fast, and once the fish is at the teaser, he must be able to keep the boat at the desired speed. It helps a great deal if the boat is slowly turned so that the wind is at the best angle for the caster—something few captains will understand unless it is explained to them.

The mate is perhaps the most important factor in getting the fish to the transom—for it's his job to tease the fish. Because he is manipulating the fish and controlling to some degree its action, *the mate should be the one who decides when it is time to cast—not the angler.*

The angler should be in the correct casting position. A right-hander should be at the right rear of the boat; the man teasing the fish on the left rear. The angler should make sure all line-catching devices are out of the way. I use two-inch masking tape over all cleats.

Finally, once the teaser rig is removed and the cast and hookup made, the captain must now chase the fish when called upon. All of this means a great deal of cooperative effort. But catching billfish has to be one of the most exciting areas of fly fishing.

There are other methods of bringing fish to the fly caster. Chumming is perhaps the oldest known method, and certainly one of the most effective. One firm rule of chumming is that once you have established a chum line you must keep it going. The fish that are actively feeding in the chum line will soon leave if the food supply is cut off.

Many people use their offshore trolling rods to tease the bait for billfish. But, a long surf-casting rod with a reel that has a large spool for speedy line recovery works better. The fast retrieve and long rod allow better control of the teaser bait.

Chumming for bluefish is an ancient art in the northeastern part of our country. The oily mossbunker (menhaden) is ground for chum and appeals to fish more than probably any other chum. Menhaden is so good for chumming that commercial outlets now sell half-gallon cans of it to southern anglers. The oily mess is mixed with seawater and dipped with a ladle. It spreads on the surface and particles begin to sink. Cutting up little fish to add to the chum slick makes it even more effective. Bluefish and many other species are attracted from a great distance to the origin of the chum. One of the best ways to take a big bluefish on a fly rod is to set up a proper chum line and have the fish come to you.

Other types of chum lines can be established. Coarse fish, or any type of fish not used in eating—scales, heads, everything—can be ground into small bits and frozen in half-gallon cardboard milk cartons. These can be kept aboard the boat frozen in ice. When needed, the chum is torn from the milk carton and deposited in an open mesh bag or old onion sack. It takes about an hour in a warm sea to melt a five-pound block. It's a good idea to give the sack an occasional yank as it hangs in the water.

If there are no fish where you set up a chum line and you decide to try another place, simply deposit the remaining frozen chum block in a bucket, then motor to another location.

If no chum is available, cutting the throats of fish already taken will produce blood, which, added to water in a bucket, can be slowly fed overboard. Oatmeal is an old standby. It can be used alone, but is better when mixed with the existing chum slick.

One of the neatest tricks for chumming, which I have seen practiced only in Bermuda, is the open-end chum basket. A cage with four sides and a top is constructed of quarter-inch hardware cloth. The bottom is open, and a sinker is suspended beneath the bottom. The Bermudians fish on the Argus and Challenger Banks, where the water is well over 100 feet deep. They can bring fish right to the surface with a chum basket.

Here's how it works. The basket, approximately six inches long and four inches square, open on the bottom, is held upside down, and hogmouth fry (small baitfish) are packed into it. A six- or eight-ounce sinker is attached to the open end of the basket. A cord, marked at twenty-five-foot intervals, is tied to the upper or closed end. When the basket is full of little baitfish, it is turned over rapidly and allowed to plunge into the depths. Line is fed continuously as the basket descends. When the basket hits bottom, the mate pulls on the cord, flushing the contents. The swiftness of the descent keeps the bait within the basket. However, when the rope pulls the basket upward, all bait is flushed from the open bottom end. Naturally fish on the bottom congregate at the area where food has been dispensed. Another basket is filled and allowed to descend, but not as deep as the first one. It, too, is flushed. Then another basket is flushed even closer to the surface. Dumping each basket closer to the surface draws the fish from the depths to boatside. I've seen wahoo, blackfin tuna, even huge mackerel sharks come right to the boat.

Once the fish are near the boat a steady feeding of either more small baitfish or ground chum will keep them within the fly caster's reach.

In the Gulf Coast areas and the lower Keys, as well as Mexican waters, the angler has a built-in chum supply. Shrimpers ply these waters at night, usually making three drags along the bottom. Naturally, they recover all sorts of fish life from the sea floor in addition to shrimp. Crabs, small fish, and many other forms of fish food are piled on the deck during the night hours, where they're separated from the shrimp. At dawn the shrimpers shovel the collection overboard.

Often you can get permission to tie your boat to a shrimper who has anchored and is about to remove all this chum from his deck. Or you can carry a lightweight plastic garbage can, or even a large plastic garbage-can liner bag, and approach the shrimper. He has had a long, hot night of work, and for a six-pack of cool beer he'll load your boat to the gunwales with chum.

Aside from a bonanza of chum, you'll also have many fairly large, three- to eight-inch fish in the "gold" that the shrimper has deposited in your boat. Many fish will respond to this type of chum. King mackerels especially like the larger tidbits. If you find kings in your chum line and are having trouble getting them to hit, there are several possible solutions. Often the bigger kings will be deeper. Then a sinking line must be used, and a cast made up-current and allowed to tumble back toward the chum line— it'll go deeper that way.

If you're chumming with large pieces, you'll probably get more strikes if you use a fly the approximate size of the chum, and if you allow the fly to drift dead in the current. Chum moves solely by current action and often a fly that is zipping along is ignored. Sometimes, when fish seem to get wise in a chum line, you can switch to a big, slurping popping bug, which makes a tremendous noise and can't be seen too well by the fish because of all the surface disturbance it makes. Often the best fly is one that resemble the drifting chum—a slightly weighted hook, with a bit of red chenille and several plumes of dark red marabou is frequently the best pattern.

The dead drift seems the best way to fool some fish working a deep chum line. However, bonito, kingfish, albacore, and tuna often like a swiftly moving fly. Two retrieves will accomplish this. One is to point the rod tip directly toward where you think the fish may be. Then with a side-sweeping motion of the rod hand, and a fast strip with the other, you cause the fly to dart forward eight or nine feet. The fish will often strike such a fast-moving lure before it realizes the fly is a phony. Another fast retrieve can be maintained over a fairly long distance. Place the rod between the inside of both knees and use the knees to hold it there. Take both hands and one after another bring the line back in as fast as you can. This retrieve allows you to take fish that will only strike a fly that moves swiftly over a long distance.

Anyone who has fished from a California party boat knows about the four- to six-inch fish called anchovies that are carried aboard by the thousands for use as chum. Special live-bait tanks are used for such purposes.

The author with a Pacific sailfish.

Blackfin and other tuna can easily be led into chum lines.

The boats head to sea, and often travel many hours before arriving at the yellowtail and albacore grounds. A mate is assigned to throw live anchovies overboard when fish are suspected of being nearby. This draws the yellowtails and albacore right to boatside. Special spinning rods with flexible tips are normally used to toss a baited hook at the frantic predatory fish. However, the fly caster can get off to himself and with a Hi-D or lead-core shooting line bomb a five-inch streamer fly into the depths and hang these magnificent game fish. Trips on such boats can be made for a few dollars, and in addition to yellowtails and albacore the fly rodder can expect to find bonito, barracudas, and other fish.

Using a similar trick, Mark Sosin, one of the great saltwater fly rodders, managed to land what I regard as one of the finest catches ever made in the salt with a fly rod. Mark was fishing on the edge of the Bermuda Challenger Bank with Captain Boyd Gibbons and Pete Perinchief. Mark waited anxiously as a school of Allison tuna were chummed up by the use of anchovies and hogmouth fry, along with chunks of mackerel. He was using a twenty-six-foot shooting head (floating line) with 100 feet of fifty-pound monofilament backing; this was attached to nearly 300 yards of thirty-pound Dacron. He used a polar bear hair and Mylar streamer fly that he and noted fly tier Bub Church had created for the situation, and a Seamaster reel.

The Allisons were chummed right to the surface, where Mark made a forty-foot cast and hung one of the fish. After many long and scorching runs, and a problem with the line and anchor rope, Mark fought and landed one of the greatest catches ever taken from the sea on a fly rod—a fifty-six-pound, six-ounce Allison tuna.

In 1973 Jim Lopez boated an eighty-one-pound Allison on fifteen-pound-test line. Pete Perinchief, Bermuda fishing expert, claimed it was the best catch ever made on a fly rod.

Chumming and great rod handling were responsible for these world-record catches.

OFFSHORE SHARK FISHING

Deepwater fly fishing for sharks has become popular the past few years, especially in California, where several species including Pacific blue sharks can be regularly caught. Bob Edgely and Lawrence Summers pioneered the sport and developed the basic techniques, which are easily understood and mastered—but landing a shark is something else. Its bull-like power and ability to carry on the fight for extended periods makes it a tough trophy.

Two basic methods are used offshore. One is to cut chunks of bait and have them ready while cruising and looking for sharks on calmer days. Once the shark is spotted, motor ahead of the fish and throw pieces of the bait. If the shark sees the chunks of meat it will take them. After it has accepted the bait, throw a large, weighted fly (a Lefty's Deceiver on a 5/0 hook is popular with many anglers). Sometimes a slow retrieve of the fly is good, other times a dead drift is better—you have to experiment.

The better method most of the time, for it draws not only visible fish but unseen sharks cruising well below the surface, is to drift with a chum bag hung over the side in areas where sharks are known to be. Ground, frozen chum is deposited in the bag and the up-and-down motion of the rocking boat will slowly peel off the melted chum. If possible, grind up fish that have a great deal of oil—this produces a more effective chum slick. Material for the chum line can be obtained from fish-cleaning houses. Some people use a wire cage to hold the chum, but on several occasions I have had sharks in a frenzy attempt to take the chum bag from the boat. I now use a large mesh bag that is tied to a light rope, making it easy for the shark to take the rig—if it really wants it. It's scary watching a shark pound against the thin side of your boat while it attempts to remove a metal cage full of chum.

You'll need your stoutest rod (size 12 to 15) with a powerful butt to fight big sharks. Incidentally, *never* put a shark in the boat, even when you're sure it's dead—they have a habit of "coming back to life." If you want to bring one home, tow it behind the boat. A flying gaff is best used, too. Sharks twist and roll and trying to hold a conventional gaff at such times can be difficult.

Fast-sinking or lead-core lines are generally best, and you'll need a wire shock leader of at least sixty pounds test. Sharks will take popping bugs fished on a floating line, but because of the mouth being set back so far, they frequently push the bug away on the strike.

 # Boats

Today most saltwater fly fishing is done from boats ranging in size from twelve-foot skiffs to fifty-foot oceangoing crafts. But, for many years saltwater fly fishing was confined to inshore waters; rarely did anyone take a fly rod to sea. In the late 1940s, J. T. Herrod, a Miami bonefish guide, had a skiff that was powered by two twenty-five-horsepower motors. It was considered the hottest thing afloat, and the ultimate in small, fast fishing boats.

In those days, after you decided to fish a particular area and found the fishing poor, you were stuck with it. Today, a fourteen- to twenty-foot outboard-powered inshore or flats skiff may have a range of more than 150 miles and a speed in excess of forty miles per hour—many go as fast as fifty. For shallow water, however, fishing boats with a capability of more than forty miles an hour are really not necessary.

It's just as important to fly fishermen that today's boatbuilders are finally designing and constructing boats for our needs. Protruding nails and screws, seats that trip anglers, gas tanks with entangling devices, and similar frustrations are gone. Now we have tanks that are hidden, and no visible cleats, nails, screws, or other gadgets. Poling platforms are standard on most flats boats today—although they may be a drawback at times.

Most modern, saltwater fly-fishing boats have a platform for the angler to stand on and drop his fly line. Perhaps an even better innovation is to have a small forward platform for the angler to stand on, and a larger plat-

Modern flats boats are a joy to fish from. The decks are clear of line-tangling devices. The guide is elevated to see the fish better. Equipped with good power, the boats are capable of covering a tremendous distance during the fishing day.

form behind to drop line. Having only a single casting platform often spells disaster, because the angler may stand on the line he wants to cast.

On modern boats there is ample storage for tackle, food, extra gear, and ice; all built-in refinements—and all out of the way. Rod holders have

Modern flats skiffs also offer secure, out-of-the-way rod holders, where the gunwale protects the tackle from salt spray.

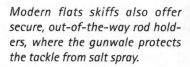

reached new pinnacles of design. Today the better-designed boats can carry four to six fly rods and as many as ten additional spin- and plug-casting outfits—ready to be cast.

Hull designs have improved radically. Many of the new flats skiffs can skim across a choppy bay at thirty-five to forty miles per hour in solid comfort. You can take them to sea in moderate weather, they pole well in the shallows, and they use gas economically. Usually made of glass or Kevlar, these boats are relatively maintenance-free, and carry a CB or another sophisticated radio, trim tabs, and a good depth finder. Reliable compasses, which stabilize well in rough water, are available. The GPS (Global Positioning System) units are super-efficient and some are hand operated—run-

A console-mounted or handheld GPS (as shown) is invaluable to saltwater fly fishermen.

ning either on the boat's battery or a few AA batteries. With the GPS you can plot courses. It will give you pinpoint accuracy, tell you how fast you are going, allow you to navigate in dense fog and arrive accurately at a difficult-to-find wreck, and perform a host of other important functions. For boaters in the salt, a GPS has become as valuable as your anchor.

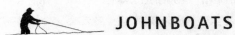 ## JOHNBOATS

The newest innovation has been the emergence of the johnboat for use in salt water. This boat can get around the shallows of the backcountry and let you fish where conventional flats-type skiffs simply can't go. With the johnboat you can prowl tiny creeks and flats that are barely wet. Many have poling towers, which are okay if you want to fish the open water. But, to thread through overhanging mangrove trees and get into many small creeks, it is wise not to have a poling platform that can catch in the branches. These flat-bottomed boats are effortless to pole—even in inches of water.

They are extremely fuel efficient. But, they have a drawback—which can be surmounted. Because the front of the bottom is made of metal and

Modern johnboats—with a poling platform in the rear, a casting surface on the front, and a clear interior—have revolutionized fishing in the shallow waters of the backcountry.

is flat, poling into a chop or small waves can create excessive noise. Captain Steve Huff has an answer for that, which I have tested. It's simple, easy to install or remove, and reduces any noise that may frighten fish. Steve uses a piece of lightweight outdoor carpeting to form a skirt around the bow and a few feet along the sides. The upper portion of the carpet is attached to the boat; the lower portion is slit to form many "fingers," which dip just below the surface when the rig is installed. This virtually eliminates any noise from a light chop. If you design it so that the fingers only reach the surface or just below it, it creates little drag, so poling is not a problem. When not in use, it can be detached and stored away.

 ## ANCHORS

Small boats should carry three anchors. One is light and used for holding in slow water, or when making a lunch stop. The other anchor should have plenty of holding power. Most of us now place three to six feet of rub-

Modern flats skiffs are swift, comfortable, easy to pole, and very quiet when approaching fish.

ber- or plastic-coated chain in front of the anchor; the coating prevents rusting, and the chain enables the anchor to grip better. The third anchor is, strangely, one that few consider, but it can be invaluable if you fish in waters less than ten feet deep. This is a drag anchor. There are many fishing situations where you would like to drift with the boat but not be constantly turned around, like drifting and casting for seatrout, striped bass, and many other species. The drag anchor can make life easier. It was developed in Arkansas back in the early 1900s. Bass fishermen used it to drift the White, Current, and other great smallmouth rivers of the area. By paying out a length of chain tied to a long rope, they could place enough resistance at the rear of the boat so that the boat never spun around, but instead drifted with the bow always forward. For saltwater fly-fishing boats, three-eighths-inch chain link seems to be the best bet. For a sixteen-foot johnboat or light skiff, a chain about four feet long is about right. Larger boats will need either a longer length of three-eighths-inch chain or a chain of larger-diameter links. The length and weight of the chain have to be determined by your individual fishing conditions.

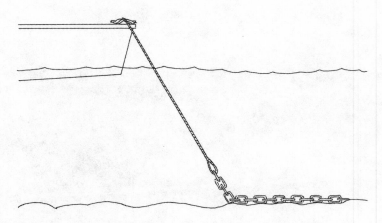

Using a drag anchor can help control the boat's direction when drifting and casting. The text explains how to use this valuable and often disregarded fishing tool.

Here is the way the drag chain works: tie a length of rope to the end of the chain. When you want to make a drift, determine which way the current or breeze will cause the boat to travel. Lay out a length of the chain and some rope. If the boat doesn't drift, you have too much rope out. Sometimes, as on a near calm day, you will only have a tiny bit of the chain caressing the bottom. When the current or wind is swifter, you may have to lay out more rope. *The more rope is paid out, the more resistance is created by the drag anchor.* You may think that the anchor would snag on the bottom, but in my many years of using one there have been only a few times when this has happened. The drag anchor is very helpful when you are fishing by yourself, or when you and a friend are both trying to cast and must maintain a controlled drift. If you haven't tried a drag anchor, I urge you to—it's very inexpensive.

RELEASE BUOYS

Always carry a release buoy. A release buoy is especially useful when you have a good fishing location and you want to be able to return to it with a minimum of effort. This float can be snapped to the anchor line so that, if a large fish is hooked, the anchor line will be loosened from the boat and the buoy will keep the line afloat while you chase the fish. Once a fish is landed, you can quickly return and set up again in the exact same position. A lobster pot float made from plastic foam is a perfect buoy.

An option on some of the bonefish/tarpon skiffs is a short tower for the fly caster to stand on to obtain a better view.

Some people have a little difficulty standing on such a platform. Captain Mike Hewlett has developed a folding platform that offers superb stability. Note that while Mike is casting, he is completely at ease.

This shows Captain Mike Hewlett's front platform folded down when not in use.

At the Deep Water Cay fishing club in the Bahamas they installed a removable "leaning post" years ago. The author can attest that if the post is not too wide, it is a great asset for the angler to rest against while standing on a bonefish platform.

There are some areas along the upper East Coast where it is feasible to pole shallow flats and search for cruising striped bass. A twenty-foot bonefish-type skiff, with some minor modifications, has become popular. Here Captain Paul Dixon, who pioneered this idea in the Long Island, New York, area, poles Sam Talarico for stripers.

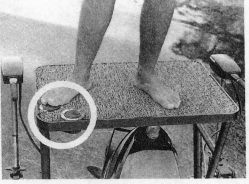

Air-activated switches are now used to run electric motors. This frees the captain to pole the boat with his arms and operate the motor with his feet.

Many more anglers are fly fishing inshore, but sometimes the seas can build to a few feet. This requires good, serviceable boats that give a dry ride. Two such models that are becoming very popular are the Jones Brothers Cape Fisherman and the nineteen- or twenty-three-foot Sea Craft.

The interior of such a boat should be free of line-tangling gadgets.

A bridge platform like this one gives easy entry to work on the boat while abroad on the seas.

STRIPER BOATS

Striped bass fishing has led a number of boatbuilders to come up with hulls that meet its exacting conditions. The flats-type skiff has low sides. The reason is that most flats skiffs are poled and the higher the sides, the larger the "sail area" and the harder the boat is to pole, especially in a breeze. The best striper boats have high enough sides to buck swells and waves of three feet and still keep the occupants fairly dry. The entry of the boat should be soft so that running in a heavy sea doesn't produce too much pounding.

The inside of the boat should be clean and devoid of line-grabbing devices. Cleats that can be pushed flat with the boat's surface and popped up when needed are a real asset.

A small pulpit allowing the angler to stand right in the bow is a decided asset on boats where anglers prefer to fish the foamy white water crashing against the shoreline where stripers often feed.

For more information on specific striper boats, see pages 144–146.

Cleats catch fly lines and spoil casts. This one is specially designed not to.

It can be depressed flush and raised again easily.

This pulpit on the bow allows the angler to cast without fear of falling into the water.

 ## OFFSHORE BOATS

Offshore fishing boats have evolved as well. Today the modern off-shore boat carries an excellent depth recorder, a multichannel radio, radar, Loran, GPS, and other navigational equipment. The hull keeps you dry and comfortable as you cruise at high speeds in relatively rough seas.

The angler who doesn't own a boat may still have to fish on a charter boat that is not designed for fly fishing in salt water (most of them aren't). If it is a large oceangoing craft, you would be wise to cover any cleats with masking tape; tape over anything else that will catch the line, too. I also ask the captain to fold back the outrigger on the side where I plan to throw my backcast. It pays to take these precautions before you leave the dock. If the boat is small, netting can be thrown over the gas cans, seats, and other gear; line dropped in the netting hardly ever tangles.

Draping a small mesh net over the motor and other line grabbers can make life easier for the caster. Small sinkers distributed along the net's edge hold it in place. Netting has holes in it, so the wind can't blow it around like it can a piece of canvas.

PRECAUTIONS AND EMERGENCY GEAR

If you buy a small boat, I suggest that you buy a small motor for emergency use. I once spent two days on a sandy, mosquito-infested beach in the Everglades with Vic Dunaway and Nelson Bryant, and learned a number of vital lessons. *One was to carry a small motor that is powerful enough to push your particular boat against the tide and wind.*

Think about survival gear, which can be kept in the kind of plastic battery cases used for storing batteries in the boat. They offer dry storage with ventilation. In those battery boxes I suggest carrying at least three suits of rain gear—one for every passenger. A flashlight, with the batteries stored separately in sealed plastic bags, is good insurance. I carry a dozen packs of matches in a sealed glass jar, as well as a cigarette lighter and extra fluid.

A small cooking pan is vital, as well as a pot to boil coffee or cocoa. Cans or jars of potted meat, corned beef, peanut butter, and similar products need no refrigeration and can be stored indefinitely. I seal all cans in plastic bags with a rubber-band closure to prevent rust. I don't worry about spare water; I always carry ice in the cooler.

The Coast Guard insists that you carry some basic equipment. You must have aboard wearable devices that will support an unconscious person upright in the water—one for every passenger. And you must have a throwable device immediately available. A seat cushion will answer for this—but it mustn't be stored; it must be in easy reach.

An oar is required on many boats, and a horn or whistle in case you need to sound a distress signal. I carry a fire extinguisher, one that is actually overrated for my boat. The dry-chemical type is best but not always required by the Coast Guard. Don't forget to have several lines, one at least 100 feet long for anchoring in storms and in deep water, as well as several others, for which you will find many uses. You should check with your local Coast Guard and Department of Natural Resources for specific requirements not mentioned here.

I lost a propeller one time and was lucky that it fell on white sand, where it could be retrieved. However, I did not have a spare shear pin and washer, so I had to jury-rig the prop with a 9/0 hook and some leader wire to get us home. Now I carry the washers needed to fit the splined shaft, the nut, and the shear pins—and a spare prop. An extra gas hose is also something you should never be without. The best toolbox I've found is a battery box. Plastic tackle boxes and similar containers seal in moisture and cause your tools to rust. I simply spray all tools with a light coating of rust preventive. Since I began using the battery box, my rust problems have ceased.

There are a few first-aid items that should be carried aboard. The Johnson & Johnson kits are excellent. If you ever fish far from shore, the cheapest and best insurance you can carry is a small, stainless steel signal mirror. They are sold by army-navy stores, outlets that furnish pilots' gear, and some camping stores.

With all these items it may sound as if you are overloading the boat—but each one is a mark of good seamanship.

TRAILERING

Most saltwater fly rodders trailer their boats to their fishing spot. But, many of them violate rules of trailering—a practice that may endanger them or at least cost them money.

Trailering is a science. Those who know the ropes make it look easy. It requires application at several times: before you go fishing, while on the road, and at the dock when putting the boat back on the trailer. Then, when you return home, there are additional procedures that should be followed for a maintenance-free boat and trailer.

To prevent accidents and get quickly and safely to where you are going you should make a number of checks before leaving. Carefully inspect your winch. Be sure the cable is not rusted or frayed. Tiny broken wires protruding from the cable can leave steel splinters in your hands, or cut deeply. If you use a rope, make sure it is not frayed; it could let go and hurt someone. Gear teeth can be broken off, leaving you with a dangerous piece of equipment. Such gears should be replaced.

This unfortunate angler did not lock the brakes on his car when putting his boat in the water, therefore submerging his car.

If you have an electrically driven winch, make certain all connections are free from corrosion. Make sure that they fit tightly, too. Have a manual handle, in case of power failure. Don't carry the handle on the winch; it may jiggle loose or be stolen.

You should carry a spare tire. Most anglers I know prefer to mount the tire right on the trailer. It must be locked to prevent theft. The most useful jack I've seen is one that resembles a half-moon gear, with a notch in one end that can be placed under the axle. When you use the jack, position a block of wood on the ground under it to prevent it from sinking into the soil. Place the jack under the axle and move the car slightly forward. The axle rides up on the half-circle jack, holding the wheel well off the ground. There are no moving parts to fail. When the tire has been replaced or repaired, the driver simply moves the car forward and the jack turns over and down, gently depositing the wheel on the ground. A hole can be drilled through one of the jack's supports so that it can be bolted directly to the trailer frame.

Perhaps the most common offense against good trailering practice is tire abuse. Almost all fishermen disregard their trailer tires—even though they support the entire rig. Tires low in pressure flex violently on the road, building up tremendous heat, which destroys the rubber. Bear in mind, too, that the trailer tires are traveling faster than your car's tires, since their diameter is smaller. Only in unusual circumstances should you use trailer tires of twelve inches or less at more than fifty-five miles an hour for any length of time. Ideally, your trailer should have tires the same size as those on your car (you will have a spare with you all the time if it does). Some trailer tires take fifty or more pounds of air. Since few gas station attendants carry a gauge that reads that high, it's advisable to buy one that reads to 100 pounds. They're inexpensive and will save you money on the first set of tires.

Let's assume that your tires call for forty-five pounds of pressure. *All tires should be checked cool, before running!* While your boat is still in the yard, check the axle tires and the spare. If two tires read okay, and the third reads thirty-five pounds, that means it is ten pounds below recommended tire pressure. Stop at the first station and check the tires! Read what the pressure is now. Then *add* ten pounds to that number, since you are ten pounds low. The boater who follows these rules will get several additional years of life from his tires. He'll also be a safer driver as his chance of a blowout is lessened.

Here is a manufacturer's chart giving recommended tire pressures:

Tire Size	Ply Rating	Max Load	Inflation Pressure
8-inch tire			
4.80/4.00	4	600	65
5.70/5.00		710	50
12-inch tire			
4.80/4.00	4	790	65
	6	960	90
6.90/6.00	4	1010	40
	6	1290	60

Most trailers carry a pair of safety chains that are hooked into holes for that purpose in the trailer hitch. All states require that they be hooked up; this does *not* mean draping the chain across the ball. You can get a little more safety if you hook the right chain in the left hole and vice versa, forming an X directly below the trailer ball and tongue; should the trailer jump from the ball it will fall into the X cradle instead of onto the road.

Another piece of chain should be installed on all trailers. Your winch has a gear that prevents the boat from slipping backward off the trailer. Most trailers have only a rubber bumper to prevent the boat from moving forward onto your car in case of a sudden stop. You should install a short section of chain to the tongue of the trailer near the winch, with a stout eye that can be snapped to the front of the boat, immobilizing it. Properly positioned, the chain will come tight when the boat is correctly drawn up on the trailer.

Before you leave home, you should tilt the motor slightly to prevent the lower unit from striking a curb or high spot in the road. One of the best devices for this is a half-inch commercial aluminum trailering brace. It costs little and fits most motors. When you are trailering, it will hold the motor at a slight angle; when you fish it can be dropped flat against the transom.

If your trailer rig weighs more than half the weight of your car, the trailer should have its own brakes. Separate brakes offer insurance against many kinds of accidents, relieve your nerves, and prevent jackknifing. Load levelers are another important factor on heavy boats. These are mechanical devices that distribute the load throughout the trailer and car, and are vital in pulling a really heavy boat.

Careful anglers always make sure that their straps lie tight against the boat before they leave the ramp. The straps that reach across a boat should have at least one twist in them on each side of the boat. Flat straps flutter badly in the wind, sometimes cutting through the metal holding hook or eroding the strap. A twisted strap remains stationary.

LAUNCHING YOUR BOAT

The most frequent offense by people trailering boats—next to disregarding proper tire pressure—is committed at the launching ramp. Most ramps will accommodate one to three boats. Yet, during a peak morning hour, scores of boats will want to use the ramp. Don't tie up the ramp preparing to launch. Note the experienced fisherman. *He'll stop a hundred yards back, load all his gear, remove his strap, put in the plug, and tilt the motor—he's ready and needs only a few minutes on the ramp surface.*

There are some safe and practical hints about launching a boat. First, all your electrical fittings are designed primarily for automobiles. You certainly would not deliberately immerse your auto headlights in water, and you should not do it to your trailer lights, either. If you have trailered your boat a long distance, you'll have heated the grease and bearings in the wheels. When you back down the ramp, keep the rims and bearings out of the water. If those hot bearings hit cool salt water a vacuum will be created and water will be sucked right into the bearings. Only your tires won't rust—they're all that should go into the water.

Have your companion stand at the end of the runway, and when the boat nears the water ask him to spread his hands apart to indicate how far the wheels are from the water. This is a much better method than waving the driver toward the water then suddenly saying, "Stop!"

Put the car in park—and leave the driver's door open, in case you have to get back in quickly. Place a chock under the wheels to prevent the car from sliding into the sea. A strap on the chock allows your companion to pull it away quickly and easily as you drive off.

If the winch is manual be careful not to get hit by the whirling handle. I know of two people who have broken an arm that way. Attach a rope to the bow eye, and, as the boat slides back, you'll have it under control.

RETURNING THE BOAT TO THE TRAILER

Putting the boat back on the trailer at the days' end can be accomplished easily with a little know-how. Attach a rope to the side of the boat at the rear and bow from which the wind is coming. After the trailer has been positioned, the driver of the car can walk to the end of the trailer and connect the cable to the bow eye. His companion, with a rope for the front and one attached at the rear of the boat on the windward side, can control the boat's approach to the trailer. As soon as the boat is on the trailer, move off the ramp to give someone else a chance. Then, at some practical distance you can attach straps, remove drain plugs, batten down, and be ready to roll homeward.

MAINTAINING YOUR BOAT AND TRAILER

When you get home, you'll wash the boat—and don't forget to wash the trailer, too. Both should be washed with warm soapy water. At almost any hardware store you can buy an attachment that hooks to your garden hose and dispenses soapy water or a fine, cutting rinse that will take all salt water from the boat and the trailer.

Get a can of touch-up paint and spot the areas where the paint has chipped. To prevent springs from rusting and to make them operate better, you can apply a solution of 50 percent STP and 50 percent kerosene. Take a paintbrush and sop the springs with the watery oil. It will penetrate between the springs. The kerosene will evaporate, leaving the STP to lubricate and protect the springs.

I carry a small jar of grease and a soldering brush (any small brush will do), and after I put the boat in the water I frequently dab grease on all my rollers. At the same time, I grease and oil the winch and gears.

 ## CHARTS

Every fly fisherman must become familiar with charts. The first thing to learn is the difference between a chart and a map. A map tells you where to go on land—a chart tells you where not to go on the water.

Charts indicate surface and underwater hazards—shoals, wrecks, drop-offs, reefs, and flats. Properly used, a chart will tell you at any time during your trip exactly where you are.

Few books will give you half the information a chart can. Depths of water, heights of lights, unusual bottom contours, mouths of rivers, and other fish-producing bits of information are yours if you pore over charts. With a good chart you can safely plot a course to unknown waters, having a thorough understanding of how to proceed and how long it will take you to get there. You can determine a good anchorage and locate possible good places to fish—all before you leave home.

Charts are put out by several agencies of the federal government. Different agencies are responsible for different areas and types of charts. Most boaters use charts prepared by the National Ocean Service (NOS) of the National Oceanic and Atmospheric Administration. NOS charts cover the Great Lakes and the coastal waters of the United States, including rivers and harbors extending inland to the head of tidal action. The NOS publishes five free chart catalogs, each covering a specific region and each having diagrams delineating specific areas covered by each NOS chart for that region. The fisherman should order the chart catalog of the area that he intends to fish. The specific charts needed can then be selected from that chart catalog.

NOS shows the land on its charts as a buff color; water areas are blue-white. You should clearly determine when you look at the myriads of numbers indicating water depths on a chart whether those figures refer to feet or fathoms. (Six feet is equal to one fathom.) Here is the NOS address where you can obtain information and charts: NOS Distribution Division, 6501 Lafayette Avenue, Riverdale, MD 20737.

If you have a depth sounder or recorder, and a working knowledge of a chart, you can discover new fishing areas. Use of the chart and a compass will allow you to return to any hot spot. Don't forget to replace old charts with new ones. Learn to trust your chart and you'll catch more fish and get there safer and faster.

The datum plane, or reference point, in the Atlantic and Gulf of Mexico waters is mean low water—an average of the two low tides. Half the time the depth of the water will be slightly lower than indicated. The Pacific Coast charts show the datum as mean lower low water—the average of the lower of the two daily tides, making these figures a little closer to the actual low tide. Always allow yourself a safety factor, for unusual local conditions could cause you to run aground.

Never mark a chart with a pen or marking pencil—unless the ink is permanent. At some time during their use all charts get water on them, and important chart notes could be marred. A number two lead pencil is good for such work. Protect your charts from weather and water. Several containers work well. One of the handiest is an old rod case, especially one made of a plastic tube, which can be shortened to the proper length with a hacksaw. PVC pipe with push-on caps is also a watertight container great for storing maps. The charts are rolled and inserted into the tube. But store the tube off the deck, since most tubes allow some seepage.

Some commercial charts now come with a clear plastic coating on them. You can also spray charts with acrylic plastic to give them a flexible, clear coating.

Index